Models of Cognitive Development

Ken Richardson
The Open University
Milton Keynes, UK

Psychology Press
a member of the Taylor & Francis group

Copyright © 1998 by Psychology Press Ltd., a member of the Taylor & Francis group.
All rights reserved. No part of this book may be reproduced in any form by photostat, microform, retrieval system, or any other means without the prior written permission of the publisher.

Psychology Press Ltd
27 Church Road
Hove
East Sussex, BN3 2FA
UK

British Library Cataloguing in Publication Data

A catalogue record for this book is available from the British Library

Library of Congress Cataloging-in-Publication Data are available

ISBN 0-86377-852-6 (Hbk)
ISBN 0-86377-853-4 (Pbk)

Cover design by Joyce Chester
Typeset in Palatino, by Facing Pages, Southwick, West Sussex
Printed and bound in the United Kingdom by TJ International Ltd., Padstow, Cornwall, UK.

Contents

Preface

Waddington (1966, p.v.) claimed that there could be "Nothing...that is both so apparently simple and spontaneous...yet so mysterious" as the process of transformation from a "simple lump of jelly" into a recognisable organism. Much of the research he largely inspired, however, has slowly eroded that mystery, so that, over the last two or three decades, we have been presented with ever more remarkable descriptions of the progression from egg to embryo to infant and adult, even in humans, and of the processes by which such transformations take place.

Such, at least, has been the case with the *physical* structures of the body and its organs, appendages, and systems. But one great scientific mountain remains: although the assault upon it has been at least as vigorous, description of the development of the mind and its *cognitive* system has by no means been as clear. The paradox is that although cognitive development is, perhaps, the most intensively researched and theorised area in the whole field of psychology, coherence and theoretical agreement — the most sure signs of scientific progress — remain uncertain here.

The main symptom of this backwardness is an ever-increasing proliferation of theories and models, and a segregation into specialist groups committed to this or that "approach", with little cross-communication between them. The problem has been lamented by many recent authors. In his introductory editorial to the most recent edition of the *Handbook of child psychology*, Damon (1997, p.79) notes how it shows "yet more glorious profusion" and warns of the "formidable models and approaches that the reader will find". Overton (1997, p.103) notes wryly how "I have often told my students that perhaps the only thing developmental psychologists agree upon is that their discipline is about change, and some seem ambivalent about that". Goodnow (1997, p.91), while acknowledging the "profusion of mini-theories or perspectives", laments "the scarcity of attempts toward integration."

Elsewhere, Markovitz (1993, p.131) says that there is "consistent lack of consensus both on the theoretical and on the empirical level", even for something as basic as the development of logical reasoning, and that theories "range from views that logical rules are genetically encoded to theories that claim that there is no such entity!" Scholnick (1994, p.728) argues that there is no common view of contents of cognition, or of cognitive development, and that "The current cognitive map consists of fractionated territories, each inhabited by processors who use specialized and untranslatable languages." Finally, Beilin (1987, p.37) complains of

> ... a bewildering variety of developmental theories. There is social learning theory, schema theory, rule learning theory, skill theory, information processing theory, componential theory, activity theory, dialectical theory, neo-Piagetian theory, ecological theory, modularity views, and much more ... To some observers, theoretical discourse in developmental psychology has the sound of the Tower of Babel: many tongues and little communication among the speakers.

Little wonder, therefore, that many students I speak to, while saying how much they enjoy courses and books on cognitive development, become worried about the lack of coherence or general principles within them. This is especially the case for those who come to psychology from the natural sciences like biology or chemistry, where they find the Darwinian framework and the structure of the atom such comforting anchor points for theoretical evaluation. For the sake of the discipline and of students, then, academic psychologists need occasionally to look up from their own favourite models, to seek to diagnose this general problem and discover how to remedy it.

One of the main reasons for this fragmentation, in my view, is that even the most recent models are rooted in "big" assumptions and presuppositions which are rarely made explicit, and equally rarely made the targets of criticism. Courses and books on cognitive development usually favour a particular approach, or consist of unsystematic "selections" from the theoretical salad, often without, in my view, a sufficient scrutiny and comparison of the roots of those theories. If they lack a grasp of the assumptions of which such roots are made, students are deprived of critical purchase on what they are asked to study, and will fail to have a clear picture of the theoretical forest, being left somewhat desperately trying to make sense of a clutter of individual trees. In other words, without clarity and understanding of the *roots* of theories, students will fail to grasp the strengths and weaknesses of models, and how they are similar or different. In the long run this means that students will be disabled from making their own critical contribution to the discipline; they will continue to feel forced into premature specialism, or will just attempt to memorise disorganised chunks of knowledge for regurgitation at exams. All of this will ensure that *future* progress in the discipline is that much retarded.

In this book I offer some effort towards a remedy for this situation. My approach is to attempt to show how the vast variety of contemporary models can be grouped, distinguished, and compared by their having roots in a much smaller number of "deep" assumptions (some, in fact, very old indeed). I also try to show how they can be criticised precisely by evaluating those underlying assumptions. Such an approach, I think, helps to distinguish the whole theoretical field as a smaller number of hills or "bumps" on a topological landscape. With such a cognitive map of their own, I hope that students and others will better be able to find their way around the whole, and in exploring one "bump" will know where they stand in relation to all the others. It is my fervent hope that such a wider view will help to provoke the earth movements necessary to bring about a more unified landscape in future.

Note that this approach is not *primarily* about authors, or even about whole models or theories (although it could be about some of them): rather the emphasis is on thematic *assumptions* and how these figure as particular — although not necessarily the only — ingredients of particular theories. Although chapters are entitled "Nativist Models", "Associationist Models", and so on, for brevity and convenience, each chapter is really about illustrations of nativist, associationist (and so on) *assumptions* in particular models, without implying the necessary exclusion of others in the same model. Indeed, there are probably few, if any, "pure" models, and the final chapter tries to emphasise how these basic assumptions have become "mixed" in many models. Again, I hope that by being able to isolate and identify such assumptions in models, and knowing how to criticise them, students will end up with a much better understanding of those ingredients, a clearer picture in the mosaic, and perhaps the kind of critical stance that will lead to better theory-making in the future.

Such an approach, of course, carries dangers as well as advantages. One of these is that not all psychologists may agree with the distinctions I have made, although these, too, are open to criticism. Another problem is that, in a fairly short work, there is not the slightest possibility of being comprehensive in coverage of models and theories. Instead, I have simply attempted to provide ranges of examples that illustrate the character of *types* of model, the assumptions on which they are based, and how they have been criticised. This has been an inevitably selective process, which may, again, be open to criticism (as well as to suggestions of more germane examples).

There is, however, no doubting the importance of the general aims of a book like this. The cognitive system itself is the most complex and intricate structure that nature has yet produced, and while we are still struggling to understand it, the disparate assumptions and partial knowledge we have continue to inform or misinform both general social attitudes and major decisions about, for example, the disposal of children in the institutions concerned with education. As Chapman (1988, p.364) has noted, there has been an all too common tendency to look prematurely for "causal" accounts of developmental outcomes, when those outcomes are themselves very poorly understood: "Many controversies in psychology have resulted from attempts to apply antecedent–consequent explanatory schemes before any general agreement has been reached about the nature of the consequents for which antecedents are sought." Again, I hope this book will help identify what we "really" know, and what, instead, remains a challenge for the future.

Assumptions underlying models may be so disparate, in fact, that theorists who use terms like "cognitive," "development", and "models" may not actually be referring to exactly the same thing. Just how seemingly bewildered inquiry has made us is, perhaps, best seen in *The Penguin Dictionary of Psychology* (Reber, 1995), which defines *cognition* as follows:

> A broad (almost unspecifiably so) term which has been traditionally used to refer to such activities as thinking, conceiving, reasoning etc. Most psychologists have used it to refer to any class of mental "behaviours" (using the term very loosely) where the underlying characteristics are of an abstract nature and involve symbolizing, insight, expectancy, complex rule use, problem-solving ... and so forth.

I would like to try to be a little more definite than that! Indeed *The Concise Oxford Dictionary* (Allen, 1993) defines cognition more straightforwardly as the "action or faculty of knowing...as opposed to emotion or volition." The term cognition, in fact, derives from the Greek word for "knowing" — but most philosophers have added "reasoning" or "thinking" as part of this definition. For the moment I will leave it as simple as that, and hope that the rest of the book will make clear the various nuances the term has acquired.

Most popular views, and dictionary definitions, of *development* include a number of ideas, some of which receive greater emphasis at different times. One of these involves change in a simple quantitative sense; i.e. growth, or just getting bigger. A related idea is that of maturation: the realisation or "filling-out" of some potential already immanent in that which is developing. Other ideas, however, stress development as *qualitative* change over time, rather than just growth or expansion. Coupled with these may be notions of progress or improvement of some sort, usually implying increasing complexity (differentiation) and reorganisation, and thus becoming functionally more competent or efficient.

The modern psychological definition of development is close to a combination of these ideas: growth and differentiation involving improvement of organisation and function. But this definition belies other difficulties. As already mentioned, it is difficult to "see" cognitive development directly, in the way that we can see aspects of physical development. We have great difficulty in describing "what" develops, "how" it does so, and what factors are involved in it and how. Little wonder that Rutkowska (1993, p.22) can claim that "Developmental psychologists ... do not agree about even the broadest characteristics of the 'development' that they are aiming to explain." If *they* can't agree, heaven help our students!

Most of the time, of course, we just infer what we can from outward symptoms, and try to integrate our inferences into a working model. As in much of science, we operate on the basis of "constructs" of the forces at work. More often than not these will utilise metaphors borrowed from everyday social experience or other domains such as information processing in the computer, the "bursting" of buds and blossoms, the ladder view of ranks of cognitive ability, the dichotomy of the sexes, and so on. Although often the route to important progress among scientists, the use of such metaphors has just as often led to their downfall. At the end of the day we need to go beyond these to a realistic description of a system and its development "as it is".

It is these constructs, at any rate, that the terms "theory" and "model" are about. Often the terms are used interchangeably, as I have largely been doing so far. I'd like to make one distinction, however. This is that a theory may be extremely vague, and personal. We all have informal theories about things like the weather, the workings of a car engine, human nature, the origins of children's personalities, etc., and, of course, how people think. These emerge as abstract "working models" in the course of our ordinary experience. They are important to us because they help us in making predictions, and reaching explanations, about everyday experience.

However, scientific theories/models differ from our everyday informal theories in two main ways. First they attempt to model parts of nature beyond the here and now, or the immediate conditions — i.e.

to be "generalisable". Second, and perhaps most important, they are *explicit*, in the sense of clearly identifying components with precise (preferably quantitative) description of relations between them. Indeed, it has been argued that the modern scientific revolution only got off the ground in the 17th century when scientists started to meet in conferences and publish their results and ideas in such explicit form. Because of this explicitation, scientific theories can be criticised, refined, tested, and more or less agreed, through the empirical *methods* of science, honed over two or three hundred years of scholarship. In these methods, a clear model is induced from careful, replicable observations. Clear predictions yielded from the relations so modelled are then put to the test in the classic design of experiments — the so-called hypothetico-deductive process.

This, at least, is the view of models found in most of the theory to be described herein. I am aware, of course, of recent "post-modernist" views that eschew such tradition — or even blame it for the fragmentation that remains the prevailing scene — and instead urge a more "interpretative" approach of observations-in-context. It is too early to say whether that approach will yield more unified theory. My only worry is how, without the very social, public, and historically honed "logic of confirmation", we will evaluate one set of conclusions against another. The danger, always, is that of a return to Authority (of particularly powerful groups or individuals, for example) as the last word on these matters, which empirical science was intended to overthrow in the first place.

Certainly I hope that the review of models in this book will help students to stand up to Authority in the future, and that, critically armed, they will help us all face up to the enormous challenge that the field of cognitive development still presents. In the process, I hope students will come to feel some of the excitement of exploration of this, perhaps the greatest, outstanding challenge for modern science. For my own part I acknowledge the immense pleasure provided by the "ideas makers" on the backs of whom this book is written. I would like thank all those friends and colleagues who made clear the need for such a book, for encouraging me to write it, and for commenting on earlier drafts. Thanks are also due to Sue Abel for drawing some of the illustrations. Specific mention should be made of the generous and knowledgeable suggestions, and corrections of errors, of three reviewers of a previous draft. I have tried to accommodate as many of those suggestions as possible in this final version. Needless to say, though, the many defects that remain are entirely my own.

Nativist models 1

Introduction

Whether in the living world or in that of artefacts, we are generally very quick to assume that almost any organised entity has predetermined form and structure. We see a building slowly taking shape, and automatically infer some basic plan, an agent who drew it, and the resulting structure as the gradual realisation of that plan. We see a complex blossom unfolding from its bud, or an infant from its embryo, and infer that the form must have been there all along in seed or egg, and its development is an automatic materialisation. In the case of physical structures, this view has been around for a very long time. During the exciting early period of microscope development in the 15th–17th centuries, biologists were quick to "see" all manner of structures in their "preformed" states, and the microscopist Hartsoeker duly provided us with a drawing of a little man — a homunculus — with all its little parts, curled up in the head of a sperm (Fig. 1.1). The added implication, of course, is that such homunculi have somehow been copied and passed through the generations in the sperm since the beginning of time.

Much the same views have arisen about the origins and developments of our cognitive abilities, as in knowledge and reasoning. The very complexity, scope, and coherence of these seem strongly to bespeak preformed or predetermined plans, and more or less automatic

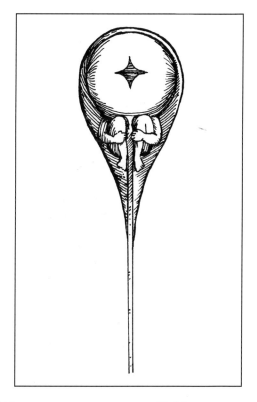

FIG. 1.1.
Hartsoeker's drawing of a homunculus in the head of a sperm.

unfolding. And here, too, such views have a very long history. Although spoken with a modern — even scientific — conviction, they were heard over two thousand years ago in Ancient Greece, when the philosopher Plato argued that knowledge could not possibly be derived from experience, which is unreliable, fragmentary, and incomplete. Instead he said it must be there from conception, put there by the hand of God, and "brought out" by a proper education based on rational discourse (the theory became known as classical rationalism). Over the centuries these Platonic views became expressed and re-expressed by generations of philosopher–psychologists. Indeed, Leibnitz (1646–1716) (quoted in Dobzhansky, 1962, p.25) provided the mental parallel to Hartsoeker's homunculus when he said that all "the souls which will one day be human souls have been present in the semen of their ancestors down to Adam, and consequently existed since the beginning of time."

These basic ideas (in various guises) still form the most popular models of human cognitive development. There have been some adjustments, of course. The most significant of these is that the genes have replaced God as the fundamental "designer". There have also been various other changes in terminology: in particular, modern theorists tend to use the label "nativist" rather than "rationalist" to describe such models. However, the basic principles survive. In this chapter I want to offer an overview of such models, hopefully in a way that will reveal those common basic principles and assumptions. Then I will try to show how the models have been questioned and criticised *through* questions and criticisms of those assumptions.

Contemporary nativism

Nativist models of cognition and its development have once again become very popular in the last 20 years, and their role in reinstating a genuine, "mentalistic", psychology is well known (Gardner, 1984). Around the turn of the 20th century, psychology had "lost its mind". This was due to a "positivist" philosophy, popular in the second half of the 19th century, which insisted that psychology should emulate the physical sciences, and should view the control of *behaviour* (rather than modelling of mysterious "mentalisms") as its primary goal. Behaviourism, as it came to be called, insisted that we should ignore unseen processes and focus only on observable behaviours, and the purely statistical rules governing the connections between stimuli and responses (see Chapter 2).

Behaviourism dominated psychology between the wars, but afterwards created increasing dissatisfaction. This, in turn, was due to the gathering evidence for the role of "central processes", mediating and moderating relations between stimuli and responses (e.g. Hebb, 1949). In the late 1950s and 1960s psychologists once again dared to speak of minds and mental processes, and cognitive psychology was "reborn" (although, in truth, it had never been completely dead). Renewed nativist theorising enlivened this rebirth in several classic forms of expression.

The first expression entailed the re-assertion of *predeterminism*, and appeared first in Noam Chomsky's theory of language (Chomsky, 1959). In pointing out that most of what a child hears in everyday language experience is highly diverse, faulty, and piecemeal — that a child actually produces numerous novel sentences that he or she has not heard before — and thus utterly rejecting the idea that the child learns grammar by imitating sentences heard, Chomsky returned to the idea that all the child's abilities in grammar must be inborn, in the form of a set of innate rules coded in our genes and biologically inherited.

This entailment was based on what has long been known as the *argument from the poverty of the stimulus*, first put by Plato in Ancient Greece. As with Plato, the essential point is the seeming incredibility of any suggestion that complex, organised mental structures and reliable knowledge can be condensed from unreliable, changeable sense experience. A distinction between *perceptual* processes and *cognitive* ones is necessary: there is typically more information in our thoughts and responses than in the perceptual input, which must involve the contributions of the mind itself. According to Chomsky (1980, p.39):

> Innate factors permit the organism to transcend experience, reaching a high level of complexity that does not reflect the limited and degenerate environment ... we find structures of considerable intricacy, developing quite uniformly, far transcending the limited environmental factors that trigger and partially shape their growth.

Noone argues that our physical organs and their functions come from experience, so why should we imply this for language and cognition, asked Chomsky (1980, p.33).

> We may usefully think of the language faculty, the number faculty and others, as "mental organs", analogous to the heart or the visual system or the system of motor coordination and planning. There appears to be no clear demarcation line between physical organs, perceptual and

motor systems and cognitive faculties in the respects in question.

And, thanks to biological natural selection (of which more later) these "organs" are common to humans, presenting *universals* of structure and form in cognition. For example, Chomsky has detailed aspects of language that are found in all languages all over the world, developing in children with remarkable uniformity, and he extends this idea to cognition and its development. How could such uniformity of structure arise from the disparate experiences of children all around the world, he asked.

The metaphor of unfolding physical organs thus became a compelling model of cognitive development itself. As Chomsky (1980, pp.33–39) states:

> My own suspicion is that a central part of what we call "learning" is actually better understood as the growth of cognitive structures along an internally directed course under the triggering and partially shaping effect of the environment ... Our biological endowment permits both the scope and limits of physical growth ...When we turn to the mind and its products, the situation is not qualitatively different ... here too we find structures of considerable intricacy, developing quite uniformly, far transcending the limited environmental factors that trigger and partially shape their growth ...

Of course, these "organs" require environmental substances, conditions, and stimulation for them to materialise: but "the environment" in such models, formal or informal, only works as a "trigger" or "fine-tuner" — the medium of activity and exercise, assisting or retarding development, but not substantially altering its course and final form. The evidence for a developmental "plan" or "genetic program", whose expression is buffered against external perturbations, seems insurmountable. According to Gardner (1984, pp.56–57): "The plan for ultimate growth is certainly there in the genome; and, even given fairly wide latitude (or stressful circumstances) development is likely to proceed along well-canalised avenues."

These are the general principles of modern nativism. In what follows I offer some slightly more detailed models: in basic information processing using the computational metaphor; in the flow of Chomskian and information-processing ideas into models of more complex aspects of cognition; and how these have more recently been laced with biological (evolutionary) principles to produce another view that has become popular in recent years, that of the "modular" mind.

Natural mechanics and natural computations

Notions of knowledge as parcels of experience, and of reasoning as the logical rules by which these are moved, shuffled, interrelated, converted, or combined to produce more complex parcels, are old ones, and the idea of "natural mechanics" pre-dates the recent resurgence of nativism. Thus, Gruber (1974) notes how Charles Darwin had to theorise about the evolution of complex behaviours in the teeth of Natural Theology, which had declared all complex behaviour as endowed by God, and deterministic machines such as clocks, music boxes, and Babbage's calculating engine (a famous Victorian computer), as the best "natural" models of cognition.

The advent of the *modern* computer, which operated even more explicitly for the manipulation of parcels of information, according to pre-programmed rules, thus furnished a potent metaphor for cognitive science in the 1960s and 70s. This signalled a transition from natural mechanics to "natural computations". In the modern computational models, parcels of information, their more detailed fragments, and their more general composites, are identified and labelled as "symbols", and then sorted, stored in memory, retrieved for problem solving in a "working memory", and so on.

By the 1980s, the computer metaphor had inspired a "standard" model of cognition. According to Vera and Simon (1991, p.34): "Sensory information is converted to symbols, which are then processed and evaluated in order to determine the appropriate motor symbols that lead to behaviour". Gilhooly (1995, p.245) states:

> In the standard model, thinking is seen as the manipulation of symbols both within working memory and between long-term and working memory. "Manipulations" of symbols are viewed as consisting of elementary information-processing operations such as comparing symbols, copying symbols, deleting and adding symbols; appropriate combi-nations of elementary operations may form complex manip-ulations. The manipulations are presumed to be in accord with rules stored in long-term memory.

A simple information-processing model is shown in Fig. 1.2. Information is input at sensory registers and encoded in some form (usually in symbolic form, such as a letter, word, or image). It is conveyed to short-term or working memory where it is analysed, compared, transformed, or whatever, according to various processes and rules, at least some of which are retrieved from long-term memory. The result of this activity is some motor action (including, possibly, some more active search of input, some strategy for gathering further information, and so on), which creates further sensory input, and so the process continues, until some criterion state has been reached.

Before I go any further it is important to point out that the "cognitive revolution" of the 1960s encompassed almost all of cognitive psychology, including cognitive associationism, which I deal with in the next chapter, and cognitive constructivism, which I deal with in Chapter 3. A number of contemporary models stress learning, development, knowledge-acquisition, and even self-modification (Siegler, 1991), as aspects of developmental change within an information-processing framework, and I will be returning to such aspects in Chapter 2. Here I deal only with nativist aspects of cognition as commonly arising in models of information processing.

The point is that the use of nativist assumptions in information-processing models is not always clear. On the one hand, as Bates and Elman (1993, p.628) point out, the computer metaphor of the mind is "by its nature a strongly nativist approach to learning ... Everything that really counts is already there at the beginning." On the other hand, we cannot be too categorical about this, because many information-processing models are *implicitly*, rather than

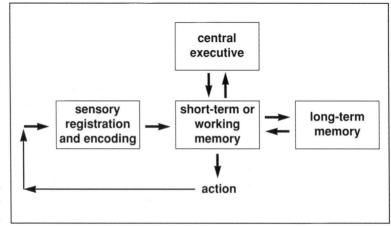

FIG. 1.2. The main components of a simple information-processing model.

explicitly, nativist, and many adopt nativist elementary processes themselves *as the basis of learning* (a "dual" system, which I will be returning to in Chapter 2).

Quite simply, nativism has entered into recent models whenever it has been assumed that, in order to carry out cognitive functions, a number of elementary and more complex processes, as well as some overall controlling or executive function, or even aspects of knowledge itself, are *preformed* for them. In the strongest expressions, some or all of these processes — encoding, comparing, combining, transforming, mapping, inferencing, and even the "rules" — are "built-in" aspects of our cognitive architecture, present from birth, and functioning like that throughout life. We may describe these aspects in various ways but "Ultimately", as Klahr (1992, p.151) puts it, "we are forced to make assertions about what I have called the *innate kernel*" (emphasis in original). Here I will attempt to illustrate how such kernels have been conceived, while describing their implications for cognitive development as we go along.

Such an innate kernel has been hinted at in many models. For example, although the well-known ACT* model of Anderson (1983) is essentially a "learning" model, he nonetheless acknowledges a number of innate principles and processes underlying its operation. These include a set of rules for identifying causal relationships in experience; a set of inductive principles for constraining the causal inference; and a set of other methods (such as using analogies) for applying causal inferences in problem solving. Although Anderson (1983) has proposed modifiable processing rules – so-called "production rules" — as the basis of learning (and I will therefore be dealing with them in Chapter 2), he also notes (1983, p.26) how the system has "... a set of mechanisms to account for acquisition of productions." And the "cognitive units" that rules deposit in, or tap from, long-term memory assume specific "types" of representation (images, propositions, or temporal strings) as a product of human evolution. Each of these is "intended to facilitate a certain type of computation", just as there are different "hardware types" built for different functions in the computer world.

Under such assumptions, cognitive development consists of the elaboration and/or increased efficiency of these "hardware" processes with age, together with the increased capacities and knowledge representations that result from their application. In the most extreme views there is no true development, in the sense of the appearance of new structures at different ages or times, and Fodor (1983), for example, has actually suggested this. As Oakhill (1988, p.178) put it:

Information processing theorists regard cognitive development as a continuous process, and view adult thinking as qualitatively similar to that of the child. Development is seen as *quantitative* in that it depends on an expansion of knowledge structures and an increase in the efficiency with which processes can be executed.

One example is that of memory development in children. It has been known for over a century that, in tests of digit span in which subjects are asked to memorise and then recall lists of digits, performance improves up to about 18 years of age (Henry & Millar, 1993; see Fig. 1.3). Many recent theories of cognitive development have implicated this "capacity" improvement as a basic factor in more general cognitive development (e.g. Case, 1985), although the reasons for it have been far from clear. One popular contender (Murray, 1996, p.334) has been "alterations in the nerve structure as determined by genetically-timed growth processes." In addition, Case has implicated improved *allocation* of capacity, perhaps as a function of more rapid identification of items, itself arising as a result of *faster* information processing.

Improvement in speech rate has also been implicated as a major factor in development of digit span. This idea is based on Baddeley's (1990,1992) model of working memory (Fig. 1.4). One aspect of this model suggests that visually presented items are automatically encoded in phonological (speech-like) form, and then maintained by sub-vocal rehearsal in an "articulatory-loop" (otherwise their traces

FIG. 1.3.
Typical development of digit span with age (data from various sources).

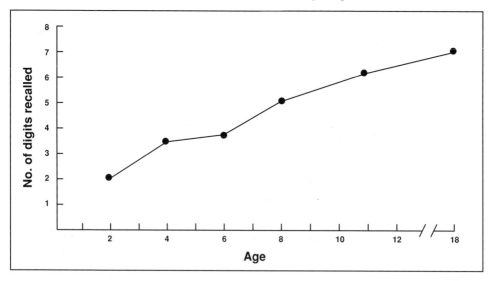

decay). Children's speech-rate increases with age: so, the faster the sub-vocal rehearsal, the greater the number of items that can be maintained. The idea is supported by the fact of a close relationship between speech rate and memory span over different ages, although a causal connection is still a matter of some dispute (cf. Gathercole & Hitch, 1995; Henry & Millar, 1993).

There have been many attempts to reduce development in reading skills to the maturation in speed, efficiency, or capacity of such basic processes (e.g. Just & Carpenter, 1992; Wagner, Torgesen, & Rachotte, 1994). And there have been attempts to relate arithmetic/mathematical ability to speed/capacity in working memory, executive processes, articulatory loop, or visuo-spatial scratchpad (Ashcraft, 1995). More generally, it is worth noting how Logie and Pearson (1997, p.253) describe working memory as "a group of specialised components offering support for temporary storage and on-line processing", and improvement with age (p.254) as due to "developments in the under-lying cognitive architecture."

The idea of innate computational processes forming the basic archi-tecture of cognition has flooded the field over the last 20 years. For example, it has been suggested that humans possess an innate "face-processing" mechanism (see Beale & Keil, 1995), and various models of "face-recognition units" have been proposed in recent years, each based on dedicated neural mechanisms (e.g. Bruce & Young, 1986). These can

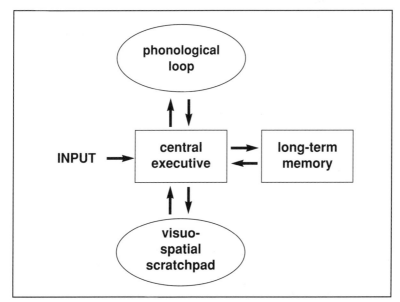

FIG. 1.4.
One view of
Baddeley's model of
working memory.

encode different faces (and different aspects of faces) but are "hard-wired" to carry out an essentially fixed function upon those encoded "parcels'. Holland, Holyoak, and Nisbett (1986) posit cognitive "operating rules" as "innate system manipulation procedures": neither learnable nor teachable, they call up the relevant cognitive rules for reasoning, changing the knowledge base, and initiating action.

By their nature, innate computational rules or procedures are rarely if ever specified in detail. But just the positing of a few innate principles such as simple rules, a working memory, and a long-term (knowledge) store, has resulted in models of cognition of remarkable power. Newell (1980) argued that any system of "general intelligence" can be reduced to such a "physical symbol system". Indeed the discipline of Artificial Intelligence has produced complex problem-solving programs on the basis of such assumptions — most famously for playing advanced chess, but also for complex decision-making in engineering and medicine — thus cementing the computer metaphor in the minds of cognitive theorists, and in those of the media and general public.

Using similar mechanical or computational metaphors, traditional theories of intelligence (Carpenter, Just, & Shell, 1990, p.404) have postulated "general" innate reasoning processes – "the ability to reason and solve problems involving new information, without relying extensively on an explicit base of declarative knowledge derived from either schooling or previous experience." These are assumed to have basic biological form, perhaps subserved by other, more specific, processes (verbal, mathematical, visuospatial, and so on) having equally innate form (Vernon, 1979). There have been major efforts in recent years to pin these down to identifiable (and presumably equally innate) information-processing mechanisms (see, for example, contributions in Vernon, 1987; and Deary & Caryl, 1997).

Sternberg (1984) has suggested that intelligence consists of the operation of executive processes and discrete mental operations which he calls "components". These are part of the system's hardware, and universal across cultures. Development, in this view (Sternberg, 1982, p.413), consists of "changes in the availability, accessibility and ease of execution of a variety of kinds of information-processing components." Differences in intelligence consist of differences in the relative efficiency of these components: thus Sternberg (1984, p.308) speaks of "different levels of power in the execution of the various kinds of components."

For example, part of Sternberg's research has consisted of analysing the way children deal with problems like analogical reasoning tasks, using reaction time or latency of response measures. Analogical reasoning problems consist of simple "relational mapping" tasks of the form "A is to B as C is to ?" (where D has to be selected from five or six alternatives). One such task might be:

> Teacher is to Pupil as Doctor is to .....
> (hospital, nurse, patient, medicine, child).

Sternberg has suggested that cognitive components involved in such tasks include encoding, inference, mapping, applying, evaluation, and response-production. Through correlational analyses he has tried to show how improvements in efficiency of some of these are involved in development. For example, children who do relatively well on them tend to spend more time in the *encoding* component but less time in other components. Although Sternberg (1984) hedges a little on the origins of these components, I think there appears to be a nativist element in them.

Case (1992) has augmented his earlier view (see earlier) with a postulated set of innate information-processing capacities. These comprise (1992, p.54) a "central conceptual structure ... a system of semantic nodes and relations ... [each] applicable ... to experience within some particular domain." These assist the identification of goals, the strategies for attaining those goals, and for integrating them into more effective responses. In Case's view, development depends, in part, in biological maturation of these capacities.

In this section I have considered more or less implicit nativism in the modelling of elementary processes underlying cognition. In the next two sections I look more closely at how these notions, together with other biologically inspired notions, have been expressed in more complex aspects of cognition.

Development of concepts and categories

Systematic, "rule-like" clustering of an almost infinite variety of sensory inputs into a smaller number of more-or-less equivalent forms (categories) has long been seen as an essential form of mental economy. This is most obvious in certain aspects of perception. Take the colours of the rainbow as an example. Although containing a continuous range of light frequencies, what we perceive are fairly discrete *bands* of colours. Experiments also show that any pair of colours (e.g. green and yellow) of fixed frequency *difference* are actually easier to discriminate when they cross a colour boundary than when they fall within one. Neurophysiological evidence supports the idea that, at this level of sensory processing at least, these are "innate mechanisms" (Beale & Keil, 1995).

Analogous studies have shown that humans display similar categorical perception with speech sounds: although experienced as combinations of continuous acoustic variables, the combinations tend to be identified as one or other of the 30 or so common phonemes. It has been suggested that infants exhibit such categorical distinctions soon after birth, thus further strengthening the idea that they must be innate (Eimas, Miller, & Jusczyk, 1987).

Similar ideas have long been entertained with respect to concepts. In most models, the word *concept* has been used to refer to the internal representation of a category of objects and events (usually associated with a verbal label). The word *category* then refers to the "extension" of the concept, i.e. all the actual and possible instances of it in the real world. Although there have been many new models of concepts in recent years, most of which I will be describing in Chapter 2, the centrality of concepts in cognition has remained undisputed. As Fodor (1994, p.95) explains: "The nature of concepts is the pivotal theoretical issue in cognitive science; it's the one that all the others turn on." And they have been described as the "building-blocks" of knowledge and cognition (Harnad, 1987).

As mentioned earlier, in traditional Platonic psychology knowledge consists of the "pure" concepts placed with us at conception. In a similar vein, many recent authors have claimed that there is "more" in a concept than can possibly be derived from experience alone. This has been said to include properties like "beliefs", recognition of "kinds" and "essences", "deep understandings of causal relations", theoretical "cores", "raisons d'être", and so on (see Jones & Smith, 1993, for a critical review). Hampton (1997) calls this "essentialism": Medin & Ortony (1989, p.135) suggest that humans are born "with a bias for thinking that things that are superficially similar are alike in deeper, more principled ways".

Such essences or "deeper ontological structures" in concepts have been implicated in many studies. For example, Carey (1982, 1985) told 4-year-olds that people have an organ called a "spleen". She then presented them with a real earthworm and a toy mechanical monkey, and asked them which one was most likely to have a spleen. In spite of the greater visible association between the monkey and people, the children tended to select the earthworm. Somewhat similarly, experiments by Gelman and her colleagues (e.g. Gelman & Markman, 1986, 1987) have indicated how even 3-year-olds make inferences about objects on the basis of their deeper properties, rather than superficial appearance.

In a typical study, children would be presented with a drawing of a snake (the target) and told that "this snake lays eggs" (Fig. 1.5). Their attention was then directed to a drawing of another, cobra-like snake, which differed markedly from the target in appearance, and also a worm which looked much more like the target. They were then asked: "Do you think this worm lays eggs like this snake?"; "Do you think this [other] snake lays eggs like this [target] snake?" The children tended to respond according to the category name rather than the superficial similarity of appearance.

In an intriguing set of studies, Keil (1986) told stories to children about animals that weren't quite as they appeared. For example, one type of animal had all the appearances and outward behaviour patterns of raccoons. But when scientists examined them inside, things became more complicated (Keil, 1986, p.184):

> The scientists found out that they had the blood of skunks, the bones of skunks, the brains of skunks, and all the other inside parts of skunks rather than those of raccoons. And they found out that these animals' mommies and daddies were skunks and that when they had babies their babies were skunks ... What do you think these really are, raccoons or skunks?

The children tended to over-ride appearances and to maintain that the animals were skunks rather than raccoons. Other studies on 2- or

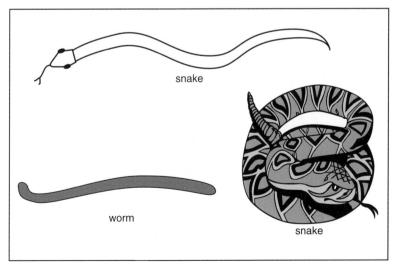

FIG. 1.5. Children appear to make inferences about object properties on the basis of principles "deeper" than superficial appearance.

3-year-olds have suggested that children can understand the logic of taxonomic class inclusion (in which, say, two concepts such as car and bike can belong to a superordinate concept such as vehicle) (Markman 1984); or, given suitably arranged procedures, can show almost all aspects of mature causal reasoning (Bullock, Gelman, & Baillargeon 1982). These results have been taken to emphasise children's "early competency" in knowledge and cognition, and that development and learning have more to do with how to *access* and *apply* these competencies in different contexts, rather than fundamental changes in their form and nature.

Keil (1988, p.85) probably offers a consensus view:

> I have interpreted research along these lines as suggestive of a constraints oriented view of cognitive development of the sort that Chomsky (1980) has proposed in linguistic theory. Under this view, acquiring complex knowledge would be impossible, if all of us did not share certain a priori constraints that restrict the range of hypotheses to be made about the structure of what is learned. [These] represent a kind of competence that is always present, namely the set of possible, or natural, knowledge structures in a domain.

As for what these constraints consist of, Keil (1988, p.92) envisages a "conceptual core" that "lays down a skeletal framework within which the periphery differentiates. Thus, the constraints are rarely if ever overridden by the periphery: nonetheless, dramatic shifts can occur in the periphery provided they honor the general boundaries of the skeleton."

Much the same has been said about the detection of causal relationships in experience, which are, of course, crucial for making predictions in the world, including the consequences of personal actions and interventions. Research in this area has produced a puzzling picture (see Chapter 2), but theorists have, in recent years, increasingly turned to nativist assumptions.

As Cheng and Novick (1992, p.367) point out:

> Although covariation is a necessary criterion for causal induction, it is not a sufficient one. There clearly are innate and acquired constraints on the selection of potential causal factors with respect to a given effect. On theoretical grounds, the problem ... requires that there be some innate biases in the inductive process.

Corrigan and Denton (1996) claim that causal understanding is a "developmental primitive", and can serve to constrain development of knowledge of natural phenomena and of categorisation.

The increasing respectability accorded to nativist models in recent years means that some innate content is now seen as almost self-evident. Thus Sperber (1986, p.1308) argues that:

> ... the more basic abilities, the linguistic ones for instance, must be to an important extent, genetically determined; the construction of abilities from within, or the internalisation of culturally-constituted abilities, can only take place on some well-developed innate foundation.

The modular mind

Recent years have witnessed a dramatic increase in models which stress that rules are innate and have arisen evolutionarily through natural selection, and acting as "Darwinian algorithms" (see Gigerenzer, 1995). The idea of the evolutionary-based computational "module" has become very popular in cognitive developmental theory in the last decade or so. Based on Chomsky's theory, that of Fodor (1983) has been very influential: it suggests (like others) that representations enter the system in the form of symbols or symbol strings (e.g. features, digits, or letters) which are analysed, stored, rearranged, recalled etc. by computational processes that are "hard-wired" by genetic instructions into discrete sub-systems called modules. According to Fodor (1985, pp.3–4):

> A module is an informationally encapsulated computational system ... largely innately specified ... and characteristically associated with specific neuroanatomical mechanisms.

Fodor's theory is one of *limited* modularity, in that it is confined to perceptual, or "input" systems. These are essentially systems that interface with external reality, and are innate, neurologically distinct, domain-specific, and automatic. They carry out preliminary analyses on sensory input characterised, according to Fodor (1985, p.4), as of specific informational or perceptual types, such as number, language, spatial information, and so on. The modules are thus:

> input driven, very fast, mandatory, superficial, encapsu-
> lated from much of the organism's background knowl-

edge, largely organised around bottom-to-top information flow, largely innately specified ... and characteristically associated with specific neuroanatomical mechanisms (sometimes even specific neuronanatomical loci) ... (and) domain specific.

The results of modular analysis are then passed on to more central systems which carry out "higher-level" cognitive tasks. The latter systems are, according to Fodor (1985, p.4), ones that we actually know little about, although:

> they are everything that perception is not: slow, deep, global rather than local, largely under voluntary...control, typically associated with diffuse neurological structures, neither bottom-to-top nor top-to-bottom in their modes of processing.

Although Fodor's model restricted modularity to perceptual systems, the temptation to extend it to *cognitive* systems has been widely indulged in recent models (for recent reviews see contributions in Hirschfeld & Gelman, 1994). These have been inspired by certain biological evolutionary ideas, namely "selectionism" and "adaptationism", which I describe later. But the upshot of them is that human cognitive abilities evolved to deal with certain *kinds* of problems, so we should have evolved cognitive modules of correspondingly constrained capabilities.

This neo-Darwinist underpinning of modular models (sometimes called Psycho-Darwinism) has been expressed in a number of recent collections (e.g. Hirschfeld & Gelman, 1994). Cosmides and Tooby (1994, p.86) state that: "Natural selection operates through the testing of alternative designs through repeated encounters with evolutionarily recurrent situations" and that (p.96):

> Natural selection shapes domain-specific mechanisms so that their structure meshes with the evolutionarily-stable features of their particular problem-domains. Understanding the evolutionarily stable features of problem-domains — and what selection favoured as a solution under ancestral conditions — illuminates the design of cognitive specializations.

As Keil (1988, p.97), argues, such specific problems "have been of sufficient importance in evolution" to have led to "specific predispositions" for cognition to occur in specific ways. In a recent paper, Cosmides (1997) likens the mind to a Swiss army knife — a bundle of functionally specialised neural circuits for dealing with specific, recurring, cognitive problems.

Note how this position also constitutes an attack on the notion of "domain-general" thought processes, which a number of other models have proposed (see earlier, and also Chapters 3 & 4). As cognitive modules deal with specific kinds of problems with specific kinds of structures, they use "domain-specific" processes. Sperber (1994, p.46) asserts that:

> Therefore, from a modular point of view, it is unreasonable to ask what is the general form of human inference (logical rules, pragmatic schemas, mental models etc.), as is generally done in the literature on human reasoning.

Accordingly, Sperber continues (p.47): "We are now envisaging a complex network of conceptual modules: Some conceptual modules get all of their input from perceptual modules, other modules get at least some of their input from conceptual modules, and so forth."

Gardner (1984) has proposed a somewhat similar set of modules in his well-known theory of "multiple intelligences". Again, the basic presupposition here is the existence within the cognitive/neurobiological system of discrete information-processing operations or mechanisms that deal with the specific, but different, kinds of information that humans encounter in the course of their regular activities. As Gardner (1984, p.64) suggests:

> One might go so far as to define a human intelligence as a neural mechanism or computational system which is genetically programmed to be activated or "triggered" by certain kinds of internally or externally presented information. Examples would include sensitivity to pitch relations as one core of musical intelligence, or the ability to imitate movement by others as one core of bodily intelligence.

Among these different modules Gardner includes: linguistic intelligence; musical intelligence; logico-mathematical intelligence; spatial intelligence; bodily kinaesthetic intelligence; and personal intelligence (access to personal feelings; relations with others, and so on). As just mentioned, their operations are conceived to be essentially genetically constituted, although subject to some developmental flexibility (and thus amenable to cultural specialisation and to educational assistance). For example, with respect to object conceptions (Gardner, 1984, p.129), "... such knowledge has been internalised through evolution so that it is now 'pre-wired' in individuals and governs how they apprehend objects in space." As grounds for these conjectures, Gardner includes a wide range of considerations such as the organisation of the nervous system, the consequences of brain damage, the existence of individuals exceptional in a particular "intelligence", and many others.

Of course, the view lends itself to wide speculation about modular identities, and candidate modules become largely subjects of informal judgement. Thus Leslie (1994, quoted by Elman et al., 1997, p.125) proposes a slightly different range:

> To the extent that there are mechanisms of domain-specific development, then a deeper notion of domain is possible — one that is less software dependent, less profligate, and more revealing of the design of human cognition. This kind of domain-specificity reflects the specialisation of mechanisms in core cognitive architecture ...Vision is an obvious example of a specialised subsystem with a specialised internal structure. The language faculty is another [p.120] ... a mechanics module ... the infant's processing of the physical world appears to organize rapidly around a core structure representing the arrangement of cohesive, solid, three-dimensional objects, embedded in a system of mechanical relations, such as pushing, blocking and support.

Smart infants

One consequence of nativist theorising in recent research has consisted, not of describing developmental change "forward", with age — as developmentalists might be expected to do — but of "going back", to seek "earlier and earlier" cognitive competence in children: ideally, what cognitive abilities humans have *at birth*. This search has itself been inspired by the emergence of two major methodological tools; "recovery from habituation" and "preferential looking" in infants. Infants, as young as a few hours or days in some studies, are sat down in a small room with blank walls and an image of an object is projected onto a screen in front of them (Fig. 1.6). They will tend to look for a

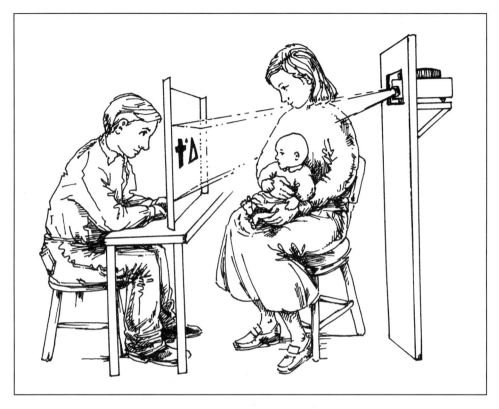

period, and then their attention appears to wane, so they look away —
they are said to have habituated to the stimulus. If the same stimulus
is switched off for a few seconds and then switched on again, further
looking is stimulated, but for progressively shorter times as the presentation is repeated. If, at some time following this experience, a *different*
image is projected, the infant will look for a period as long as they did
with the original — they are said to have dishabituated (Fig. 1.7).
Alternatively, infants may be presented with two or more pictures
simultaneously, and the time they spend looking at each one — i.e.
preferential looking — is measured.

Either separately or in combination, these simple techniques have
been said to afford investigators quite deep insights into the nature of
infant cognition. For example, Slater and Morison (1985) habituated
newborns to a single object presented with different degrees of tilt, and
then presented the same shape in a novel tilt, paired with a *new* shape.
The infants looked more at the new shape. This has been taken as good
evidence of "shape constancy" at birth — i.e. the rather complex ability

FIG. 1.6.
Laboratory set-up for
investigating
preferential looking or
habituation and
dishabituation in
young infants.

FIG. 1.7.

Typical "recovery from
habituation" curve in
studies of infant
cognition
(data from various
sources).

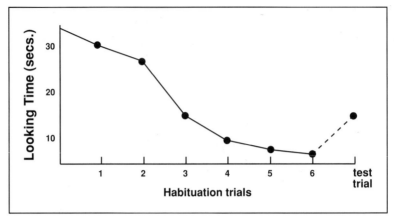

to maintain a conception of an object as the same object despite transformations of its retinal image. The same techniques also suggested
"size constancy" at birth — i.e. the ability to maintain a conception of
constant size of an object over changes in its distance from the viewer
(and again changes in the retinal image; Slater, Morison, Town, & Rose,
1985).

The technique has also been employed in studies at the conceptual
level. For example, Antell and Keating (1983) habituated one-week-old
infants to displays of three dots, and then found that the infants readily
dishabituated to displays of two dots. This has been taken to suggest
that a primitive concept of number may be innate (see also Wynn, 1992).
Another classic study is that conducted by Kellman and Spelke (1983),
using a display like that in Fig. 1.8, in which 4-month-old infants were
habituated to a rod moving back and forth behind a block occluder.
Following habituation to this arrangement, they were exposed, in turn,
to the two stimuli shown at the bottom of Fig. 1.8. The question was
whether they would dishabituate more to the one on the left or to the
one on the right. The latter, in fact, appeared to be preferred, even
though the image is much closer to the original than the one on the left.
In order to *be* preferred, so the argument goes (1983, p.483), the infants
must have been "seeing" much more than just the *image* in the original;
they must have been inferring a whole rod — and this depends on them
having "an inherent conception of what an object is."

Baillargeon and colleagues (e.g. Baillargeon, 1987; Baillargeon,
Spelke, & Wasserman, 1985) have examined infants' reactions to
surprising or impossible objects or events, in what is sometimes called
a "violation of expectation" paradigm. Such reactions are taken to
indicate whether infants possess the kinds of constraints that adults

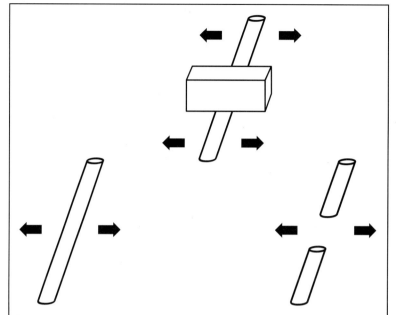

FIG. 1.8.
Test of infants'
knowledge of objects
and object relations
(adapted from
Kellman and Spelke,
1983).

have in *their* conceptions of objects and events. For example, a screen falling over backwards, through 180°, on a table would present a series of images that would be natural and unsurprising to an adult. But exactly the same full sequence occurring when a box was clearly visible behind the screen (as if the screen moved straight through the box) would be very *unnatural* and *surprising*.

In Baillargeon's studies, infants of 4.5 months were first habituated to the "natural" screen (Fig. 1.9) and then were tested with each of two alternatives after a box had been clearly placed in the trajectory of motion. In the first alternative, the screen stopped in its tracks, as adults would expect it to, on contact with box. In the second alternative, the screen apparently passed straight through the box (the experimenter having covertly moved it). Looking times were then compared: the infants spent longer looking at the familiar but inconsistent motion than at the novel but consistent motion, as if the former was more "surprising". This was taken as evidence that the infants had a clear representation of the continued existence of the box and of the relationship between it and the screen.

Again using the violation of expectation paradigm, Baillargeon and Graber (1987) habituated 5-month-old infants to the kind of events shown in the top half of Fig. 1.10: a short and then a tall rabbit passing

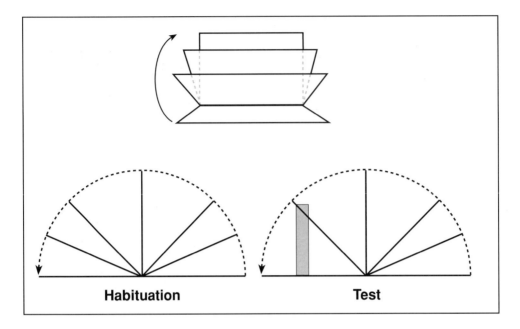

FIG. 1.9. Baillargeon's test of infants' knowledge of objects and object relations. Top: how the screen might appear to the infants in habituation trials. Bottom: the habituation (left) and "test" stimuli showing the "obstructing" object in place behind the screen (right).

behind a screen before re-emerging on the other side. In the test phase a window was cut in the screen, low enough for the short rabbit to *remain* unseen during this passage, but not for the tall rabbit. The rabbits were duly passed behind the screen, such that *neither* of them appeared in the window, before re-emerging on the other side. The infants looked more at the "impossible" event (the non-appearance of the tall rabbit in the window) than the other.

A wide range of other experimental situations have been devised (some rather complex), all producing similar results (Baillargeon, 1994). As Baillargeon (1994, p.31) concludes, the set of results "grants far more physical knowledge to infants than was previously done", and infants' interpretation of physical events involves "a conceptual analysis similar to that engaged in by older children and adults." Thus has emerged what in recent years has come to be called the "smart infant" thesis — that infants know far more, and are cognitively far more advanced, than was previously dreamt of.

On the basis of such data, Spelke (1994) and her colleagues have been among the advocates of a relatively "strong" nativism in cognitive development. Spelke (1994, pp.431&439) states:

> Although debates continue, studies of cognition in infancy
> suggests that knowledge begins to emerge early in life and

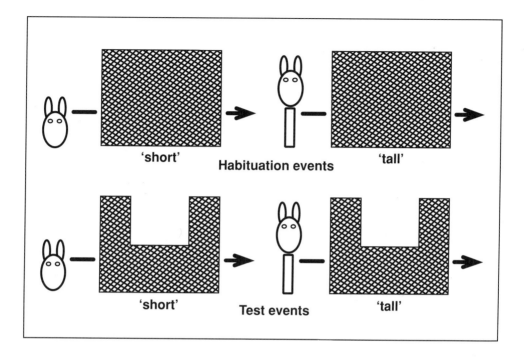

'short' **Habituation events** 'tall'

'short' **Test events** 'tall'

constitutes a part of humans' innate endowment ... Innate knowledge may emerge through maturation or be triggered by experience, but learning and processing do not appear to shape it.

FIG. 1.10. Adapted from the events in the Baillargeon and Graber (1987) studies.

Thus, in the context of knowledge and reasoning about objects, for example, infants are said (Spelke, Brienlinger, Macombre, & Jacobson, 1992, p.60) to be born with four constraints:

continuity (objects move only on connected paths; they do not jump from one place and time to another); *solidity* (objects move only on unobstructed paths; no parts of two distinct objects coincide in space and time); *gravity* (objects move downward in the absence of support); and *inertia* (objects do not change their motion abruptly and sponta-neously) (emphases in original.)

Objects or events are "surprising" to the extent that they violate these principles, and this, Spelke et al. claim, is what the research has shown.

In a recent summary, Spelke (1994, p.433) argues that "young infants appear to have systematic knowledge in four domains: physics, psychology, number, and geometry." Or, as Mehler and Dupoux (1994, p.98) put it, "From space to objects...the baby seems to come equipped with a rich model of the world" which is "the cognitive expression of the genetic heritage proper to the human species." As mentioned earlier, a simple biological rationale for this nativist view exists (Spelke, 1994, p.438): "If the constraints are highly reliable ... then natural selection may have favoured the evolution of mechanisms that give rise to this knowledge."

By using similar methods, various other innate abilities or inherent conceptions of young infants have been said to be revealed. Infants appear to have a preference for speech sounds over other acoustic stimuli (Mehler & Dupoux, 1994). Human infants, it is claimed, are born with certain social predispositions or with "innate interpersonal abilities" (Trevarthen, 1979b); "humans are provided with an innate mechanism for social learning" (Meltzoff & Gopnik, 1993, p.352; see also Chapter 4).

More recently, this idea has been expanded to include the innate cognitive structures that infants require to "know" that other humans also have minds, and the "intentionality" that goes with this. Infants are born, it is said (e.g. Wellman, 1990) with an innate "theory-of-mind." According to Hobson (1993, p.121) the infant can perceive the "outer-directedness" of people's attitudes because "there are 'hard-wired' mechanisms that guarantee this ability." Leslie (1992, p.20, quoted by Elman et al.) argues that "the normal and rapid development of theory-of-mind knowledge depends on a specialised mechanism that allows the brain to attend to invisible mental states ... The mechanism is initially innate and in some sense, a specific part of the brain."

As mentioned earlier, face processing has suggested another candidate module. As with a number of other recent models, much of its inspiration comes from studies in infancy, suggesting that infants are either born with special processing capabilities, or with an enhanced facility for handling "face" data. For example, neonates appear to prefer looking at schematic faces, rather than other patterns of similar complexity, or inverted schematic faces. And they seem to develop face representations extremely rapidly, being able to distinguish their mother's face from that of a stranger quite early after birth. So Carey (1994, p.95) argues that "Evolution has provided the baby a running start in face recognition." Johnson and Morton (1991) have suggested that infants are born with an innate face perception mechanism — a special predisposition (not a general ability applied to the specially complex stimuli of faces) to attend to faces, and so facilitate further learning about them (on the basis of a more general learning ability that subsequently develops). The result (1991, p.23) is that "our ability to process information about faces is greater than that for any other class of visual stimuli."

One of the most intriguing and controversial cases has been that of imitation in infancy. Piaget (e.g. 1972) reported imitation of hand movements in 8-month-old infants. However, imitation of facial gestures did not (he claimed) appear until around 12 months, because it requires the more complex process of matching what can be seen (other's face) with what cannot be seen (own face). This requires a much more complex system of coordination between visually perceived variables (the other's facial gestures) with kinaesthetic/motor ones (the infant's own facial movements). However, in a number of studies, Meltzoff and Moore (e.g. 1992) have claimed that imitation of mother's tongue-protrusion, mouth opening, and lip-protrusion occurs in infants only hours (or even minutes) after birth! They suggest (1992, p.482) that this is an "innate capacity", and functions as a means of enhancing knowledge of others by re-enacting their actions, and as a means of social communication. Connecting this evidence with face perception, Slater and Butterworth (1997, p.232) argue that, "the finding that infants imitate facial gestures from birth provides the clearest evidence that they come into the world with a rudimentary knowledge about the face."

A similar suggestion is made about sensitivity to certain sorts of dynamic structure or movement. For example, it was shown long ago that people can identify "a person walking" from a display in which reflective material has been attached to the main joints of a real person walking in side view and filmed with a light shining on them. The resultant display of 11 light points is then shown to people, who very quickly identify it (Johansson,1985; Richardson & Webster, 1996a). A study by Bertenthal, Proffitt, and Cutting (1984) suggested that infants showed preferential looking at such a stimulus compared with a display of the same number of lights moving randomly. Oates (1994, p.113) suggests that "This reinforces the notion that infants are specially attuned to the perception of events in the world that have particular sorts of dynamic qualities."

In sum, a wave of such studies, data, and their interpretations have led, over the last decade or so, to renewed convictions about the gene-based cognitive preparedness of infants. The fact that even young infants *appear* to have such well-formed abilities has been very influential, radically switching theoretical perspectives about cognition and its development. Karmiloff-Smith (1992, 1993) suggests it has been quite decisive (1993, p.595, italics in original): "The neonate and infancy data that are now accumulating serve to suggest that the nativists have won the battle in accounting for the *initial structure* of the human mind."

Hard and soft nativism

Note that, as already mentioned, there is a tension in this contemporary nativism about the degree and / or nature of preformationism involved. Whereas some, like Spelke, appear to believe in hard-wired knowledge, others may refer to genetic "constraints" which *facilitate* the development of knowledge along certain lines with certain predisposed forms. As mentioned earlier, Keil (1988, p.92) envisages a "conceptual core or core competency that is defined by sets of rigorous constraints and which is supplemented by a periphery that is governed much more loosely". Geary (1995, p.27) suggests that "knowledge or skeletal principles of the domain ... appear to orient the child to relevant features of the environment and guide the processing of those features." These skeletal principles are then fleshed out in the course of subsequent experience. Keil (1990) has made this distinction in the kind of diagram shown in Fig. 1.11. With reference to brain structures, Elman et al. (1997, p.30) argue that:

> In this form of nativism, knowledge is not innate, but the overall structure of the network ... constrains or determines the kinds of information that can be received, and hence the kinds of problems that can be solved, and *the kinds of representations that can subsequently be stored.* (Emphasis added.)

Accordingly, Elman et al. (1997) argue *against* modularity as something pre-wired. Rather, modularity arises as a product of development itself, under the "guidance" of genetically-specified constraints. According to Karmiloff-Smith (1994, p.699), "The skeleton outline involves attention biases toward particular inputs and a certain number of predispositions constraining the computation of those inputs." Karmiloff-Smith (1993, p.595) also argues that the human cognitive apparatus has "some innately specified information that allows it to attend to persons, space, cause and effect relations, number, language, and so forth"; and suggests that humans have "a number of innately-specified processes which enable self-description and self-organization", together with "mechanisms for inferential processes, for deductive reasoning and for hypothesis testing".

The bedrock of this position is the infancy data, as mentioned earlier. But Karmiloff-Smith also claims that there are other (innately constrained) processes that "redescribe" the representations that humans initially create, making them more explicit. Through this process, four levels of representation emerge in the course of development. For example, the first level consists of information "encoded in procedural form", sequentially specified, and stored independently, with no links with representations of other domains. These become redescribed and re-represented by "system internal dynamics", into progressively more abstract and "explicit" forms, under conscious awareness, and capable of verbal report.

Karmiloff-Smith appeals to data from several areas of cognition as evidence in support of her claims. Take, for example, the area of graphic representation or drawing. Children between 4½ and 10 years of age were asked to make drawings of a house, and then drawings of a

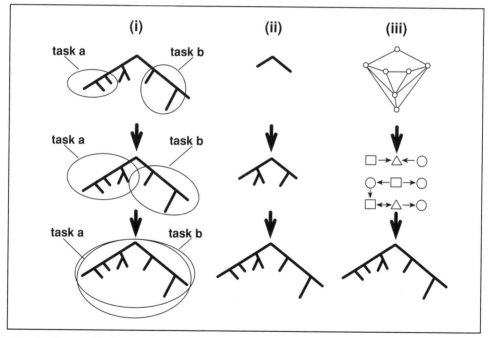

FIG. 1.11. Some models of cognitive development (following an idea in Keil, 1990).
(i) Fully prestructured knowledge/cognition, development consisting only of increased access over time to corresponding task structures (task a and task b).
(ii) Early constraints permit freer development, but only along certain lines.
(iii) Early structures undergo periodic transformation/reorganisation (this is a constructivist view, which will be discussed in Chapter 3).

house (or man) "that doesn't exist". A few of the young children simply drew a stereotyped house. Slightly older children showed a little more flexibility in that they drew the objects with some changes in size or shape or in deletion of elements. The older subjects, though, showed much more flexibility, inserting new elements (sometimes from a different category), or changing the position or orientation of elements, and overcoming the sequential constraints apparent in the younger children, in the process. Karmiloff-Smith suggests (1993, p.611) that this indicates redescription of representations: the very young seemingly tied to a sequential "house drawing" procedure "which runs off more or less automatically"; the older ones seemingly able to interrupt the sequence with more flexible permutation and alteration of components. Karmiloff-Smith argues that the various innate constraints are necessary for the early potentiation of such learning.

Practical applications

The metaphors of growth, of what is "already there", or of innate guidelines or constraints, import into modern scientific psychology what have been common assumptions in philosophical and informal psychology for a very long time. This is most clearly seen in their manifestations in theories of education. It has long been part of the Socratic and Platonic legacy that the knowledge be "brought out", and the mind strengthened, through critical analysis and dialogue, as in the rigours of Latin, still in widespread use in the 19th-century academies and universities.

In keeping with the analogy with physical growth, more recent educationists have urged us to respect a "natural" maturation of innate abilities promoted by suitable action or exercise. Froebel, for instance, (Smith, 1979, p.165):

> agreed with Pestalozzi that children are born in possession of specific mental faculties, but he asserted that growth, power and self-fulfillment develop from the child's inner impulses, through spontaneous activities ... As plants grow from within, aided by nature, so the child will unfold and grow if aided by parents and teachers to express his instincts and utilise his native powers.

Maria Montessori similarly believed that education should be such as to permit "a development of individual, spontaneous manifestations of the child's nature" (quoted by Isaacs, 1966, p.156)

Likewise, in more recent versions, a role for development as such is limited. Fodor (1983) even suggests that development from one state to another of greater complexity, is impossible — all is there already in the blueprint for the modules (Fodor, 1985, p.35): "Deep down, I'm inclined to doubt that there is such a thing as cognitive development in the sense that developmental cognitive psychologists have in mind." The environment of experience has merely a triggering and fine-tuning role, as already mentioned.

Those whose nativism is based on constraints rather than detailed structures do allow a greater role for experience in development (Karmiloff-Smith, 1994, p.706): "development goes far beyond the triggered unfolding of a genetic program." But this is always within the general form determined by those constraints. As a result, development is seen as largely automatic, and so long as adults offer a basic range of experience and opportunities for exercise, there is little to be done in terms of intervention.

Nativist models tend to be disappointing, therefore, with regard to opportunities for intervention to promote development. To Scarr (1992, p.16) the message of a nativist model is that:

> it is not easy to intervene deliberately in children's lives to change their development, unless their environments are outside the normal species range ... for children whose development is on a predictable but undesirable trajectory and whose parents are supporting a supportive environment, interventions have only temporary and limited effects.

Finally, it is worth noting how information-theoretic models have inspired a search for basic mechanisms that can be diagnostically isolated in order to explain children's developmental defects. The putative "defective" component is identified through specific tests (e.g. sensory or memory or comprehension tests) and possible remedies then considered. For example, deficiencies in specific information-processing components have been invoked to account for the reading deficiency of dyslexia, or of specific computational difficulties in dyscalculia (Murray, 1996).

Criticisms of nativist models

Nativism is the oldest and most durable form of attempt to account for the way that our cognitive abilities come into being. The fundamental assumption of the account is that there is "knowledge" (and with it, cognitive processes) preformed in some way, by some potent agent initially outside the cognitive system, and thus dictating, guiding, or constraining the course of development within it — "a ready made faculty for knowing", as Piaget (1977) put it. Since the Ancient Greeks, the source of this knowledge has switched from preformed knowledge deposited by God, to predetermining forces in "germ plasm" and the modern conception of the gene.

My hope is that you will now be able to recognise nativism when you see it. However, I have been at pains to point out that there have been strong and weak forms of nativism, and not simply "pure" nativist models conjectured by "pure" nativist authors. This has meant distinguishing models in which the fundamental structure of knowledge and/or cognitive processes are predetermined in genes, from those that indicate constraints together with a structuring role for other developmental processes (which I move on to in the chapters that follow).

In this section I want simply to raise awareness of the most prominent criticisms of nativism in cognitive developmental models. There are certain to be many more, and students and other readers are encouraged to find them. In addition, however, because recent nativism has derived much strength and support from Darwinian evolutionary theory, I want to extend the section a little by considering these, and some theoretical difficulties with it. I hope this, too, will help generate further criticism.

Theoretical vagueness

Without doubt the main problem with nativist models has been their common theoretical vagueness. In scientific models we need to see explicit components and variables, with explicit — ideally quantified — relations between them. But nativist models tend to be based on hunches or *metaphors* of formative forces, rather than substantive identifiable structures, variables, and relations. In consequence we are rarely provided with details about how they actually work in development. As Johnston (1994, p.721) points out:

> ... nativist accounts are usually silent on the question of how ... [innate] elements come into being. The strategy has been criticised by several generations of developmental theorists ... on the grounds that invoking the concept of innateness amounts to abdicating responsibility for explaining development.

And as Cain (1992, p.76) notes with reference to Gesell's maturationism, "The precise mechanism by which genes work, in Gesell's day as today, is still mysterious."

The *contents* of what is innate, and what develops, thus remain shrouded in mystery. Rather we are expected to put our faith in implicit, unidentified, formative agents (such as genetic codes or genetic constraints) which are only described intuitively. For example, innate "constraints", "attentional biases", "potentials", "predispositions" and "rules" are commonly envisaged (see contributions in Carey & Gelman, 1991, and in Hirschfeld & Gelman, 1994), without specification of what these are. Sperber (1994, p.51) says that "All that the internal structure provides is...a mode of construal, a disposition to organise information in a certain manner and to perform computations of a certain form." Karmiloff-Smith (1992, p.595) posits innately specified information that allows the infant to "attend to persons, space, cause-and-effect relations, number, language, and so forth", together with innately specified processes and mechanisms that "enable self-description and self-organization" and "inferential processes, for deductive reasoning and for hypothesis testing."

But what *is* the innately specified information? What are the innately specified processes (in terms other than metaphoric)? Terms like "construal", "organise", "disposition", "computation", "information", "enable", "mechanisms", and so on, are all mere metaphors devoid of explicit substantiation, as is the term "innate" itself. As descriptors of a system, of how it works and develops, they are singularly unhelpful. They could be applied to any system of the human body. Yet I suggest that we would be very unhappy if, after decades of research, digestion in the gut or excretion in the kidney came to be described in such ways by physiologists or medical practitioners.

This problem is not overcome by the common descriptive tool frequently used by cognitive nativists, namely the flow-chart of information passing from module to module, or, more recently, "architectures", which are assumed to do the essential work by virtue of simply being part of our genetic endowment. As Dennett (1978, p.123) complained, "each box specifies a function without saying how it is to be accomplished (one says, in effect: put a little man in there to do the job)." In whatever area of cognitive development (concepts, face processing, reasoning, etc. etc.) it is not enough that psychologists "explain" it by telling us that it is a biological "given".

As described earlier, some theorists have proposed a weaker form of nativism, arguing in favour of early genetic constraints, and subsequent "epigenetic" cognitive development within those constraints.

Again, though, such proposals appear to be based on rather loose metaphoric reasoning. For example, Keil (1988, p.92) argues that "... dramatic shifts can occur in the periphery provided they honour the general boundaries of the skeleton. Because the core is only a skeletal framework, it does not completely constrain the structures within it ...". But real life structures, anatomies, and architectures that are associated with an underlying skeleton remain closely tied to and determined by it. Dramatic changes in animal anatomies do not occur without changes in the skeleton; and we can hardly argue that dramatic changes in the shape of a building, say, can change without a change in its foundations. Yet such dramatic changeability is precisely what most characterises human cognition.

Part of the problem in debates may have been the haste, or even tendentiousness, with which theorists seem to have adopted nativist interpretations of data. Take, for example, the Karmiloff-Smith "drawing" data described earlier, in which older children displayed greater flexibility of use of representational resources. In the first place this is very indirect and non-compelling evidence for innate constraints: developmental progression in all domains (e.g. computer programming and use) may well go through such a sequence, but it would be difficult to argue that this was due to constraints put there by evolutionary selection. There may be perfectly plausible non-nativist explanations for this kind of development. Indeed, in studies on children's strategy choice in problem-solving tasks, Siegler and Crowley (1994, p.223) show how apparent "constraints" can be conceptual rather than innate:

> The key factor determining the degree of constraint appears to be the degree to which understanding of goals and causal relations is veridical and available, rather than whether the domain is evolutionarily important, the age at which learning occurs, or whether understanding is produced by domain-specific or general learning mechanisms.

In other words, rationalist theorists are extremely vague about the nature of innate form, or genetic constraints. They seem to be accepted largely on negative grounds: i.e. because they appear to be rendered logically necessary by the argument from the poverty of the stimulus, or the absence of — or reluctance to look seriously for — alternative accounts. The main current exception to this, the early infancy data, is an area I turn to later. Many authors have, indeed, suggested that nativist arguments stem from inadequate investigation, and that the claim for innate knowledge "is shorthand for an unexplained developmental process" (Thelen & Smith, 1994, p.34). Theorists proposing alternative models (see Chapters 2–5) argue that nativist psychologists have simply underestimated the rich structure of human experience and action, or of the developmental system itself, because they have rarely tried to describe it. I hope you will be in a better position to judge this for yourself after reading those chapters.

Spelke et al. (1992, p.629) are quite candid about the dilemmas created by a nativist model:

> It rejects several classes of explanation for the foundations of cognition, but it offers no explanation in their place. The apparent emptiness and arbitrariness of nativist proposals in psychology are characteristic, and they lead characteristically to discontent ... If cognition is part of humans' psychological beginnings ... psychologists cannot contribute to the explanation of its origins. That explanatory task falls entirely to other disciplines.

But Thelen and Smith (1994, p.33) complain about the dualism inherent in such attributions:

> We believe that developmental psychology is in grave danger if it gives itself the right to say "innate" whenever there is as yet no developmental theory and then frees itself from saying what innate "means" by saying that solving that problem is someone else's job.

Theoretical fragmentation

One consequence of theoretical vagueness is theoretical fragmentation — the lack of shared conceptions of the constituents of cognition and processes of development. In a general context this has been noted by numerous authors. Scholnick (1994, p.728), for example, complains that "The current cognitive map consists of fractionated territories, each inhabited by processors who use specialized and untranslatable languages"; Beilin (1987, p.37) of "... a bewildering variety of developmental theories" with ... "the sound of the Tower of Babel"; and Hirst and Manier (1995, p.89) of a "stuffy windowless room, shut off from the 'real world'."

The extreme idiosyncrasy of models is seen especially in the information processing approach to development. As Thelen and Smith

(1994, p.38) point out, the proliferation of highly specialised models seems to have reached an impasse:

> The processes and mechanisms postulated in models are closely linked to the experimental paradigm they seek to explain. The literature is thus replete with seemingly unrelated models; models of analogy ... contain no overlapping mechanisms with models of naive physics ... which in turn contain no overlapping mechanisms with models of perceptual classification.

Early competency and infancy data

Many contemporary convictions that there is "something there", predetermining the form of knowledge and cognition, stem from studies suggesting early competency in infancy. Karmiloff-Smith (1992, 1993) describes how such studies have "won the battle" in accounting for the initial structures of the mind. Although many if not most theorists have found the infancy data compelling, the data are not immune to criticism, either in terms of their empirical sufficiency, or in terms of how they are collected and interpreted.

I cannot engage in a detailed critique of all studies here, although it is true that results have often been replicated and may well point to something very interesting. On the other hand, investigators admit that the procedures of data collection are extremely difficult, and in a typical investigation 50% or more of infants will have to be rejected for "fussing". Cohen (1991, p.1) admits to never having "had the courage to run a full-blown experiment with human new borns." As Seigal (1997) notes, habituation techniques are not perfect measures of cognition in infancy, and interpretation of them is far from unambiguous: even if infants *do* look at one display longer than another, this does not necessarily mean they are doing so because they "prefer" it or are "surprised" for the same reasons that adults might be. Spelke et al. (1992, p.627) suggest that, given their visual and perceptual immaturity, "It may not be possible to investigate knowledge of physical objects in newborn infants." The visual acuity of newborns is, indeed, quite poor ("about 30 times poorer than the adult", according to Slater, 1989, p.44); much development takes place between birth and four months; and no-one really knows *what* newborns are looking at or preferring in such studies.

It may be that what infants are preferring in their preferred looking are hitherto unrecognised *perceptual* differences arising from stimuli. In criticising the leap into nativist speculation, Bickhard (1997, p.240) notes how, "*Perceptual* alternative hypotheses to the favoured *cognitive* interpretations of results have frequently not been considered and control conditions for them not used" (emphases in original). Elsewhere I have argued (Richardson, 1992; Richardson & Webster, 1996a; see Chapter 5) that what a cognitive system particularly needs to be sensitive to, in order to be maximally adaptable, is the nested covariation structures with which the world of objects and events is replete. If this is the case, then what infants need to be born with is not preformed cognitive structures, but acute sensitivity to in-depth covariations in the environments they actually experience. The kinds of stimuli that infants appear to prefer — faces and other social events; speech sounds compared with other sounds; the "broken" as opposed to the continuous stick in Fig. 1.9 — all exhibit such complex covariation structures. The danger is, of course, that the flight into innate structures may lead us to neglect the possibility of alternative, *developmental*, stories.

As Bremner (1997) points out, it is one thing to show that infants are responding *as if* they have prestructured knowledge and cognition, but quite another to prove that they *actually* have it. Most of the infancy work has been based on looking time, and we have no exact way of demonstrating that this is directly related to the variable in question — for example, that infants who prefer to look at a novel shape, compared with an old one, do so *because of* an innate concept of shape constancy. Munakata, McClelland, Johnson, and Siegler (1997, p.687) make similar points. After reminding us of the variability and "task-specific" nature of results, they point to the dangerous tendency of accepting a description of behaviour as one of the mental system used in its production. They stress the need to move from such "shorthand descriptions" to an understanding of actual processing mechanisms, and propose an alternative, representational, view of increased looking time at unexpected events.

Basically, this consists of two levels of representation (Fig. 1.12). Sensory inputs create one kind of representation of spatial relations in the world. Over repeated experience these contribute to a higher level of representation about relations between objects. The latter may or may not be present in any *current* input, but the representation permits predictions or expectations about them, a property that only requires that measure of activation about objects be maintained after they have disappeared. A discrepancy between such predictions and actual events in the current array triggers an increase in looking time.

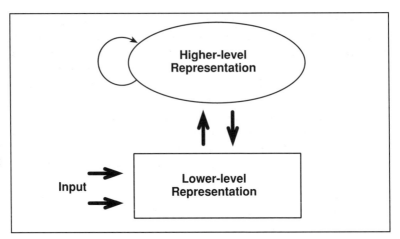

FIG. 1.12. Adapted from Munakata et al.'s (1987) model of representational discrepancy (which they call an "adaptive process" model) to explain looking-time results in infant experiments.

In fact, in most studies, differences in the major dependent variables of looking time or preferential looking across contrast groups or treatments tend to be probabilistic and marginal, rather than categorical. For example, mean looking time for the preferred stimulus is often only around 10–20% greater than that for the comparison stimulus. The same point applies to the imitation data, which indicates that many subjects did not show a preference at all (or did not imitate). It seems reasonable to ask why, if the ability is supposed to be "innate" and therefore universal, many infants do not demonstrate it. Of course it can always be argued that it is due to constraints of experimental design, including fatigue or distractability of infants. But this is only to admit that, in spite of efforts to control for known variables, many imponderable ones remain.

Bremner (1997) also argues that although the infancy data suggest that infants may be sensitive to differences in stimuli, this may not amount to knowledge in the real sense — in the sense of knowledge for guiding action in the world. Thelen and Smith (1994, p.234) have proposed a "dynamic systems" interpretation of typical infancy data – ones which, they claim, will "take the 'magic' out of demonstrations of infant competence and begin to make scientific sense of the truly amazing things that are infants' and adults' minds".

I turn to dynamic systems theories in Chapter 5, but basically, Thelen and Smith argue that what is present at birth is a composite of a developing system and a structured environment. Infants may be simply responding to complex correlations that vary across stimuli, rather than cues that trigger innate knowledge or constraints. In the case of "innate" shape constancy, for example, it may be argued that what an infant is habituating to in successive experiences of an object under spatial transformation is its characteristic covariation structure, as between corners, edges, and surfaces. Any successive experience that pairs a new view of the same object with a view of a different object will present covariations, rather than a specific configuration, that match the set habituated to. So it is hardly surprising that infants prefer to look at the new one. But this is due to an *induced* covariation structure, not innate shape constancy. Certainly, more recent studies have shown the importance of *perceptual* similarity and variation for the formation of concepts in infants (Jones & Smith, 1993; Oakes, Coppage, & Dingel, 1997).

These are all problems of interpretation. But there also appear to be substantial methodological problems. In the preferential-looking paradigm, Mix, Levine, and Huttenlocher (1997) have shown how the apparent "concept of number" in young infants can be explained away when elementary (but previously unrealised) controls are added to the design and procedure. In the "violation of expectation" paradigm, based on looking time, Bogartz, Shinskey, & Speaker (1997, p.420) have pointed to lack of certain controls in the procedures. When these are introduced, results are readily interpreted in terms of simple perceptual distinctions, rather than innate knowledge:

> In considering one study after another purporting to demonstrate young infant knowledge ... we have found repeatedly that the same simple ideas of motion capturing attention, tracking and scanning of objects, and longer looking to displays dependent on their relationships to previous displays, has had great explanatory value in providing an alternative interpretation.

In a review of all the imitation studies up to 1989, Poulson, Nunes, and Warren (1989, p.292) stated that:

> Meltzoff & Moore's ... thesis that neonates exhibit complex cognitive processes that enable them to imitate visible and non-visible actions is seriously jeopardised by the methodological flaws of their studies, by the difficulty in ruling out rival hypotheses, and by failings to replicate consistently their findings.

Anisfeld (1996) pointed out that in studies following the work of Meltzoff and Moore (1977) there had been 28 positive findings and 48 negative findings. Anisfeld (1996, p.149) has analysed the infant imitation studies more recently, and generated similar scepticism:

> a critical examination of nine studies...demonstrates that the claims of early imitative abilities are not well founded...a close examination of these studies suggests that in contrast to the TP [tongue protrusion] effect, which was clear and consistent, the MO [mouth opening] and HM [head movement] effects were weak and inconsistent and in some cases derived from the TP effect. Because the matching behavior found is restricted to a single gesture, it is best explained as a specific, directly elicited response, rather than imitation.

Finally, it is worth drawing attention to the seeming self-contradictions that emerge in the nativist literature. Although "babies are born with determining biases", yet "human knowledge is acquired through construction and reconstruction in forms that still have bewildering variety" (Kessen & Resnick, 1992, p.111). Also, although we are told (Elman et al., 1997, p.354) that cognition and its development is "self-organising", in which "(t)here is no need for genes to encode and control these interactions directly", yet we are told, by the very same authors, that "The gene is like the conductor leading an orchestra" and that (p.321), "the role of the genetic component — call it the innate component if you like — is to orchestrate these interactions in such a way as to achieve the desired outcome." In other words it seems as if theorists have great difficulty in relinquishing the idea of some ultimate "controller" even when they want to (see also Oyama's, 1985, critique).

The computational metaphor

As mentioned earlier, one of the aims of the information-processing approach has been to model learning and reasoning in ways that can be implemented in a computer. This has invariably entailed assumptions about "hardware" (read innate) processes and architecture. Although popular for a long period, there have been increasing worries about the appropriateness of the computer metaphor for cognitive development. Bates and Elman (1993, p.627) mention some of the important differences. First inputs to a computer are discrete, static and "clean", whereas real experience is often, if not usually, partial, fuzzy, and dynamic. Second, the rules that apply in computers are rigid and inflexible, whereas human thinking is creative and often "rule-forming". Third, "learning" in a computer is "programming", often consisting of wholesale intervention by the programmer, resulting in discrete jumps in performance which are unhuman-like. Finally, human reasoning is highly context-sensitive: for example, in letter and word recognition it is well known how the same input can be ascribed different symbolic identities, depending on its context (Fig. 1.13; Smyth, Collins, Morris, & Levy, 1994).

A major problem with the symbol-system view is that it does not indicate the origin of the symbols in human (as opposed to computer) experience. Envisaging symbols as input from a keyboard (e.g. features, or object names) is one thing; how they are derived in real minds from the degenerate data of real experience, is another. This is known as the "symbol-grounding" problem (e.g. Harnad, 1990), and it remains unresolved. Oakhill (1988, p.185) expresses doubts about the relevance of the information-processing approach for the understanding of development:

> ... the two fundamental questions in developmental psychology are about the psychological *states* that the child passes through, and the *mechanisms* by which development occurs. However, very little work has been done to address this second question, and it is likely that theoretical progress has been hindered by the lack of understanding of the mechanisms by which children's thinking develops.

Recent years, then, have witnessed a waning of confidence in the cognitive revolution of the 1970s and 80s. Chief among the doubts has been that it has merely substituted one set of metaphors with another, equally mechanistic, set: i.e. "natural mechanics" with "natural compu-

FIG. 1.13. Context-sensitivity of inputs is a problem for traditional symbolic models: the same input is ascribed different symbolic identity (top); "event" or "went" depending on the context (bottom) (adapted from Smyth et al., 1994).

tations". It has been suggested that the essential characteristics of "mind" seem to have been as much lost in the latter as in the former (Bruner 1990, 1992). This explains why a "second cognitive revolution" has been launched in recent years in order to attempt, once again, to rescue key ingredients of the mind like "meaning" and "intention" from the dust of raw mechanism (Harré & Gillett, 1994; cf. Brockmeier, 1996).

Developmental disappointment

In the strongest nativist models, the only or main changes in knowledge and cognition over time, within the individual, consist of growth or maturation, rather than development as such (the latter implying something that improves and progresses, usually by becoming more complex, over time). Even the weaker nativist models, however, imply some preformed structure, and thus some correspondence between initial structures or constraints and each stage of change (see Fig. 1.11). Many theorists, especially those who have observed (or think they have observed!) complex developmental changes in children's reasoning and knowledge, have railed against the absence of a developmental story in this scenario. They point out that the way in which knowledge and cognitive processes are actually supposed to emerge from "dumb", innate, computational processes is rarely specified in any detail.

Evolution and nativism

Because so much underpinning for current nativist psychology derives from neo-Darwinian theory of evolution, and its enshrinement in genes, I want to divert a little here to consider that argument, and suggest why it is suspect. Although the origins of whatever it is that is said to be innate have been switched from mystical (including deistic) forces to the gene, the conception of the gene entailed, even in modern nativist stories, may be far too idealistic.

In the standard picture, genes are codes for characters or "parts" of characters which are then "selected" by the kinds of environmental problems encountered, resulting in progressive "shaping" of the character and its successful "adaptation" to the problem. However, it is now well known that the contribution of genes in the development of evolutionary-important characters is very indirect, and depends on a range of other considerations. The first is that the only product of a gene is a protein, not a "character, or even "part" of a character. How this protein becomes involved in the "making" of knowledge and cognition can be modelled in various plausible ways — but the idea that genes can code *directly* for knowledge or cognitions, like a blueprint, program, or set of instructions, is not one of them (Richardson, 1998).

This applies even to weaker nativist models which propose genetic constraints, rather than well-formed innate knowledge (e.g. Elman et al., 1997). The simple fact is that prestructuring, even of this kind, which is still enshrined in genes, would only be adaptive to environmental problems that remained unchanged over many generations. Natural selection is a trans-generational regulation, and can only "shape" a character or constraints across generations if the target problem remains relatively unchanged. The problem is that most aspects of the environments of advanced organisms are *constantly* changing, either through the exertions of various natural forces, or through the actions of organisms themselves on the environment. This has been particularly the case with humans, who appear to have evolved in highly changeable, unpredictable circumstances, but have also added an even more complex changeability in the form of social cooperation.

The paradox is that development itself (as opposed to simple maturation of pre-formed structures) is an evolutionary solution to changeable environments. Instead of a simple "two-layer" expression of genes into pre-adapted characters, developmental regulations are found on at least four levels, increasingly remote from direct products of structural genes, depending on the speed and complexity of environmental change (Plotkin & Odling-Smee, 1979; Richardson 1998). Let us look at each of these in turn.

Genomic regulations

On the first level, where a crucially specific endpoint is desired (e.g. wings of specific size and structure in flies), but the egg and embryo have to withstand considerable environmental change and buffeting, this seems to have become more assured through the evolution of regulatory genes. These react to the products of the environment (temperature, availability of nutrients, physical shocks, etc.) to regulate the activities of the basic structural genes — sometimes, in effect, *changing* the latter's products and their incorporation into the emerging embryo. So important are these "genomic" regulations, even in the development of fruit flies, that up to 90% of genes, and 95% of DNA, may be regulatory in function (Lawrence, 1992).

Moreover, such is the nature of the regulations involved in the development of the crucial characters that no fundamental locus of control is evident; rather a dynamic, self-organising system appears to have evolved, using genes as *resources* for development, rather than being, as Elman et al. (1997, p.354) put it, "like the conductor leading an orchestra". Indeed, it is now clear that, at least for critical characters — and thanks to genomic regulations — variable genetic resources can be used to obtain required developmental endpoints. Whereas nativists speak of the genotype as constructing the structures of the mind and body, it is now becoming commonplace to speak of the the developing system as *constructing its own genotype*, as it activates or suppresses genes, and amends gene products, in the face of an environment constantly threatening to throw development off course (Oyama, 1985; Rollo, 1994).

Note that, in this organisation, the constraints in the structural genes laid down by natural selection have been "opened up" by these new regulations, so they form a more adaptable, and more durable, whole.

Epigenetic Regulations

Even this system of genomic regulations will be dysfunctional, however, if the environment changes in the generation time between parents and offspring, such that a formerly crucial developmental endpoint becomes redundant, and new challenges are presented. This would be like having a highly intricate production process for a jacket that is in fashion just before it is made, but is right *out* of fashion by the time production is complete.

In the living world, this problem has been overcome by developmental plasticity — or changing adaptively *in the course of development*. For example, certain snails (*Thais lamellosa*), which are predated on by crabs on certain sea-shores, gain protection by increasing the thickness of their shell. However, this step is inevitably energy-costly and material-costly, and would be wasted if the snails end up on a crab-free habitat, as is often the case. The problem is compounded by the fact that such invertebrates disperse their young very widely, and so cannot predict in advance where they will end up. The problem is solved by a developmental plasticity for thick shells or thin shells which, and in turn, appears to be triggered by the presence of some substance produced by crabs in the neighbourhood. According to Stearns (1989, p.442) "It makes sense to leave the choice of shell morphology, and with it an entire trajectory of growth and reproduction, until after the adult habitat has been reached."

Such *variable* epigenesis is well known, and this kind of plasticity is prominent in the development of nerve cell connections in the brain (for review see McGaugh, Bermudez-Rattoni, & Prado-Alcala, 1995). Note how such epigenesis "opens up" the genomic constraints (committed to a particular endpoint), making more variable outcomes possible.

Cognitive regulations

The problem with this kind of epigenesis, however, is that it results in a permanent structure at the end of development, so that it, too, is dysfunctional in situations in which radical environmental change may occur *throughout life*. Behaviour and its regulation (i.e. cognition) evolved precisely to deal with such problems. But we need to think carefully about what the problems entail. Nativists tend to see the environment as relatively structurally impoverished, and this biases their view of the role of cognition. But, *because it is rapidly changing,* the environment of advanced organisms can be structured in deep and complex ways.

A hypothetical example I have suggested elsewhere (Richardson, 1998) is that of a monkey that feeds on fruit in the upper canopy of a rain forest (having discovered a covariation between elevation and food abundance). The monkey also learns that nearer the forest margins the fruit lies lower down (a height/abundance covariation conditioned by location). But those marginal locations, at certain times of the year, are also more frequently scanned by monkey eagles (the conditioning itself conditioned by a correlation between predator presence and season). This whole covariation structure — which makes the environment predictable through its "deep" contingencies — may change completely when the monkey troop moves to another forest because of fruit depletion (i.e. its own activity).

Clearly, in order to survive in situations like this, organisms need systems that can represent this kind of covariation structure — and *re*-represent it whenever it changes. This is what the cognitive system seems to be for. Learning, and the cognitive system required to regulate it, only evolved when the environmental structure that is a critical source of predictability changed significantly within the lifetime of an organism. Such life-long change cannot yield predictability via stable genomic regulations, nor even by epigenetic regulations that reach a fixed endpoint. Just as the evolution of epigenetic regulation "opened up" genomic regulations, so cognitive regulations have opened up epigenetic regulations to make them responsive to ever-changeable patterns of covariation complexity throughout the lifespan. This, of course, occurs chiefly in the cerebral/cognitive system, allowing plasticity in cortical connectivity *throughout the lifespan* (e.g. Weinberger, 1995).

In this need to cope with increased degrees and complexities of change *throughout life*, initial "constraints" could be a major handicap.

FIG. 1.14.
Nested regulatory
systems contributing
to cognitive
development. Note
how products at one
level become
resources for
development at the
next level (right-hand
arrows), under
regulation from that
level (left-hand
arrows).

The evolved regulations just mentioned seem to be systems for overcoming such constraints, and they have done this by nesting the old in the new, and turning them into "provisions" or "furnishings" rather than constraints. As Cairns (1990) explained, this puts development in relation to psychology where evolution is to biology.

Such "nested hierarchical" models of development (see Fig. 1.14) have become very popular in evolutionary biology in recent years (Depew & Weber, 1995; Rollo, 1994), and are drastically changing traditional views of genetic determination of characters. Later, in Chapter 5, I will put the view that this is not the end of such "liberation from constraints". In sociocognitive models these cognitive regulations have, in humans, been further nested in a new, social, level of regulation. Such models try to explain how social regulations vastly extend cognitive regulations; how humans "adapt" through cultural tools rather than physical organs; and thus how, by overcoming constraints "lower down" in the hierarchy of regulations, humans largely adapt the world to themselves rather than vice versa.

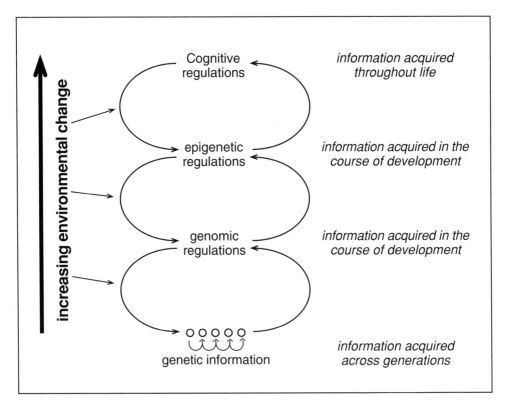

The upshot of these last few paragraphs, however, is that there is something paradoxical about an insistence on innate structures or constraints in the face of highly changeable environments, which require a far more flexible and creative kind of environment-management.

Associationist models 2

Introduction

A second major branch of developmental cognitive theory also has its roots in Ancient Greece, and is usually traced to Aristotle, who was Plato's student. Aristotle agreed with Plato and his followers that reliable knowledge consists of abstract ideas, but disagreed about the impossibility of these being derivable from sense experience. Aristotle was an acute and practised observer — as a naturalist who systematically catalogued the features of living things; as an embryologist who followed the development of chicks in their eggs; and as an anatomist who dissected human bodies. From these many activities Aristotle had acquired immense knowledge: different from sense experience in the sense of being universal or abstract, as the Platonists had insisted; but nonetheless derived from it. Far from being an illusion, not to be trusted, sense experience seemed to him to be the very meat of knowledge. In direct contradiction with his former master, Aristotle propounded a connection between facts and general principles.

This was not to say, however, that sense experience forms knowledge, as it were, "by itself". To construct this knowledge, Aristotle postulated a special faculty, the faculty of intellect or reason. Although the faculty is innate, the concepts themselves are not; they are abstracts from sense experience. Whereas Rationalists like Plato argued that innate knowledge is realised through rational thinking and discourse, Aristotle's version, based on induction of knowledge from sense experience, is often called Empiricism.

As for the mechanism and content of this induction, Aristotle introduced the notion of mental associations. This consists of the registration and storage in memory of associations (such as shared attributes, co-occurrences, and sequences of events) in the real world. These are the real sources of the Platonic concepts or universals, he argued. For example, as a result of repeated sense experience with dogs, the associated features of furriness, four legs, barking, and so on, become abstracted by the intellect and placed in the memory as the concept of

Dog. Associations can form between objects or events that commonly occur together, such as a horse and saddle, or in reliable sequences, such as the seasons. Similarly, long chains of associations are formed in memory, and we recall them by finding the beginning of such a sequence. The strength of such memories is increased by repetition (habit) and by association with pleasure and pain. Aristotle wrote at some length about the "laws" of association of this sort, most of which have been reiterated in theories of learning and behaviour in the 20th century.

Aristotle's theory of cognitive development was a much more *developmental* one than that of the Rationalists. As Robinson (1981, p.88) notes:

> Aristotle ... willing to accept the facts of everyday experience, advanced a dynamic theory of psychological development. As an associationist, he recognised the role of practice and rewards and punishments in learning and memory. As a social observer, he noticed differences among the young, the mature and the aged as regards emotion, reason, courage, loyalty, motivation.

The principles of associationism were, again, passed down the ages, becoming resurrected by the Empiricists/Associationists of the17th and 18th centuries such as John Locke and David Hume. These writers, however, accorded to associations a far more determining role in knowledge construction and reasoning than had Aristotle. Rather than being a *resource* for knowledge and reasoning, to those new philosopher-psychologists associations comprised the very substance of cognition, the structure of the mind itself Thus they attempted to show that even the most complex of concepts and thoughts "remain rooted in the soil of experience" (Robinson, 1981, p.218). Or, as Anderson and Bower (1973, p.16) put it, "The British empiricists extended the domain of associationism from Aristotle's original concern with human memory to encompass all mental phenomena."

Over the next 200 years, psychology became filled with various metaphors of mental associations. Locke likened them to "animal spirits" so that associations

> seem to be but trains of motion in the animal spirits, which, once set going, continue in the same steps they have been used to, which by often treading are worn into a smooth path, and the motion in it becomes easy and, as it were, natural. (Yolton, 1977, p.45).

Hartley used the metaphor of "vibrations" exciting each other. Hume discussed the nature of inner connections, and mentioned "traces" and "cells" which were "rummaged" by "spirits" (Laird, 1967, p40).

By the 19th century new metaphors could be borrowed from physics, chemistry, and biology. John Stuart Mill based associations on a "mental chemistry" in which "ideas fused into one." James Mill, and others of the Radical movement, took pleasure and pain as the twin activators determining exactly which associations should stick in the mind, and which should be ignored: "Nature has placed mankind under the governance of two sovereign masters, *pain* and *pleasure* ... They govern us in all we do, in all we say, in all we think" (Bentham, 1789/1966). Thus was born the doctrine of Utilitarianism.

In his round-up of psychology towards the end of the 19th century, William James (1890/1950, p.597) noted how, "These authors traced minutely the presence of association in all the cardinal notions and operations of the mind." Whereas the Rationalists had sought to describe various innate ideas and faculties, now "the several faculties of the mind were dispossessed; the one principle of association between ideas did all their work."

By the end of the 19th century, the discovery of the cellular constitution of the brain led to the notion of real connections or bonds between neurons as the basis of associations. James (1890, p.563) described the "Law of Association" as "an effect within the mind, of the physical fact that nerve-currents propagate themselves easiest through those tracts of conduction which have been already most in use"; and (p.566) "when two elementary brain processes have been active together or in immediate succession, one of them on recurring, tends to propagate its excitement into the other." Finally, Thorndike (e.g.1911) spoke of neurons firing and becoming connected as the basis of associations between stimuli and responses, and coined the term "connectionism".

In case you start to think that all this is a little remote from cognitive development, let me point out, before going any further, that all these theorists were very keen on the implications of their ideas for development, especially the rearing and education of children. Aristotle recognised the role of practice and of rewards and punishments in the learning and memorisation of rules or habits, and expressed these in several laws of association. Locke, too, saw mental development and the increasingly complex content of knowledge and reason, as the acquisition of associations, which subsequently would operate automatically. Training, practice and good "habits", rather than rule-learning, were necessary. Locke (quoted by Yolton, 1977, p.171) stated:

But pray remember, children are not to be taught by rules, which will always be slipping out of their memories. What you think necessary for them to do, settle in them by an indispensable practice, as often as the occasion returns ... This will beget habits in them, which, being once established, operate by themselves, easily and naturally.

Behaviourism

The new, hedonistic, associationism born of Utilitarianism — with rewards, pleasures, and pains, as the determinants of human behaviour, and thus of which associations are registered — was a significant departure from the past. It led, as Leahy (1987, p.43) puts it, to a

> completely mechanistic picture of the mind in which idea follows idea automatically with no room left for voluntary control. The exercise of will is an illusion ... Reasoning is no more than the associative compounding of the ideas contained in syllogisms. Attention ... is mechanically directed by the principle of utility.

After the turn of the 20th century, this movement led to a situation in which, as many commentators have pointed out, "psychology lost its mind". Utilitarianism, combined with an intense desire on the part of psychologists to advance their goals by emulating the physical sciences, shifted attention from the understanding of "inner" knowledge and mental functions as such, to the *control* of "outer" behaviour.

In behaviourism, as it came to be called, associations were used not to explain mental states but to explain "behaviour". It is no use looking for associations "in" the mind, the behaviourists argued, but *between* observable stimuli and responses. Taking the lead from the Utilitarians, S–R associations were deemed to be determined by the principles of pleasure and pain, now re-described as "reinforcers". And as, in the light of new evolutionary thinking, humans could no longer be thought of as *radically* different from other animals, the operation of these principles could be studied experimentally in animals such as the rat. Thus, in experiments on animals, it was soon being demonstrated, for example, that an S–R bond or connection is formed or eradicated by the "satisfaction" or "discomfort" that follows the behaviour which produced it: "The greater the satisfaction or discomfort, the greater the strengthening or weakening of the bond" (Thorndike, 1911, p.244).

Thorndike named this principle the "Law of Effect", and claimed it to be as applicable to human learning as to that of animals.

Learning and development thus became reduced to "conditioning" Two kinds of conditioning came to predominate. Classical conditioning stemmed from the work of Pavlov in Russia, and consisted of the "realignment", as it were, of reflexes such as salivation to food, from their inherent stimuli (the food) to new stimuli (such as a ringing bell). This was achieved over many trials in which the bell was presented in conjunction with the food, until the salivation became evoked by the bell itself.

The second, "operant conditioning", is most associated with B.F. Skinner, who carried its message right through to the 1980s (e.g. Skinner, 1985). In this kind of conditioning, previously non-specific or uncommitted behaviours (the "operants", such as an animal's press on a lever in a cage) become associated with particular stimuli (e.g. a red light, chosen by the "trainer') as a result of their consequences (e.g. food dropping into a tray). Training of rats to press levers (or children to read, for that matter) is thus best achieved, in this view, through the imposition of suitable "contingencies of reinforcement".

This brand of associationism came to dominate psychology between the wars. Under the broad umbrella of "learning theory", many models of knowledge acquisition and behaviour (if not explicitly cognition) emerged. With great pride in the use of "objective" experimental procedures, new "facts" and "laws" about children's learning were sought. As Miller (1993, p.180) put it:

> Children underwent classical and operant conditioning,
> solved simple discrimination-learning problems, and even
> wandered through mazes seeking prizes rather than cheese
> at the end ... It should come as no surprise that children
> learned faster than rats but more slowly than college
> [students].

Even in the 1980s Skinner was insisting, along with other behaviourists, that the only really important topic of development is the "schedules of reinforcement" that "shape" behaviour. These govern the development of all skilled actions such as numeracy and language. Thus Skinner scorned all reference to entities such as reasoning, cognition, or other inner processes of the mind, not because he denied their existence, but because they are unobservable and unverifiable. Terms like "intelligence", "mental operations", "reasoning", "induction", "thinking", "imagery", and so on, are used without definition, he claimed. So he accused cognitive scientists (1985, p.300) of "relaxing standards of definition and logical thinking and releasing a flood of speculation characteristic of metaphysics, literature and daily intercourse ... but inimicable to science."

Behaviouristic associationism persists in one guise or another to this day. For example, Bijou (1992) has attempted to describe development within a "behaviour analysis" framework, from early biological maturation in infancy, acquisition of social and academic skills in mid-childhood, and other social and vocational skills in adulthood. Some developmental research has simply been designed to show that children can form associations, and at what age. In one study, for example, an auditory cue, such as a tone, was presented to infants as young as 10 days old, and paired with a puff of air to the eye, causing the eye to blink — a form of classical conditioning (Little, Lipsitt, & Rovee-Collier, 1984; see Janowsky, 1993, for review). Another kind of conditioning has been exploited in studies on infant perception. In this "operant conditioning" the infant sucks on a pressure-sensitive dummy in order to change the focus of an image on a TV screen (to which the dummy is wired via a computer). The harder the infant sucks the clearer the image becomes, or the more likely it is to switch to a preferred image (Fig. 2.1; see Walton, Bower, & Bower, 1992). In the process the infant is, of course, forming an association between sucking strength and image quality.

These procedures have been much used as research tools, to indicate what, for example, an infant can see or hear. Apart from such uses, support for behaviourism waned sharply after the 1950s (see later). It is worth pointing out, however, that some authors, such as Miller (1993, p.178) believe behaviourism actually had a long-term beneficial effect on developmental studies because it injected them with a methodological rigour that had previously been absent: "Thus learning theory changed the course of developmental psychology. Developmental psychology remains experimental today, but the content of studies has shifted from learning to a wide range of cognitive processes, such as memory, attention and representation."

Finally, it is worth noting that contemporary behaviourists view their roots just as much in biology as do nativists. They simply argue (Donahoe & Palmer, 1995, p.37) that, "The need to survive in environments that are not stable over evolutionary time has selected a genetic endowment allowing organisms to learn", so that some have spoken of the *instinct to learn*. Instead of selecting genes, rapidly changing environmental contingencies "select" behaviours from a repertoire or pool through associationist principles.

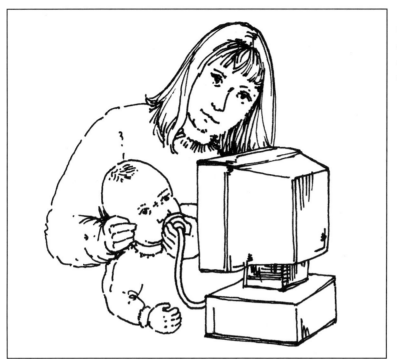

FIG. 2.1.
General set-up for association-forming in a non-nutritive sucking procedure.

Cognitive associationism

Had Skinner's attack on cognitive science prevailed, it would be paradoxical, today, to be talking about associationism in a book about models of cognitive development. But Skinner was already fighting a rearguard action when he wrote the passages just mentioned. A new associationism was already emerging as part of the "cognitive" reaction to behaviourism. By the 1960s, evidence had been accumulating for two decades that even the rat running a maze may be doing more than merely forming stimulus–response bonds. For example, a rat's familiarity with an empty maze permitted it to find its way about much more quickly when the experimenter started to introduce food in a specific location, compared with rats with no such prior experience. Rats that had been trained to swim a maze for food reward were found to be able to run it just as quickly with the water removed, even though this entailed the use of quite different "responses".

Accordingly, even before the 1950s, Tolman (1948) had been talking of "cognitive maps", and Hebb (1949) of "central processes". Thus, theorists began arguing that these are indeed crucial to mental functioning (just as Aristotle had done) — and crucial to the *under-standing* of behaviour. Whereas William James had complained about attempts to reduce all to a single principle, a new breed of associa-tionists in the 1950s adopted Aristotle's dual system: innate faculties for abstracting information from experience; but the information they abstracted consisted of associations. So the associationists found a niche within the cognitive revolution described here, and at least some co-existence with the nativists' modelling. If the latter were vague about contents of cognition, the former offered at least something to be clear about. The view of the "dual" mind that neo-associationists proposed is indicated diagramatically in Fig. 2.2, and is still very popular, if often held implicitly rather than explicitly.

In a different way, the neo-associationists have also benefited from the new metaphors furnished by the advent of the computer. As Anderson and Bower (1973, p.38) put it:

> ... the clear theoretical leaders in the past decade have been the small number of computer scientists who work on models of mental organisation. In our opinion, it is these computer simulation models of mental memory that begin to actualise the full potential of associationism as a theory of mental organisation.

Such metaphors have significantly determined what counts as the content and business of cognition, and thus models of its development.

As usual, however, progress has been dependent on the adoption of certain assumptions and strategies. Always it has been necessary to ask:

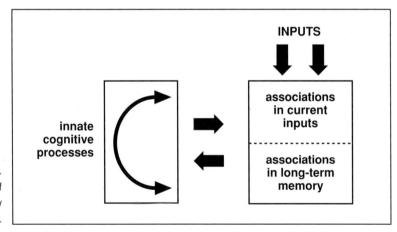

FIG. 2.2.
The dual system of cognition proposed by neo-associationists.

associations between what? The traditional associationists envisaged associations between sensory "qualities", which further converged into features of objects, and then objects themselves, and, finally, "ideas" of increasing complexity. This had the virtue, at least, of grounding cognition in real experience. In modern neo-associationism, the basic "parcels" of association are not usually direct experienced, but, as it were, at least partly finished products of processing such as:

- *Images* (or pictographic representations of experienced objects and events).
- *Symbols* (conventional representations of events such as graphic or verbal labels, i.e. words).
- *Concepts* (some — usually condensed — representation of a category of objects or events).
- *Propositions* (language-like statements of external states, such as "has four legs" or "is an animal").

These are not primitive stimuli or responses, but already meaningful "parcels" of information, and their correspondence with the flux of experience is indirect and uncertain (and, literally, *assumed*). This raises obvious theoretical problems, to which I will return later. But their enormous advantage to the cognitive modeller is that they are capable of being implemented as keyed-in instructions in a computer, and of being manipulated in any number of transformations and combinations as the modeller sees fit.

The strategic acceptance of such assumptions opened the floodgates of new associationist investigation. As already mentioned, and as described in Chapter 1, it is at least tacitly accepted that the processing which brings about these associations in the first place, and then uses them in thinking and acting, are separate entities, often considered to be "intrinsic" or "innate". Accordingly, theory has been dominated by models of memory, representation, and concepts, and how associative structures within them are reflected in cognition. It is worth considering some of the early cognitive associationist models first, in order to grasp the spirit of this neo-associationism, before turning to the more recent developmental models.

Semantic networks

The essential theoretical tool has been that of a "network" of associations — often called a "semantic network" — reflecting the co-occurrence of parcels of information (objects or properties of objects, or events) in actual experience in interconnecting "nodes" in the mind/brain. Among the best-known theories is that of Quillian (1969) who devised a network model of memory in which all information was encoded either as a "unit" or as a "property". A unit is a concept – i.e. a representation of a whole category of things such as "cup" or "shoe". A property is anything that might be said about a unit — e.g. "red", "shaggy", "belongs to John". These form clusters of associations if they co-occur with sufficient frequency in experience — as with *John's dog*, for example. But new concepts can then be created by nesting or overlapping of properties when two or more units themselves become associated in experience: for example, if Ann is John's girlfriend, we can have a concept of Ann's boyfriend's dog.

An example of a "nested network" is shown in Fig. 2.3 (after Quillian, 1969). Note how, in this case, associations are stored at various levels in an inclusion hierarchy, and properties are stored only at their appropriate level. This simplifies the structuring of associations. Generally, though, as Anderson and Bower (1973, p.81) explained, "Since there is no limit to the number and nesting of properties that can be associated to a given unit, it is clear that concepts of predicates of practically unbounded complexity could be built up and represented in the memory format."

Note that this model is based on associations in the form of "labelled relations": for example, "has a", "can", "is a" (e.g. "a dog is a mammal"). These are somewhat different from the associations of the traditional associationists. As already mentioned, their virtue is that

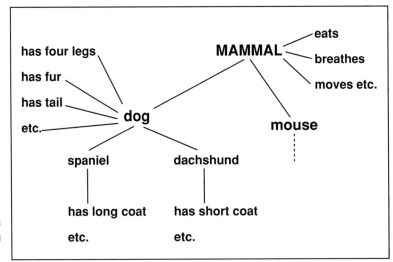

FIG. 2.3.
A nested semantic network (adapted from Quillian, 1969).

they can be entered as labels or values into computer programs, and simulations carried out. Even this superficial resemblance to computations in a real mind has generated a great deal of excitement, although it glosses over the question of how these relations are established in the mind in the first place.

In Anderson and Bower's (1973) Human Associative Memory (HAM), associations are formed between "semantic primitives" to form "complex ideas" which can be *further* associated. These "nodes" of ideas, such as "dog", or "person", linked with associations to form propositional trees, form the basic units of knowledge in HAM. Anderson and Bower (1973, p.169) explains that "HAM will attempt to store these trees in long-term memory by forming associations corresponding with each of the links in the tree." As nodes can belong to more than one tree, however, trees tend to intersect. So knowledge in HAM consists of a vast network of interlocking trees. Parts of the network are activated in specific cognitive tasks to form a short-term or working memory.

As with the Quillian model, the links in HAM are not just associations in the sense of statistical co-occurrences. They also code a *quality* of relation (for example, "causes" or "possesses"): According to Anderson and Bower (1973, p.181), this quality "... expresses a functional connection between the ideas a and b (i.e. that a can lead to b), but with the added specification that a will lead to b only if the relation X is evoked." Given a verbal, visual, or other input expressing a, say, and a desired relation (e.g. "an animal that has horns"), then the mind finds the matching node and the relation X and returns an ordered list of other nodes that are so associated.

The model of Collins and Loftus (1975) has concepts again stored in nodes, with diverse links to other nodes, but with those more closely associated sharing many links, with shorter paths (Fig. 2.4). The links can also vary in strength, so that those that are used more often will become stronger and faster. Another feature of the Collins and Loftus model is that activation of a node will "spread" along associative links (by a process called spreading activation), so activating related nodes. So when we think of "green" we may automatically think of "grass", of "pear", and so on.

Finally, in Anderson's (1983) model, knowledge consists of "cognitive units" which can be propositions (Bill loves Mary), spatial images (a visual figure), temporal strings (a number series), again connected by links, and from which more complex structures can be built by hierarchical embedding. Each node has a strength reflecting its frequency of use, and connections between nodes also vary in

FIG. 2.4.
Adapted from the
spreading activation
model of Collins and
Loftus (1975).

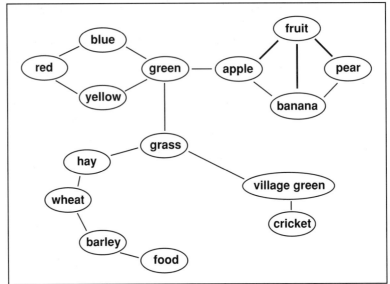

associative strength. Spread of activation occurs within these parameters or constraints, and the "matching" and "action" process of "rules" applied in working memory can lead to the induction of new rules.

Anderson (1983) called the rules "productions", or "production rules", in which action is taken when certain preconditions in the encoded input are fulfilled. Thus a typical rule might be:

> IF person 1 is the father of person 2
>   and person 2 is the father of person 3
> THEN person 1 is the grandfather of person 3

The rules may self-modify by adding more conditions, by generalising across two or more conditions, or by composing repetitive sequences into larger units. Somewhat similarly, Holland, Holyoak, and Nisbett (1986) have suggested a system of associative-like rules which can model environmental structure, be strengthened by feedback, associate with other rules to create larger knowledge structures, and so on.

Beilin (1985, p.101) has noted the stimulus–response nature of production rules ("whenever a condition is satisfied, a corresponding action is taken"), and of other rules invoked in more recent theories. But there has been continual debate about the extent to which learned rules can be described as contingency-shaped associations in this way (Reese, 1989). The approach has been used in developmental studies by devising tasks that may instantiate certain forms of association (or "rules") and then analysing children's behaviours to see to what extent they have used them (and any developmental trends in such use).

A well known example of this approach is that of Siegler (1978) who studied 5–17-year-olds' predictions about a balance beam. The beam contained equally spaced pegs on which one or more equal weights could be hung (Fig. 2.5, top). With various permutations of weights and distances from the fulcrum, the child had to predict which side would go down when a lever holding it steady was released. Siegler identified four common rules from, first, reliance on weight cues alone, then distance cues, then an additive combination of both, and finally the correct multiplicative rule. These were characterised in terms of information flow, as in a computer program, as shown in Fig. 2.5. Siegler

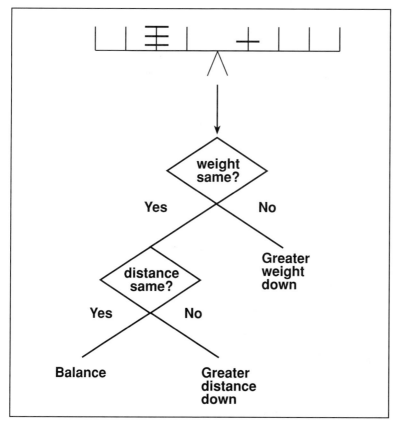

FIG. 2.5.
Top: Balance beam incorporating variable weights and distances as in Siegler's studies. Bottom: Fragments of information-processing model for solving a balance beam problem (Rule II: if weight same, greater distance operates).

interprets such results in terms of encoding of the dimensions (and thus their association with side of descent): the younger children seemed relatively unaware of the "distance" dimension, because they seemed unaware of its association with the outcome variable, even when it was pointed out to them. Only the 13–17-year-olds used the more complex rule with appreciable frequency. Siegler (1978) considers this "knowledge" factor to be more important than mere memory capacity in the development of such rules.

As with the other models just mentioned, one of the exciting aspects of this whole approach has been that it readily generates hypotheses that can be experimentally tested with real people rather than rats. One of the predictions of Quillian's model, for example, was that statements like "a dog is a mammal" will be verified faster than one like "a spaniel is a mammal", because there are fewer associative links to cross. Experiments duly verified this. Collins and Loftus's (1975) model explains, in addition, another empirical finding: statements involving more typical members of a category ("an apple is a fruit") are verified faster than ones involving non-typical members (e.g. "a tomato is a fruit"). Quillian's model cannot do this. In addition, as Reese (1989) notes, the approach, especially when computer simulations are being aspired to, encourages the breakdown of cognition into analysable units in individuals.

As we shall see in Chapter 5, a major branch (known as connectionism) has emerged from these foundations in recent years. In spite of this, neo-associative modelling has continued with topics like organisation in memory, taxonomic hierarchies, further semantic networks, depths of processing, episodic versus declarative memory, associative schemas, and so on. For example, information in hierarchical associations has sometimes been called a "schema". As Anderson (1983, p.37) explains: "One schema can occur as part of another, as a window is part of a wall schema ... Also important is a generalization hierarchy. In recognising a Labrador retriever, for instance, we call on information stored in a dog schema or an animal schema." A schema is seen to operate when information (probably partial) enters working memory. If its structure matches that in a schema in long-term memory, then the latter will activate and "fill-out" the missing details. For example we enter a restaurant and the (partial) input activates a schema that leads us to expect a table, waiter, implements, and so on. Note that such schemas are theoretically different from the "constructivist" schemas I shall be describing in the next chapter.

In sum, whereas traditional (pre-1950s) associationism focused on simple paired-associate learning, often in animal models, more recent theorists have used more fruitful ideas like the production system and working memory. As a result, as Shanks (1995, p.13) has pointed out serious attempts have been made:

> to develop procedures that are representative of real-world learning tasks such as how medical practitioners acquire knowledge of diseases from photographic illustrations ... how people learn different artists' styles ... how they learn to recognise faces ... add and subtract numbers ... and many others

All this work has been mostly carried out with adults. Throughout, however, the modern associationist view (Shanks, 1995, p.50) is that "the associative learning mechanism has been shaped by evolution to detect statistical contingency." These are the basic ideas that have inspired recent developmental models.

Developmental models

In "old" associationism, what develops consists of increasingly complex associations — sensory qualities combine to form more complex forms, or ideas; "ideas" become associated as the basis of memory, knowledge, and cognition. This progressive extension of association complexes and/or their occasional replacement by others is the central developmental metaphor in associationism. In other words development is "learning" (or "acquisition").

Indeed, some research has sought to demonstrate that, as children get older and/or experience with a particular domain increases, evidence of more extensive and more complex associations can be found, and that this is related to cognitive performance in the domain. But other recent modelling has focused on the interface in the dual model and the interactions between process and association, surrounding such issues as: (a) strategies for organising the associations; (b) mental effort (perhaps dependent on motivational and attentional factors); and (c) the influence of knowledge already *in* a semantic store. As knowledge is the key product of association-formation, let us take the last of these first.

The knowledge base

Accretions and organisations of knowledge have, of course, long been seen as central to cognitive development in the associationist view. So the basic description of such changes, and how they affect cognition, has long been a major aim of research. As mentioned earlier, one of Siegler's conclusions in the balance beam study was that knowledge of a dimension's association with an "outcome" variable was important to its being encoded in children. However, improvement was not simply a question of "weighing-up" or combining associations in an additive manner. It depended on knowing that the "weight" association is embedded in the "distance" association in a hierarchical manner, so that the information provided is "interactive". (Another way of saying this is that one association is "conditioned by" another, and I shall have a lot more to say about such interactive relations in Chapter 5.) It can also reasonably be assumed that the more organised the knowledge the more rapid and efficient access can be, and the more efficient the cognitive processing for which it is required.

Such research has often been described as memory research — and sometimes more than that. In an important sense, the knowledge base *is* memory. But the role of it in the acquisition of *new* memories or new knowledge has long been a key topic, too. For example, the accretion of associations is sometimes seen as a kind of snowballing effect within each specific domain. As Flavell and Wellman (1977, p.4; cf. Chi & Ceci, 1987) pointed out:

> Older individuals presumably store, retain, and retrieve a great many inputs better or differently than younger ones. They do so simply because developmental advances in the content and structure of their semantic or conceptual systems render those inputs more familiar, meaningful, conceptually interrelated.

And as Chi and Ceci (1987, p.112) point out, if we can think of the simplest organisation as that of a "chunk" of associations, then the younger child's knowledge base is limited in several ways compared with the older child: "first is the absence of a recognisable chunk ... the second ... is in terms of the size of the chunk ... A third difference is the number of associations, pathways, or test branches leading to a chunk." So further attention has focused on the *structure* of the knowledge base.

The structure of knowledge itself

As Chi and Ceci (1987, p.115) explain, "saying that young children have less knowledge than older children or adults borders on triviality. The sheer quantity of knowledge, although important, is not nearly as important as how that knowledge is structured." Accordingly (1987, p.116), recent focus has been on "(1) how children's knowledge is represented, that is, the structure of that representation; (2) how the structure of children's representations compares with adults' structures; (3) how the structure within a representation affects processing performance." Another concern, of course, has been the *mechanisms* of developmental change. Either way, associationism has had a dominant place in this recent thinking.

Chi and Ceci (1987) suggested changes in the kind of associative network shown in Fig. 2.6. The circles are nodes that store concepts (which may be common object nouns, images, or propositions), and the triangles store attributes. The links are associations between them. It is such links between concepts and properties that increase with development. Chi and Ceci (1987, p.116) explain that "Hence, what knowledge children have simply refers to what concepts and attributes are contained in their memory. One could also say ... that children's knowledge increases as they acquire more links about the concepts and attributes that they already have."

Thus it is easy to see development consisting of an increase of links or associations between nodes as a result of such associations in

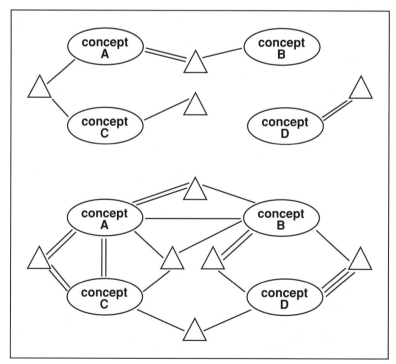

FIG. 2.6. Diagrammatic representation of relatively undeveloped (top) and relatively developed (bottom) knowledge structures showing concept nodes, attributes, and associative links.

experience. And this alone brings many cognitive benefits. As Murray (1996, p.334) points out, the older child can recognise more ways that the concepts *bucket, string, food, sea,* and *tuna,* go together than can the younger child: Murray compares the loosely woven, threadbare memory of the latter with "the intricately woven strands forming complex patterns" in the older child.

However, it isn't only the *amount* or *density* of association that is theoretically important, but (again) the way that these may be organised in clusters and/or hierarchies. The more well-formed and discrete these are, the easier it may be to make accurate inferences from concepts to attribute, attribute to attribute, or concept to concept.

In support of these notions is Chi and Koeske's (1983; see Chi, Hutchinson, & Robin, 1989) study of the structure of a young child's knowledge of a highly restricted domain — that of dinosaurs. This knowledge was elicited by asking a $4\frac{1}{2}$-year-old to do three things: (a) generate a list of dinosaur names; (b) identify a dinosaur from a list of attributes provided; (c) generate dinosaur attributes from dinosaur names. It proved possible to draw a highly structured associative network from the dinosaur–attribute links that the responses provided.

In a subsequent comparison of children who were "novices" or "experts" in dinosaur knowledge, Gobbo and Chi (1986, p.235–236) observed how novices' generation of information tended to mimic the production of a list of features, whereas experts' generation of information "took the form of a more coherent discourse, suggesting that there are greater associations among concepts within the experts' (than the novices') knowledge structures." Somewhat similarly, the development of knowledge of the spatial environment in children has been described in terms of a "hierarchical ordering of places" which "can be described by a system of primary, secondary and tertiary nodes and the paths that link them", where the nodes represent procedures and specific places (reviewed in Colledge et al., 1995, p.44). Nodes differentiate with increased experience of a location, and the links increase in strength.

Knowledge structure and memory performance

The facilitating effect of formed associations in the knowledge base has also been shown in another paradigm used by Owings and Baumeister (1979). A distinction made in much of associationist memory research is between nouns for *concrete* concepts such as "table" and "chair", and nouns for *abstract* concepts such as "truth" and "wisdom". The assumption is that it is possible to form many more associations between the former than the latter, and this can in turn affect performances in, for example, paired-associate tasks, where the formation of associations between the pairs is an important strategy.

Owings and Baumeister presented high-frequency concrete nouns to 7-, 9-, and 11-year-olds. These children were instructed to provide one of three responses to each word: a "semantic" response (describing "what is it?"); a "phonetic" response (i.e. offering a rhyming word); or a "structural" response (i.e. counting the letters). In a subsequent test many more of the semantically processed words were recalled than those processed in either of the two other ways, and more so for the older children. Again this is thought to be due to more associations being formed, particularly in the older children.

Such an interpretation is also supported by Ceci's (1980) study in which he presented lists of animal names to 4-year-olds, after controlling for item familiarity through prior instruction about the animals and their attributes. The numbers of names subsequently recalled was directly proportionate to the numbers of obvious associations between them — for example, being egg-layers or insect-eaters.

The general finding that recall from memory is improved when the material is more meaningful and/or familiar (see Chi & Ceci, 1987 for review) is also attributable to retrieval being enhanced by the available, developed network of associations. With expertise in specific domains this can be independent of age. For example, having ascertained through simple tests that a group of 10-year-olds was more knowledgeable about chess than a group of adults, Chi (1978) found that the children could recall a greater number of chess pieces from a series of presented game positions than the adults. Similarly, in the study by Chi and Koeske (1983) it was found that the structure of a child's dinosaur knowledge very much influenced categorisation and recall of dinosaur names. A subsequent study showed that the structure appeared to facilitate a variety of other inferential abilities such as the prediction of new attributes (see Chi, Hutchinson, & Robin, 1989).

Note again that an associative structure is usually taken to describe "content knowledge", and thus only part of cognition: in contemporary associationism there are usually assumed to be other cognitive processes operative over these contents. For example, although Gobbo and Chi (1986) concluded that experts can generalise and "reason analogically" in making predictions from partial information, they admit (p.234), as we still must today, that the connection between reasoning and content knowledge is still very unclear.

Associative learning strategies

As mentioned earlier, there is much evidence that children's improvement in memory with age is due to better organisation and better strategies for both acquisition and recall (Kail, 1990). In turn the role of associations in these organisations and strategies has often been demonstrated. The deliberate association of items in memory has long been commended as a mnemonic strategy, and confirmed in much research. And children's ability to "chunk" items in memory according to some associated features or properties has often been invoked as an explanation for their increase in memory span with age (for review see Henry & Millar, 1993). For example, it has been shown how adolescents spontaneously cluster or group to-be-remembered items, but also deliberately associate them more with items in memory (e.g. phone numbers with birth dates), compared with younger children (Murray, 1996).

As also mentioned earlier, a major paradigm has been that of the paired associates (for reviews see Schneider & Pressley, 1989; and Kee, 1994). In a typical experiment, children are required to learn up to 30 or so pairs of unrelated nouns such as *dog–ball, arrow–glasses, chicken–coffee*. In the subsequent test trial they are presented with one member of each pair and asked to recall the other. The research has mostly studied what factors are involved in success on such tasks, and whether they change with development. For example, "elaborative strategies" have been strongly implicated in some studies. These are "meaning enhancing additions, constructions or generations that improve memory" (Levin, 1988, p.191, cf. Kee, 1994). Thus, in the case of the pair *dog–ball*, making up a statement like "the dog is playing with the ball" might be one elaborative strategy. Generating a visual image of the dog with the ball in its mouth might be another. Encouraging people to use such strategies considerably enhances retrieval in paired-associate tasks, and this is considered to be due to the associations that are thus forged between the pairs.

It has been shown that young children below the age of adolescence, however, rarely use such elaborative strategies spontaneously — but when they do so, performance markedly improves at all ages. There has been much debate about whether verbal elaboration is better than imagery elaboration, and about the best kind of instruction in strategy use (Kee, 1994). In adolescence, the increasing *spontaneous* use of elaborative and other strategies has been attributed to the development of "metacognition", i.e. the emergence of awareness of personal cognitive powers and more deliberate use of them.

Paivio (1986) proposed a dual-coding model in which information can be stored in memory either in the form of visual images or as verbal codes. Associative connections can be formed between aspects of these codes so that activation of one can lead to activation of the other. That is, the existence of such an association provides a more durable code. This has been tested with children and students by, for example, presenting a reference map prior to reading a passage of text about it and then being tested for retrieval. Typically recall is improved compared with presentation of the map or text independently (e.g. Kulhavy et al. 1993).

Concepts

The associationist networks discussed so far posit concepts as key nodes, with associative links between them becoming richer with development. This might indicate that concepts, although the main basis of knowledge, are themselves simple, undifferentiated, "items". On the contrary, however, a long line of research over the last 30 years has revealed rich structure in concepts, and associationist ideas have frequently been invoked in attempts to describe it.

As mentioned in Chapter 1, a concept is usually thought of by psychologists as the mental representation of a category of objects or events. Common nouns are usually the verbal labels of such concepts. For most of this century, various strands of research have attempted to get to grips with the nature of concepts. One prominent line has focused on the "conceptual behaviour" of children. When asked to sort objects, say, into groups, young children tend to do so on the basis of a single perceptual attribute such as colour or shape. Older children will do so on the basis of associations of properties such as correlated attributes (e.g. has four legs, fur etc.). Such associations are also suggested when children are asked to free recall from a list or display of items to which they were earlier exposed. In a typical study children will have words read to them (in random order) from a list that can actually be divided into four categories (see Table 2.1). When asked to recall them, clustering of semantically related items occurs in the sequences of words in children's reports, and this tendency increases with age (for review see Reese, 1979).

TABLE 2.1
Categories of Words Used in a Typical Clustering Study

Animal	Clothing	Vehicle	Vegetable
horse	shirt	plane	carrot
goat	sock	car	cabbage
pig	vest	bike	potato
cow	coat	train	leek

The most prominent strand in the last 30 years, however, has aimed to describe the structure in concepts themselves. Although there have been nativist models of the basis of the structure of concepts (see Chapter 1), there have also been many associationist models of concepts. Indeed the so-called "classical view" of concepts (Smith & Medin, 1981) can be traced back to Aristotle, and simply assumes that a concept is a representation of the necessary and sufficient associated features that define the category.

The classical view came under criticism in the 1970s when it was realised that it is actually difficult to find defining features for most categories. In addition, when people were asked to rate exemplars of categories like "bird" or "mammal" for their "typicality" some were rated more highly than others (Rips, Shoben, & Smith, 1973). This should not happen according to the classical view. Eleanor Rosch and her colleagues showed that categories appear to have internal structure, not explained by the classical view. They also objected to the nativist view that concepts are prior to experience of the world and that the child "is taught to impose upon this environment a kind of discrimination grid which serves to distinguish the world as being composed of a large number of separate things, each labelled with a name" (Leach, 1964, p.34; quoted by Rosch et al., 1976).

Instead they argued that concepts are induced by *probabilistic* (rather than "all or none") associations of features or attributes that members of a category share. Wittgenstein (1958) had used the term "family resemblance" to express a similar view. Rosch et al. (1976, p.422) argued that this reflects the "correlational structure" of the world: "Children are probably engaged in learning the co-occurrence contingencies of their environment and probably categorize on the basis of their knowledge of those contingencies." The structure of inclusiveness of attributes also determines, they argued, the "taxonomic structure" of the concept.

Rosch et al.'s original studies were with adults. People were asked (Rosch et al., 1976, p.389) to list "all the attributes they could think of" of 90 named objects from 9 taxonomic categories (fruit, tool, clothing, tree, bird etc.). The names were at the superordinate (e.g. furniture), basic (e.g. table), and subordinate (e.g. kitchen table) levels. These were checked by two other groups of subjects. The lists suggested that (1976, p.392) "the basic level does appear to be the most inclusive level at which objects have clusters of attributes in common." Further studies suggested that it also appears to be the level at which a visual image is most easily formed, and which involves the most similar sets of movements in handling them. In children such clusters of associated attributes appear to be those for which the names are acquired first.

One method that has been used to support this view is the method of "triads". In the method used by Rosch et al. (1976) children from 3 years up were shown three pictures of objects and asked to put together or point to "the two that are alike, that are the same kind of thing" (p.417; see Fig. 2.7). In some triads, successful pairing could only take place at the basic level (for example, cat with cat). For others, pairing could only take place at the superordinate level (for example, vehicle with vehicle). At the former level, sorting was virtually perfect, whereas at the superordinate level (where there is less association of attributes) sorting was much more difficult for the younger children, but, again, was near perfect for 4-year-olds.

Mervis and Crisafi (1982) manipulated the associative structure of nonsense stimuli to make much the same point. The stimuli, and their hierarchical associative structure, are shown in Fig. 2.8. "Curved" versus "angular" is one associated attribute discriminating the sets at a superordinate level. Members of basic-level categories were of similar overall shape and share three other attributes. Small differences in outline shape and placement of detail distinguished subordinate categories. 2-, 4-, and 5-year-olds were presented with triads of pictures from each of the three levels, and asked to show "which pictures are the same kind of thing, which ones go together". The 2- and 4-year-olds sorted significantly more accurately at the basic level compared with either the superordinate or subordinate levels.

Another well-known method is that of "sorting'. Children are presented with objects or pictures of objects and asked to "put together the ones that go together, the ones that are the same kind of thing" (Rosch et al., 1976, p.420). The fact that Rosch et al. found that young children sort more easily at the basic level than at the superordinate level is due, they say, to the greater associative clustering of attributes at that level.

Rosch referred to such a structure of concepts as "prototypical" — as if tending towards a single "best exemplar", displaying the ideal associative structure of a category. This is one possible explanation for the graded structure of most categories, some members considered to be "good", others more marginal. Indeed, Rosch and Mervis (1975) showed that the more an exemplar was judged to be prototypical of a category, the more attributes it shared with other members of the category, and the fewer it shared with members of contrasting categories.

Thus a single associative principle gives some account of the structures of categories (Rosch et al., 1976, pp.433–434):

FIG. 2.7.   Two typical triads, the top requiring a match at the basic level (cats); the bottom one requiring a match at the superordinate level (vehicles/transport).

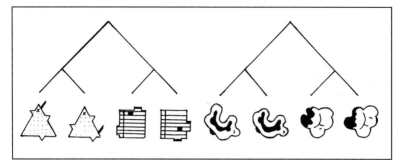

FIG. 2.8.
Stimuli used by
Mervis and Crisafi
(1982; reproduced
with permission).

> Categories form to maximise the information-rich clusters of attributes in the environment ... Prototypes of categories appear to form in such a manner as to maximise the clusters ... within categories ... [This] makes prototypes potentially useful in cognitive processes. Matching to a prototype in categorization would allow humans to make use of their knowledge of the contingency structure of the environment without the laborious process of computing and summing the validities of individual cues.

This idea of the formation of prototypes has been very popular in associationist models of cognitive development. Within a few years a number of investigators were attempting to establish at what age children could "form" prototypes. In one approach, Bauer, Dow, and Hertsgaard (1995) used a sequential touching task. They presented 13- to 18-month-old infants with objects from two categories simultaneously, and observed the sequence with which objects were touched. The assumption is that infants' sequences of touching are influenced by the degree to which they perceive those objects as from the same category. Thus inferences are drawn about their category (conceptual) representations. The results suggested that sequence of touching was influenced by the "prototypicality" of the category members, defined as the number of attributes shared with other category members, and distinct from those of members of other categories.

In another study, Strauss (1979) presented 10-month-old infants with drawings of schematic faces that varied on four dimensions. In subsequent tests the infants appeared to find the (non-experienced) "average prototype" more familiar than ones they had actually experienced before (Fig. 2.9). The conclusion was that a sort of overlaying of experienced values along each dimension led in effect to the average value becoming most prominent in conceptual representation. Other prototype models have suggested that a prototype is formed from the association of the most frequently occurring values of each dimension — a kind of multidimensional mode. Following a number of studies, Younger and Cohen (1983) concluded that 10-month-old infants have already developed adult-like categorising abilities. Note, however, that there have been other models of prototype formation that are not associationist in character.

More recent studies have examined categorisation in even younger infants. For example, using the preferential looking technique described in Chapter 1, Quinn, Eimas, and Rosenkranz (1993) familiarised 3–4-month-old infants with either pictures of cats or pictures of dogs. Later the infants were tested with novel pictures from both the familiar category and the novel category; if they looked longer at the latter it was assumed that this was because they had formed a category of the former. There was some evidence that this was the case, although it depended on the perceptual *variability* of exemplars experienced.

Some theorists have argued that infants' earliest categories are "perceptual", based on directly available global similarities of appearance, and thus associations of simple sensory values (Mandler & McDonough, 1993). In this view, later condensation into adult-like *conceptual* categories requires additional, non-associative mechanisms (although what is meant by this, and the possible mechanisms involved, is controversial — see Jones & Smith, 1993 for review; see also Oakes, Coppage, & Dingel, 1997). Some research has suggested that development of categorisation seems to be related to the availability of names or name-like labels to serve as organising "handles" (Gopnik & Meltzoff, 1992; Waxman & Markow, 1995).

Notice how the modelling of prototypes requires an independent "averaging" or "counting" mechanism that, again, harks back to the dualism in modern associationism.

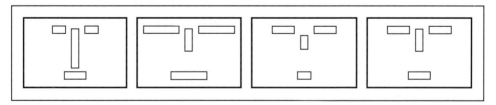

FIG. 2.9.   In studies of associative structure of schematic faces, experience of a series such as the first three faces might be expected to create the prototype (average of all dimensions) seen in the fourth face. Although not actually experienced, the latter is often rated as the "best" exemplar of the category.

Covariations, causes, rules and schemas

Apart from its importance in memory and concepts, the detection of associated or covarying attributes is required for establishing *causal* relationships. As Kareev (1995, p.490) explains:

> The ability to detect covariation when it exists and to correctly assess its strength is extremely important for cognitive functioning and adaptive behaviour. Recognition of what features "go together" is essential for category formation, whereas detection of sequential dependencies is the basis for the discovery of cause-and-effect relationships. The detection of covariation is thus the basis for much of inductive learning.

In spite of this importance, the picture presented from years of research into covariation detection has been a very puzzling one. Both children and adults appear to have great difficulty with the kinds of explicit covariation problems presented in controlled laboratory tasks: they often fail to detect covariation where it exists, and, more curiously, sometimes report it where there is none. This has led to a major debate about whether human cognition is "rational", determined by inherent biased principles, or simply erratic (Anderson, 1991; Kareev, 1995). As a result — as mentioned in Chapter 1 — many theorists have decided that the detection of causal covariation requires some innate mechanism.

The associations or covariations required to be induced in causal reasoning are, again, sometimes described as "rules", and can vary with different problem types. A popular approach has been to specify frequencies of co-occurrences of each of the values of two variables in a two-way table (Fig. 2.10): for example whether plants are "sick" or "not sick", and having received or not received some special plant food (Shaklee, Holt, Elek, & Hall, 1988). In this case, subjects have to say whether they think plants will get better with or without the special food.

One rule that subjects may use is the "*cell-a* rule" (Shaklee et al., 1988): i.e. judging the association to be positive if the cell *a* frequency is the largest in the table, and negative if it is the smallest. Another rule would compare frequencies in *a* and *b* cells (*a-versus-b* rule). A better strategy would be to compare *a* and *d* cells with the *b* and *c* cells. The best strategy of all is to compare the probability of a plant being healthy given that it has received plant food, with the probability of the plant being healthy given that it received no food: the so-called *conditional*

FIG. 2.10.

Typical contingency
table for assessing
subject's ability to
abstract causal
covariation between
food supplementation
and plant health
(numbers in cells are
frequencies of
co-occurrence).

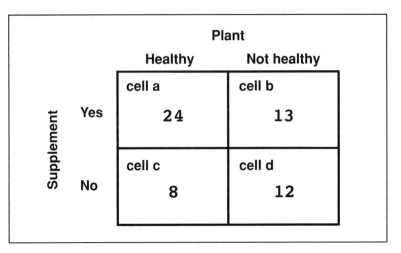

probability rule (Shaklee et al., 1988). By modifying the distributions of frequencies from problem to problem the investigators can infer which rules the subjects are using in their reasoning.

Shaklee et al. (1988) found that the conditional probability rule (which requires attention to all four cells of the table) was rare among children below college grade; that training in the rules was possible; and that responsiveness to training also improved with age. This was taken to suggest that the competence is there before the spontaneous development. So associations are captured, in this view, but inventive ways of combining the associations in novel ways, in order to make novel inferences, also develop. Training, of course, is a way of *demonstrating* such inventiveness to the subject, short-circuiting the need to discover it independently (Shaklee et al., 1988).

Other authors have questioned whether judgements from tables like that in Fig. 2.10 entail simple associative principles, or rather more complex *information integration* at a more abstract level (see Allan, 1993, for review). This indicates a more "constructivist" model of learning and development, and this is reinforced by other studies suggesting the role of background knowledge in covariation judgements (Alloy & Tabachnik, 1984). I will be returning to such models in Chapters 3 and 4. Nonetheless, associationists have continued to suggest that "rather than assuming that subjects mathematically transform real-time events into probabilities, and then arithmetically compare those probabilities ... one might look to elementary associative principles for a viable account" (Wasserman, Elek, Chatlosh, & Baker, 1993, p.183; quoted by Allan, 1993, p.439).

Such rule-learning-by-association has been amenable to description in terms of information processing. This has given further scope for computer simulation. Siegler and Shipley (1987) used a "distributions of associations" model to describe simple addition in 4–5-year-olds. The children tended to use one of four strategies, from counting with fingers through to apparently direct statement of the answer. Siegler and Shipley suggested that children tended to respond on the basis of "strengths of association" between problem and representations of answer options in memory.

For example, asking 4–5-year-olds in a pilot study just to state the answer to a problem like 3+2=? suggested tables of associative strength like that in Fig. 2.11. Such distributions seemed to account for different strategies used with problems of different difficulty. Siegler and Shipley (1987, p.80) state:

> If children do not state a retrieved answer, they proceed to elaborate the representation of the problem. They can generate either an elaborated external representation, for example one in which they put up their fingers, or an elaborated internal representation, for example one in which they form a mental image of objects corresponding to the augend and addend. Putting up fingers or forming an image adds visual associations between the elaborated representation and various answers to the already existing association between the problem and various answers.

The results of Siegler and his colleagues seemed to show a relationship between mean solution time and the degree of overt

FIG. 2.11. Fragment of a 'strength of association' table between addition problems and possible answers (from Siegler & Shipley, 1987).

Answer												other
Problem	1	2	3	4	5	6	7	8	9	10	11	
2 + 4	.01	.04	.01	.34	.39	.10	.06		.02		.02	.02
2 + 5	.01		.03	.01	.12	.33	.29	.04		.03	.01	.11
3 + 1	.01	.01	.06	.77	.02	.03	.03	.04				.02
3 + 2												
3 + 3												

strategy needed to solve the problem (in turn due to the distribution of associations). Of course, it seems unlikely that ready-made answers are being stored with a "strength of association" with all possible problems, but this model does illustrate associationist modelling in describing cognitive processes.

Curiously, there have been many reports of children's and adults' registration of associations when, in contrast with the studies just mentioned, the covariations are rendered implicit or unconscious. Levicki and colleagues, in a number of studies, have shown how people readily abstract covariation "unconsciously", when it is present in a task, but their attention is not actually drawn to it until later, when they are tested (e.g. Levicki, Hill, & Czyzewska, 1997). While performing what are actually distracting tasks on digits on a series of pictures some association is, as it were, "sneaked in". For example, some covariation between line thickness and pleasantness of a picture may be built in across the series, though without the subjects' attention being drawn to it (e.g. Baeyens, Heremans, Eelen, & Crombez, 1993). Subsequent tests show that subjects have registered the covariation, even though, when asked to describe verbally any associations in the series of pictures, they are unable to do so.

Applications of associationist models

As already mentioned earlier, psychologists from Aristotle onwards have been quick to see practical application of associationist models. Such insights have entailed a specific view of the promotion of development — i.e. as learning or training — rather than facilitation of inner, deeper, changes. And the principles of association identified by Aristotle have found much expression in the 20th century. Proper child-rearing, or socialisation, has been seen to depend on the inculcation of appropriate habits via associationist principles, perhaps with judicious use of rewards and punishments. In education, it can be argued that the rote memorising of chunks of information through principles of association, with suitable rewards and punishments, has long been *and remains* the most common pedagogical method.

Apart from these areas, associationist principles have been popular in advice about memory and remembering, which seem equally applicable to children and adults. For the most part it takes the form of strategies for encoding, as in enhancing associative links through imagery; for retrieval, as in looking for associative "hooks" (e.g. thinking of a person's first name, or address, may yield their surname); or a number of other mnemonic devices. The clustering of ideas that appears to occur spontaneously in children's memory processes can also be harnessed for instructional purposes. It is suggested that, in order to facilitate memorisation, materials should be organised on the basis of interrelations of meanings, and this will especially benefit younger children (Reese, 1979). In addition, as Murray (1996, p.337) explains, "children can be taught such memory-enhancing strategies as rehearsal, grouping items, key-word associations, acronyms and rhymes as mnemonic devices."

By far the most detailed educational application of behaviourism has been that of "programmed learning" advocated by Skinner, and popular in the 1950s and 60s. In such programmes the learning of complex material such as mathematics or reading comprehension is broken down into small steps that are easily achieved, presented to the pupil in order of increasing difficulty, and rapidly reinforced with feedback. Mastery of each step (getting the answer right) is a powerful secondary reinforcer in Skinner's view. A great advantage is that programmes can be presented on teaching machines. According to Skinner they clarify the curriculum goals, increase motivation and are self-pacing (see Murray, 1996, for fuller review).

In 1948 Skinner wrote a novel (*Walden Two*) as a way of publicising the practical implications of operant conditioning for child rearing and adult training. In it society was governed in a "scientific" and harmonious way by the principles of operant conditioning, and children were reared by a group of behaviour-engineers, skilled in the use of contingencies of reinforcement. Even in the 1960s and 70s principles of association by conditioning were being incorporated into mechanical "teaching machines" (Fig. 2.12) and "programmed learning routines". For example Whaley and Malott (1968) describe a regime for the classroom in which children are paid tokens according to the numbers of problems they get correct. The tokens could be exchanged for trips to the zoo, circuses, shopping trips, sweets, biscuits, clothing and so on from the school shop, and many other things. In all of these, development was assumed to proceed by the strengthening or weakening of S–R associations, or their incorporation into more complex chains.

The most controversial applications of behaviourist associationism have been in what are called "behaviour management" and "behaviour modification". Such principles have been widely used by therapists and teachers for dealing with learning problems, and suggested to parents as programmes for improving their children's development. According to Bijou (1984, quoted by Murray, 1996, p.191) such programmes have indicated that, for example:

FIG. 2.12.
A "teaching machine"
in use.

when a teacher pays any kind of attention to unruly
conduct, such behaviour tends to increase (reinforcement);
when she directs her attention to desirable personal social
behaviour (reinforcement) and totally ignores undesirable
behaviour, that behaviour tends to decrease (extinction).

Still and Costall (1987, p.7) argue that part of the field of Artificial
Intelligence has taken on the mantle of Taylorism (the scientific organisation of industrial production) as a form of personnel and production
management by reducing human economic and social activity to
mechanical rules.

Another broadly associationist application has been in attempts
to organise and present knowledge for teaching purposes in the
form of "knowledge maps". These are of several types (Evans &
Dansereau, 1991) but most often consist of two-dimensional line diagrams with propositions in boxes connected by different kinds of
associative links — so-called "node-link" maps. For example, a map
may summarise main ideas or concepts and how they inter-relate
(e.g. "part of" or "leads to"), or show the taxonomic structure of an
area of knowledge, or a sequence of events. Figure 2.13 shows a
prototype map of the "good student" based on characteristic links
between attribute nodes.

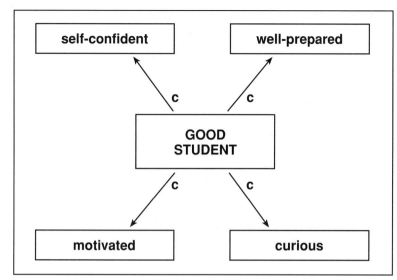

FIG. 2.13.
Example of
knowledge prototype
used in semantic
maps for educational
purposes
(c = characteristic;
adapted from
Lambiotte,
Dansereau, Cross, &
Reynolds, 1989).

As adjuncts to purely verbal presentations, such tools have been found useful in schools and colleges for purposes such as defining curriculum goals, assessing progress, improving group discussion, integrating knowledge from various sources, and so on. They are thought to work by assisting associative organisation in memory (the tacit assumption being that this is the natural structure of knowledge in memory), and reinforcing such organisation by forming visual-imagery associations with purely verbal propositions. For example, according to Kulhavy et al. (1993, p.375), the facilitating effects of using maps to illustrate texts in teaching is considered to be due to a "dual coding" in which "information from the map can be used to cue retrieval of associated verbal facts." The availability of graphics packages on desk-top computers for running programs devised by experts in specific areas has given this approach a recent boost, and much research is currently being done on what aspects of maps improve knowledge acquisition (e.g. Hall & Sidio-Hall, 1994).

Criticisms of associationism

Associationism arose as an answer to the nativist/rationalist insistence that knowledge and cognition are too rich to arise from degenerate, unreliable experience. Nativism doesn't really answer the question: where do these wonderful things *really* come from? Nativists have replied that some prior knowledge is needed simply to make *sense* of sense experience. Aristotle accepted this by postulating a faculty of reason that abstracted form from sense data. This is the position of contemporary neo-associationists — insisting on associations as the basis of knowledge organisation and storage in memory, whilst admitting the role of some innate constraints and processes in encoding, storage, retrieval and so on. This is the dual system described in Fig. 2.2.

On the face of it this may seem like a sensible compromise — but it has a number of problems. The first is the over-simplification of the conception itself. As Wilson (1980, p.105) says, "An association is simply two or more entities which are linked so that elicitation of one can lead to elicitation of the other." There is no doubt that people can come to behave in a way that appears to reflect such an association in nature, as if they had "represented" that association in some way. But to suggest that all of nature, and the most complex aspects of thought, can be reduced to such simple correlations would be misleading in the extreme.

Especially in the last 20 years or so, we have come to realise that nature is rather more complex than regular bivariate associations, and so also, therefore, is our sense experience. The world we experience as humans is constantly changing in space and time, and almost always novel. Significant direct associations are few and special, and often contrived as part of human action itself. Not only may associations involve variables with many values, they may also be non-linear: indeed they may also be "interactive", in the sense that an association between two variables may be conditioned by a third, and this three-way interactive association by a fourth variable, and so on. In this way an apparently weak and unprovidential relation between two variables may actually yield considerable predictability, *if* this "deeper" structure of association is registered. I discuss such association structures further in Chapter 5. In the meantime, it should be clear that associations in real experience can be very complex, fragmentary, "deep", time-based, and dynamic.

Most criticisms of associationism flow from this point. As indicated in Chapter 1, behaviourism was dealt a series of severe blows after the Second World War. First it was becoming increasingly clear from animal studies that some biological constraints on learning operate, or at least "preparedness" for certain kinds of learning. For example, it became clear that it is easier to condition dogs to jump through a hoop than to yawn, and that rats learn to avoid bait that is poisoned, and produces nausea, more quickly than they learn other responses. In 1949 Donald Hebb was able to state quite strongly (p.xvi) that:

In mammals as low as the rat it has turned out to be impossible to describe behaviour as an interaction directly between sensory and motor processes ... something like thinking, that is, intervenes ... there are central processes operating also.

This became particularly clear in experiments with children, who, unlike animals, tended to use verbal labels in learning strategies, so that they came to be described as "rats with language" (see Miller, 1993, p.181). Indeed, for a long period, experimenters spent considerable time and effort in devising experimental designs that would "exclude" or "control for" such "higher processes" (Kessel, 1969). In addition, it is worth pointing out that behaviourism reflected a particular philosophy of science that has always been controversial, and frequently criticised for its "behaviour-control" objectives.

The difficulty associationism has in capturing the complex structure of experience has been a particular target of criticism, and one that nativists have capitalised on, as we saw in Chapter 1. The problem is that, when sensory experiences occur in conjunction or succession, we can (socially) describe them as taking on one or other of a wide range of relationships: same location; shared features; membership of the same category; the action of one upon the other (causal relationship); and so on. The *quality* of these relationships must clearly influence our reasoning in situations involving them. But in associationist accounts *all* are described by one and the same kind of mechanism (see the quote from Wilson, given earlier).

Neo-associationists, of course, have been conscious of this problem, but have "solved" it only by *imposing* the structure through the use of labelled relations (such as "is a" or "has"). As Anderson and Bower (1973, p.61) explained, "All recent attempts to simulate human memory with an associative model have had to resort to labelling the associative links with the various relations they express." Again, this is re-stating part of what the mind must do in forming knowledge, without indicating how it is done. The problem is similar to that of the symbol grounding problem manifest in "symbolic" cognitive science generally (see Chapter 1). But it is also typical of the artificial intelligence approach, which aims, as it were, to strip away all the really difficult and complicated things that human cognitive systems do in perceiving and acting on the world, by reducing them to bald "decision rules" underneath.

Thus, the suggestion that a child's knowledge of a domain consists of the accretion of simple bivariate links, like those shown in Fig. 2.2, surely misses much of the real structure. So do arguments like those of Rosch and Mervis (1975) that a prototype made up of an association of static, perfectly formed features, is the best representation of a category of objects because it reflects the structure of the world. This is because the real structure is "deeper" and dynamic. For example, children and adults can readily recognise, and make predictions about, objects from fragments of input, such as a few moving dots or point-lights on a computer screen. Analysis of the evocative information in such displays suggests a much more dynamically structured kind of knowledge in conceptual representation (Richardson & Webster, 1996a).

Moreover, the kinds of associations *attended to* in human experience are embedded in culturally evolved activities and priorities (see Chapter 4). As Rutkowska (1993, p.61) points out, "whether biological taxa, colours or emotions are concerned, cultural *'use considerations'* regularly overrule supposedly universal perceptual gestalts" (emphasis in original). She gives the example of the Cheyenne whose category label, *vovetas,* includes vultures, hawks, two kinds of insects and tornados — all of which present a whirling, funnelling kind of motion. Rutkowska (1993) suggests that we should be thinking in terms of "action programmes", which include environmental structures and their representations, in the context of human purposes and actions.

Critics of the field of Artificial Intelligence, which has attempted to establish simple computer-implemented rules, by examining the "rules" used by experts in a domain, have pointed to the difficulty of finding such rules in real-life thought and action. Such experts don't actually appear to operate by simple production rules, but by bringing far more abstract structures to bear on each special case (Dreyfus & Dreyfus, 1987). Likewise, as children develop, their perceptions of similarity among objects also appear to become based on more abstract, relational, properties rather than simple contiguities of features. For example, young children may say that a cloud is like a sponge because "they are both round and fluffy" whereas an older child or adult would say that "they both hold water and give it back later" (Gentner, 1988; cf. Medin, Goldstone, & Gentner, 1993). This appears to involve more complex changes in knowledge structure than an accretion of associations. As noted earlier, in the context of Siegler's rule-assessment approach, the associations are not simple but are embedded in each other, hierarchically, so that the information they provide is "interactive" rather than additive (a point I will have much more to say about in Chapter 5).

Given all of this, it is perhaps not surprising that it has occasionally to be acknowledged that associationist models provide, at best, an incomplete characterisation of behaviour, although they still provide a useful heuristic for research (Baker et al., 1993). One response to this realisation has been the increasing invocation of schemas in recent years, as more abstract associative structures in representation. But this strategy, too, has problems. One of them has been "how one gets any action from them" (Anderson, 1983, p.37). This has only been possible by postulating further cumbersome computational procedures which add on or fill in courses of action, and render the system less like a "real" one. Besides, to imply some kind of complex association structure by calling it a schema has not always been helpful. According to Mackworth (1987, quoted by Klahr, 1992, p.139) the schema idea:

> has repeatedly demonstrated an ingenious talent for metamorphosis. A schema has been variously identified with a map, a record, a pattern, a format, a plan, ... a program, a data structure, a script, a unit, and an agent. Each of these concepts has, in turn, considerable variability and ambiguity.

Lakoff (1987) has argued convincingly that categories (and thus their conceptual representations) are not singular coherent entities made up of clusters of stable properties at all, but multiple representations often changing over time and place. As an example, he shows that we can simultaneously harbour at least five, potentially disjunctive, models of a mother: the person who gave birth; the person who contributed the genetic material; the person who reared the child; the current wife of the father; or the closest female ancestor. These representations are problematic for a simple associationist view of concepts and categories.

That associationism has engendered a shallow view of learning (not to mention cognitive development) is seen in attempts to demonstrate the superiority of humans compared with other species (primates, other mammals, reptiles, and fishes) in classical conditioning tasks. Although these have been accompanied by careful measurements of the most recently evolved part of the brain (the neocortex), showing the three-fold advantage possessed by humans, a corresponding advantage in learning has not been so clear. As Oakley (1985, pp.155&167) put it:

> though the idea that learning depends on neocortex has a long history, there is one serious objection to it, namely that comparative learning studies show that neocortex is

manifestly not a prerequisite for learning ... conventional learning designs of the sort employed in psychology laboratories then give rather few clues as to the unique selective advantages conferred by neocortex which might account for its emergence in the course of vertebrate evolution.

The alternative view, of course, is that there is something radically wrong with the "conventional learning designs". Similar objections apply to the alarming conclusions that people appear to have difficulty abstracting (causal) covariations. There are several objections to the conclusions, from the kind of studies portrayed in Fig. 2.11, that this reflects a general human incapacity. The main objection is that the usual experimental procedure presents a most unreal situation to subjects. People are used to dealing with cause-and-effect, and categorical, relations in meaningful contexts, in which prior knowledge can be invoked to provide interpretative "scaffolding". In everyday situations people are usually dealing with highly fragmentary (degenerate) inputs, and seem to do so very well. Levicki and colleagues, in a number of studies, have shown how people readily abstract covariation "unconsciously", when it is present in a task, but their attention is not actually drawn to it until later when they are tested (e.g. Levicki, Hill, & Czyzewska, 1997). The point is, of course, that the human cognitive system appears to be set up for the abstraction of just such complex covariation structures, not the simple bivariate relations (often of only binary values) that appear in experiments on covariation detection.

As mentioned in Chapter 1, many theorists have drawn attention to the deeper ontological structure that even young children seem to bring to problems, rather than reasoning on the basis of visible, or superficial perceptual associations. Mandler and McDonough (1993) have shown that even young children can make conceptual distinctions that have no perceptual parallel (e.g. that birds and aeroplanes belong to different categories). Studies of children's understanding of scientific knowledge (i.e. their informal versus "scientific" view of physical and other reality) suggest complex transformations of knowledge structures and cognitions, rather than simple accretions of associations among properties (Carey, 1990; Driver & Bell, 1985; Gil-Perez & Carrasco, 1990). These, and other studies, point to a more constructivist view of development, to which I turn in the next chapter. As mentioned in Chapter 1, however, some theorists interpret such observations in terms of innate constraints.

Another aspect of this shallowness is that it appears to offer only a stultifying account of human thought, quite devoid of creativity and productivity. An association, after all, only returns specific values of features or attributes, according to associations already repeatedly experienced, so how can any new thought be created? There are few indications in traditional associationism of how new knowledge can be generated from existing knowledge in a way that is so characteristic of human thought. As Anderson and Bower (1973, p.25) explained in their neo-associationist manifesto, "To this day there is still no well worked out theory of how the mind spontaneously interrogates its own knowledge to construct new knowledge." Billman (1996, p.291) and Fodor & Lepore (1996, p.254) make related points about the failure of prototypes to explain the *productivity* of thought.

Some theorists (such as Kendler, 1995) have attempted to overcome this problem by proposing a distinction between an "associative" level of thought and a "rational" level, which is more creative and flexible in forming hypotheses, making deductions, and controlling attentional resources. Development is then a slow movement from the more primitive associationist mode to the more advanced rational mode. It is reasonable to point out, however, as does Chalmers (1997, p.145), that "there is as yet no consensus as to what 'associative' and 'rational' mean in terms of task achieving behaviour."

Constructivist 3 models

Introduction

The third foundation of contemporary theory is to be found in the writings of Immanuel Kant (*Critique of pure reason*, 1781/1968). Kant tried to resolve what he saw as the errors of the other two, rival, foundations. He couldn't accept that innate conceptual powers could be used to make judgements about reality independently of the content of sense experience. And he couldn't see how the intuitions in sense experience alone could be a basis for sound judgement. As he put it in a famous passage, "Concepts without intuitions are empty, and intuitions without concepts are blind". (Kant, 1781/1968, p.73).

Kant (quoted by Walsh, 1968, p.62) argued that both are needed for proper judgement. Sense experience requires the application of concepts for interpretation, "otherwise it would be possible for appearances to crowd in upon the soul ... and consequently would be for us as good as nothing." But this does not mean that we are born with ready-made knowledge. Instead, all we are provided with, Kant argued, are some very basic, but abstract, organising concepts (of quantity, quality, relation, and modality) through which we start to make sense of experience.

Intellect and sensibility must thus work together. But the results in the mind are not simple, direct associations. When they work together the results are schemas — *constructed* representations that form our working knowledge and thoughts about the world without being direct "copies" of it. As Walsh (1968, p.82) put it, "the schema ... is, in effect, a second concept which has the advantage over the [concept] in its abstract form of being directly cashable in terms of sense experience, and can be plausibly thought to provide an interpretation of it." But this new kind of representation is neither innate, nor impressed by sense experience — it is *constructed* in personal life history.

The idea became a very fertile one for philosophers and psychologists. First, I want to offer some illustration of the range of expression of this idea in 20th-century theories, before turning to the most prominent of these, that of Jean Piaget. Because Piaget's theory has also had most to say about development, it will take up the bulk of this chapter.

Gestalt psychology

The transcendentalism that followed Kant's doctrines, most notably in Hegel and Goethe, pervaded German philosophy and psychology in the 19th century, and eventually spread to other parts of Europe. Hegel introduced the notion of dialectics to a constructivist view of human history. Both James Mark Baldwin (1861–1934) and George Herbert Mead (1863–1931) introduced the "dialectics of personal growth" to cognitive development (Markova, 1990). In psychology, however, the earliest expression of this movement was that of Gestalt psychology. This movement originated in Germany at the turn of the century, later moving to the USA, and forming a distinct school which was prominent right up to the 1950s, and still finds favourable support.

Gestalt psychology was classically constructivist in that the mind and its contents and products were not seen as either a copy of external associations *or* of innate knowledge, but rather as an agent that structures the "given" by creating new functional relations between its parts.

The movement started with observation and interpretation of some distinct perceptual phenomena. Thus, Ehrenfels had argued in 1890 that the perception of music involves a "form quality" that transcends the sum of its particular elements (described by Robinson, 1981). Wertheimer, in 1912, had students observe two stripes a few inches apart in a darkened room which could be illuminated in swift succession. Subjects tended to report a single stripe moving in the direction of the order of illumination — a common experience with any lights lit in swift succession, and known as the "phi phenomenon'. Other Gestalt theorists showed how subjects tend to "see" a single triangle in Fig. 3.1 (left) and columns rather than rows in Fig. 3.1 (right). In these, and other such cases, there is nothing in the sensory experience which "contains" the form or the movement. Instead, there appear to be built-in lawful, mental processes that impose organisation on sense data to produce the percept (or Gestalt).

In the 1940s and 1950s Gestalt psychologists turned their attentions to human problem-solving as a constructive reorganisation of problem situations, such as to aim for good and complete form in the solution. Solving a problem, they maintained, depended on "seeing" or constructing it the right way, when the solution becomes immediately

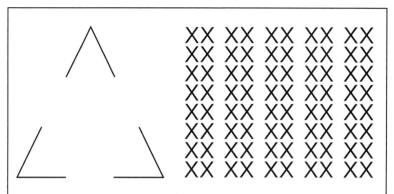

FIG. 3.1.
The Gestalt "Law of Closure" completes a whole figure (left) from incomplete parts. The "Law of Proximity" will arrange components into rows or columns according to spacing (right).

obvious (the term "insight" was frequently used). In all of these ways the Kantian undercurrent remained, in the sense of logical relations imposed on sense-data to construct a "world" in representation (for a recent review, see Murray, 1997). Note that, because Gestalt theorists do not usually explain the origins of this structuration except as general aspects of nervous system organisation, they have sometimes been described as nativist. Piaget said (1977, p.417): "Such an interpretation certainly consists in a biological apriority or a variety of preformationism." While it is probably difficult to disagree with this, Gestalt structuration is certainly of a more general or basic form than that of the discrete knowledge structures and cognitive processes reviewed in Chapter 1, and embodies a more "Kantian" constructivism, than "Platonic" apriorism. For that reason I leave it here, though some students may like to conclude otherwise.

Modern schema theory

In Chapter 2, I described how the term "schema" has been applied to complex associations, such as common scenes, situations, or sequences of events. Here (and in most of this chapter) I want to describe how the term has been used in another way. In his well-known book *Remembering* (1932), Bartlett described studies in which subjects were asked to reproduce stories and pictures experienced earlier. They typically elaborated or distorted the originals in a way that imposed their personal and social conventions over the original story line. Bartlett thus concluded that remembering is a reconstructive process — an interaction between experience and some more abstract cognitive representation of the world experienced. He used the term schema to describe this representation and is thus "the acknowledged originator of the use of schemata to describe story recall". (Thorndyke, 1984, p.144).

Bartlett's use of the term "schema" was thus broader than that of associations in memory; it incorporated social learning and cognition, and he saw its function as that of liberating us from the strictures of immediate experience. As he later put it in his book on *Thinking* (1958, p.200):

> It is with thinking as it is with recall: Memory and all the life of images and words which goes with it are one with ... the development of constructive imagination and constructive thought wherein at length we find the most complete release from the narrowness of present time and space.

The notion of the schema as the basis of knowledge and thought has become very broad in recent years, and its developmental aspects increasingly explored. According to Glaser (1984, p.10) a schema is a "modifiable information structure that represents generic concepts stored in memory." Sometimes the term "frame" has been used to indicate the development of a generalised representation of commonly recurring, but variable, objects and events in a familiar context. Schanks, and Abelson (1977) introduced the notion of a "script" as a description of the generalised representation of sequences of events following a familiar theme, but in which detailed objects and events may vary. For example, we may have constructed a script for "getting dressed" or "eating at a restaurant". In each of these scripts there are said to be sequences or clusters of slots being filled by variable — though substitutable – events or objects ("slot fillers") depending on the particular context (e.g. getting dressed for work versus getting dressed for a jog). Nelson (1986) has argued that such scripts serve as the basis for the formation of higher (superordinate) levels of conceptual representation.

There is much empirical evidence that children incorporate details of routine events into generalised representations, forgetting those details in the process. Thus they will remember, for example, that they had lunch on Tuesday last week, but not the details of the menu. When asked to report about specific activities such as shopping, baking, or the events of a birthday party, even 3-year-olds structure their reports in a stereotyped temporal sequence, "using the general pronoun and timeless present tense, 'You do X'" (Davidson, 1996, p.38). At the same time, narratives about specific events often consist of interactions between generalised knowledge and particular details, unusual details, perhaps inconsistent with the general routine, being particularly well remembered (for review see Davidson, 1996).

Another common type of schema is that of the stereotype — e.g. gender stereotypes — the existence and influence of which have also been studied in children. For example, if told stories or given descriptions of individuals, children are more likely to remember information that is consistent rather than inconsistent with gender-role stereotypes, often distorting information to *make* it consistent (for example, describing a male secretary, in a picture, as a typewriter repair-man; see Davidson, 1996). Studies in the same vein have shown how children from 6–10 years old have a negative schema of the elderly and respond on the basis of the schema regardless of the prior description of the particular character being questioned about (Davidson, 1996).

Note again that the term schema is sometimes used by associationist theorists to describe any more-or-less "abstract" set of associations. For example, a prototype (see Chapter 2) is sometimes described as a schema (see Billman, 1996), but this is a different use of the term from the constructivist usage being described here.

Mental models

A number of models suggest that the mind consists of a set of formal rules which, when applied to given premises or other preconditions, automatically produce an inference (see Chapter 1). Byrne and Johnson-Laird (1990, p.142), however, ask us to consider the following given statements which we are asked to fit into a plausible story:

> 'Lisa can have a fish supper'
> 'Lisa catches some fish'
> 'Lisa goes fishing'

What they argue is that rule-based models cannot do this based only on the information given. Rather we have to use our background knowledge, or understanding of the premises. This is brought to bear on the problem by helping to construct a "mental model" of the current situation, together with alternative outcomes and their relative probabilities. Johnson-Laird (1983, p.165) contrasts mental models, "which are structural analogues of the world", with "propositional representations which are strings of symbols that correspond to natural language", and "images which are the perceptual correlates of models from a particular point of view." Byrne and Johnson-Laird (1990) summarise studies in which they have pitted one kind of theory against the other with results supporting the idea of mental model construction.

Halford (1993, p.8) suggests that problem solving (as in the Gestaltian "insight" mentioned earlier) depends on having an internal representation or mental model "that is structurally isomorphic to the problem". Although acknowledging that sometimes associative processes operate, he argues that much of human problem solving consists of reasoning analogically using mental models based on structural regularities in common experience. For example, general experience, even in early childhood, leads to a generalised conception of an "ordered set": e.g. in sets of building bricks, in relative heights of brothers and sisters, and so on. This can be used to solve a "transitive inference" problem in which, for example, children are asked "if Bill is happier than Tom, and Tom is happier than Harry, who is the happiest?". According to Halford it is solved by mapping analogically from the (known) ordered set to construct a mental model of the current problem, when the solution becomes fairly obvious (Fig. 3.2).

Cognitive development in this perspective consists, at least in part, of the progressive registration of the structural regularities in the world of experience, and thus their extension to an ever wider array of problem types through the availability of more mental models. Such models also become more complete, more economically "chunked" (in

FIG. 3.2. Problem solving through construction of a mental model (reasoning analogically from an ordered set of building blocks) according to Halford (redrawn from Halford, 1993).

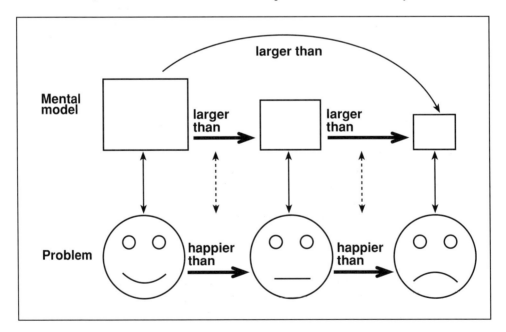

the sense of representations utilising fewer dimensions), and used more flexibly across problem situations.

Mandler's theory

Mandler starts with the reasonable assumption that we reason with what things "are" rather than "what they look like" — reasonable, because the same kinds of things are variable and/or changeable in appearance. This, then, distinguishes conception from perception. Knowledge concepts *start*, of course, from perceptual input. But from there they are transformed, or "redescribed" into meaningful categories, initially "image schemas" (Mandler, 1992) which may have little obvious association with perceptual features.

As an illustration, Mandler (1992) cites the following study. Ross (1980) familiarised 1-year-old infants with highly varied wood and plastic replicas of one of three categories (animals, furniture, or food) using the habituation/dishabituation paradigm described in Chapter 1. When an exemplar from another of the categories was then presented, the infants dishabituated to it (i.e. it was perceived as "new"). As Mandler (1992, p.275) explains, these results are difficult to explain purely on grounds of similarity or dissimilarity of appearance, because the *within*-category variability in shapes varied as much as the between-category variability. It's as if the infants are also conceiving something deeper — that the "new" objects are "different kinds of things".

Instead, Mandler (1993, p.146) argues that further cognitive processes of analysis and transformation intervene:

> What turns a pattern into a concept is a process I call perceptual analysis. It redescribes perceptual information into a conceptual format ... This process results in the description of animals as the kind of objects that start up on their own, move in an irregular way, and interact contingently from a distance with other objects. These redescriptions are based on perceptual categorisation, but they go a step further: they provide the meanings that determine the kinds of perceptual information that will receive further attention.

So conceptual development, then, is a process of increasing analysis, discrimination, and refinement about the properties of things. For example, among the earliest concepts thus being formed in early infancy are "animate" and "inanimate", based perhaps on the analysis of different kinds of motion. Mandler's theoretical model (1992, pp.276–277) for the process is typically Kantian

> It is not necessary to posit innate knowledge about objects to account for the early appearance of concepts. We need only to grant that infants are born with a capacity to abstract certain kinds of information from the perceptual displays they process, and to redescribe them into conceptual form.

Obviously such a capacity of reprocessing is no trivial one, but Mandler gives few clear details about what it might consist of. We are told (1992, p.277) that it involves "attentive analysis": "instead of merely 'looking', the infant notices some aspect of the stimulus array, and recodes into a simplified form [which] distills its meaning." This form is said to be that of an "image schema" — for example the notion of PATH of objects in space, and of animate and inanimate, as mentioned earlier. These are said to be of "analog form" (i.e. some sort of veridical copy); but there is no indication of how such analogs are formed in real brains/minds. Nor are we told anything more about the "kinds of information" that are abstracted to constitute them. Some ideas are floated, such as "contingent motion" and "linked paths" as the basis of the animate concept. Although suggestive, they are at a very general, metaphoric, level, without any indication of how they are formed in real brains/minds. Such lack of detail, however, is a very common problem in constructivist theory, as in cognitive theory generally.

Piaget's theory

The theory of cognitive development built by Jean Piaget over a period of several decades stands as a powerful exemplification of a constructivist approach, and remains the most detailed theory of cognitive development. As he emphasised many times, Piaget was an epistemologist, interested in the nature of human knowledge, and how it changes over time (as in, particularly, the history of scientific knowledge). By this he meant, as had all the philospher-psychologists before, *necessary knowledge* — knowledge that appears to be "independent of time", yet conceived by cognitive operations "that are subject to evolution and constituted in time" (Piaget, 1959, p.23, quoted by Smith, 1993, p.1). Piaget argued that this could best be understood by studying the development of knowledge in children (he was thus only secondarily a developmental psychologist). The theory stands as a bold alternative to empiricism, and, to a large extent, nativism as accounts of the origins of reliable knowledge.

Basic presuppositions: The coordination of parts and wholes

Early in his life Piaget became interested in part–whole relations, and saw the structure of those relations, and the balance or equilibrium between them, as the answer to the problem of organisation in all fields of inquiry, including psychology (Chapman, 1988). Developing intellectually at a time when logic was seen as the height of human reasoning, and logical thought as the most "correct", "adapted", "justifiable", and so on, he naturally thought that these relations underlay logical operations, too. As a result (Piaget, 1952, p.245; quoted by Chapman, 1988, p.32):

> it became clear to me that the theory of the relations between the whole and the part can be studied experimentally through an analysis of the psychological processes underlying logical operations ... Thus my observations that logic is not inborn, but develops little by little, appeared to be consistent with my ideas on the formation of the equilibrium toward which the evolution of mental structures tends.

For Piaget, human intelligence is neither a hypothetical, general, mental strength or power, nor the operation of specific cognitive processes. Rather, it is the process of adaptation that characterises so much of life as a whole. But, unlike the maturation of pre-adapted physical processes of the body, adaptation at the mental level cannot be predetermined. The evidence for this is that, in the emergence of knowledge and reasoning powers in individuals, "there is a continual construction of novelty" (Piaget, 1970, reprinted in 1988, p.11). It is this (ultimate) creativity or inventiveness of thought that stands out as the strongest assumption in Piaget's theory. Thus he valued other constructivist theories, such as the structuralism of the Gestalt theorists, but criticised the lack of transformation, creativity and development within them (Van der Veer, 1996). By the same token Piaget had little room for *a priori* categories or structures in cognitive development, and thus has only a rather weak connection with this aspect of Kantian philosophy (Chapman, 1988), though similar to it in other respects.

Another basic assumption is of the role of action in "revealing" the world to which organisms adapt. Thus according to Piaget, intelligence arises neither from the "inside" nor from the "outside", alone, but from external actions, not only on physical objects but, more importantly, on or with other human agents.

Basic constituents

The most basic constituents of intelligence are the coordinations that are revealed in such actions, and which become represented in mental structures or operations. Indeed, in his early works *(The language and thought of the child; Judgement and reasoning in the child)* Piaget noted an inability in the under-7s to understand relations because they lacked reversibility at a representational level — i.e. the ability to move mentally from one state of a transformation to another (e.g. parts into wholes), and back again. When this does occur the representations are in *equilibrium*, and it is such equilibrium that Piaget saw as the developmental pre-requisite for logical and scientific thinking.

Different degrees of equilibrium characterise three stages of development in Piaget's theory. Readers of Piaget have commonly construed an age-related sequence in these, promulgating something like the following picture. In the first eighteen months of life children acquire reversibility at a sensorimotor level, but this is not yet represented in thought. Such reversibility in representation develops very slowly up to the age of 7, but even up to the age of 11 years is only expressed in thought and action with concrete objects and situations, immediately present in experience. Only after 11 years can full reversibility in thought be found, applied to imagined or hypothetical situations, and thus the child takes on the qualities of mature logical and scientific thinking. However, it needs to be stressed that age has simply been a convenient descriptive marker and is not itself an actual criterion of developmental stage: rather the latter is determined by other criteria of "level" (cf. Smith, 1997).

According to Piaget, the properties of stages depend on the internalisation of coordinations revealed in the world by action upon it. Take, for example, a ball of clay rolled out into successive shapes (Fig. 3.3). According to Piaget, the actions of the subject on the object reveal simple coordinations. First, the length and the thickness are not independent dimensions. There is a necessary connection between them — as one changes so does the other; that is, they vary together, or covary. In other words they are *coordinated*. But this coordination is itself only part of a wider system of coordinations of which even a simple action like this consists – coordinations between the visual appearance and the motion of the ball, for example, and between these and the sense-receptors in muscles and joints.

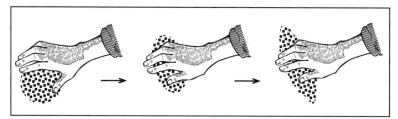

FIG. 3.3.
Coordinations in
rolling a ball of clay.

But the really exciting prospect is that, when these coordinations have been represented in the sensorimotor system, a set of new powers becomes available which vastly increases our predictive abilities (our intelligence) about the world. For example, there is now *compensation* (or reversibility by reciprocation) between the variables. We can predict that reducing the length will increase the thickness proportionately, and vice versa:

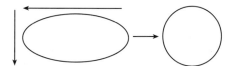

This also illustrates *reversibility by inversion*. Given a transformed shape, we can predict what effort would be required to return it to its original shape. This illustrates two of many operatory structures: the one expressing reversibility by inversion; the other reversibility by reciprocation.

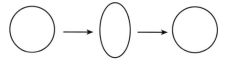

In everyday thoughts and actions like digging, riding bikes, lifting objects, and so on, in which the myriad permutations of sensations and motor actions in each specific task are almost always novel, we take these powers for granted. But they would not be available without the representations of coordinations being constructed. This is why coordination is such an important idea in Piaget's theory. As Piaget (1972, p.22) put it, "... intelligence derives from the coordinations in action ... higher mental processes are internalised actions."

This derivation is most explicit in the passage from sensorimotor to representational intelligence. Because it is the stage that has been most clearly described I will dwell on it at some length here, and then deal with the others more briefly. However, it should already be clear that the main problem of cognitive psychology from Piaget's point of view is "to understand the mechanism of these internal coordinations, which imply both invention without trial and error and a mental anticipation closely related to mental representation" (1972, p.105).

Sensorimotor intelligence

Infants enter the world with a set of simple coordinations which we call reflexes. These include such phenomena as the grasping reflex, the plantar reflex, the looking reflex, the sucking reflex, and so on. Apart from these, the infant has no "knowledge" of the world, and is incapable of making any "cognitions" about it. No distinction can even be made between stimuli arising from the inside world and from the outside world. The individual does not yet form a "subject" with an identity separable from the world in general.

However, the innate schemes are not fixed, isolated responses. They ensure actions on the world — actions which encounter frequent *disturbances*, and, through the coordination needed to adapt to them, the schemas modify and develop. Even within the first few days of life, for example (Piaget & Inhelder, 1969, p.7), "the newborn child nurses with more assurance and finds the nipple more easily when it has slipped out of his mouth than at the time of his first attempts". Over a similar period, sucking of other things, such as covers, clothing, or thumb, becomes assimilated to the same schema. In the process the schema accommodates to the new shapes and forms. Take, for example, the scheme (or palmar reflex) of grasping — the tendency to grasp anything placed in the palm of the hand. Studies in infancy show how the original "tight" grasping pattern slowly accommodates to a range of shapes of objects (Fig. 3.4).

Piaget (1975, p.88) states: "A similar pattern expresses the activity of looking; if an object sighted by the subject is moved out of the visual field, a slight movement of the head or eyes displaces this field until the

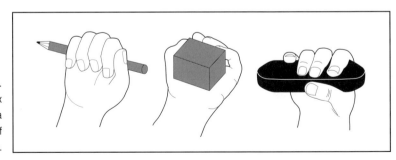

FIG. 3.4.
The palmar reflex accommodates to a variety of shapes of objects.

object is again found in its centre." To the child the initial disappearance of the object is a disturbance. There is compensation and re-equilibration of the existing coordinations in the scheme, and the infant very soon develops the power of following a moving object in the visual field. This power is, of course, based on *new* coordinations involving the direction and speed of motion, the motor commands to the eye and neck muscles, and so on (Fig. 3.5).

So even "innate" schemes are modifiable, and must not be thought of as fixed responses. New coordinations are constructed from those present at birth by sequences of "re-equilibrations", and the development of "compensated" schemes:

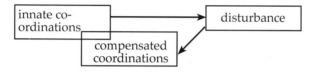

Similar sequences apply to all the innate coordinations — including seeing, hearing etc. — starting from the first moments of birth.

Piaget called the repetition of compensated reflexes (e.g. putting hand to mouth to suck it), common over the first 10 weeks, "primary circular reactions". The separate sets of coordinations in developing schemes, such as looking and grasping, then become *inter*-coordinated. The infant typically tries grasping everything in the visual field. When,

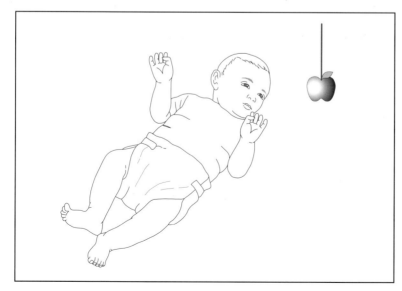

FIG. 3.5.
Visually tracking a moving object requires development of suitable coordinations of vision and motor actions.

as is often the case, certain effects are produced (e.g. pulling a cord over the pram shakes some rattles), this will be repeated over and over again. Piaget called these "secondary circular reactions", which are common in the 4- to 8-month period. But, although there is coordination of vision and grasping, the *effects* are not yet coordinated with them — rather they are seen as a "magical" result. Put any object over the cot and the baby will look for the cord in order to make the sound. Such "means–end coordination" is only shown to appear when, for example, the infant begins to pull one object as a means to obtaining another, usually in the 8- to 12-month period (Fig. 3.6).

As a result of these developments, important new powers emerge, including the concept of object-permanence. In one famous demonstration of behaviour prior to this stage, an infant is presented with an object. Just as reaching commences, however, the object is covered with an inverted cup. Thus concealed from sight, the object has no further existence as far as the infant is concerned (Fig. 3.7).

FIG. 3.6.
Means–end coordination appears in the 8–12-month-old period.

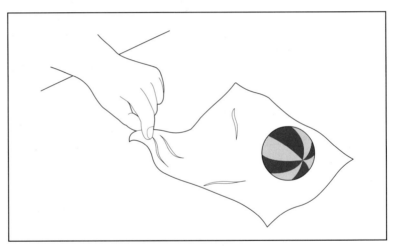

FIG. 3.7.
Lack of appropriate coordinations means that an object placed out of sight literally ceases to exist.

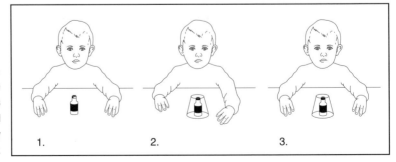

1.   2.   3.

With the development of appropriate inter-coordinations, one object no longer simply "replaces" another when covering or screening it; the infant now appreciates that what is seen or not seen is a consequence of *relations* between objects in a coordinated system, rather than one set of fleeting stimuli replacing another (Fig. 3.8). This is what Piaget called the concept of "object permanence" — a new operational structure which involves not just the idea that a body "exists", but also a whole system of spatial awareness from which a new range of predictions can be made on the basis of the spatial relations among objects (see Piaget, 1954). In particular, the infant can now conceive of him or her self as an "object" distinct from those in the outside world, a momentous development which Piaget called a "Copernican revolution".

This dynamic continues, according to Piaget, with even more remarkable consequences between 12 and 18 months. New powers and new confidence arise with the coordinated schemes just described. Instead of merely reacting to disturbances, the child now begins to act upon and manipulate objects simply to produce disturbances: banging and throwing objects in various ways; breaking up crusts of bread, and so on. These are called *tertiary circular reactions* and appear as a drive to know objects through experimentation.

These developments produce a kind of logic of action, according to Piaget. For example, the concept of space as we know it (so-called Euclidean space) is seen in the concept of object permanence, but involves logical structures. Piaget referred to these (after the mathematical theory of logic) as the "group of displacements", in which the world near and far, and objects in it, are inter-related as a coherent set of coordinations (a group being an inter-related set of operations which make up a logical structure).

The power and economy of such structures are easy to demonstrate. For example, in the diagram below, the path from A to B and then to C is seen as equivalent to the path from A to C. If a child rolls a ball from A which bounces off a chair at B and then rolls under another chair and

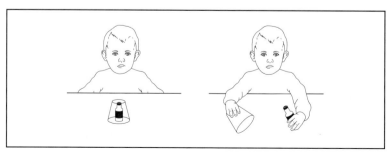

FIG. 3.8.
With the intercoordination of schemes the world becomes one of relations between objects, rather than fleeting appearances and disappearances.

out of sight at C, he/she will not slavishly follow the perceptual route ABC but go direct to C. Moreover, the possibility of the ball returning to its original position via CBA (reversibility) becomes understood. Understanding of these properties of space allows for various forms of detour, diversion, and other predictabilities in "route planning": e.g. that AC + CD = AD. And because these displacements in space are coordinated as ordinal, step by step, variables, so a concept of time begins to be constructed at this point.

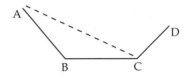

These are nascent "operations of thought" of which there are many others emerging at this stage. In this stage, too, "the child becomes capable of finding new means not only by physical or external groping but also by internalized combinations that culminate in sudden comprehension or *insight*" (Piaget & Inhelder, 1969, p.12, emphasis in original). Thus solutions in problem solving begin to flow. This leads to a transitionary phase and the advent of the

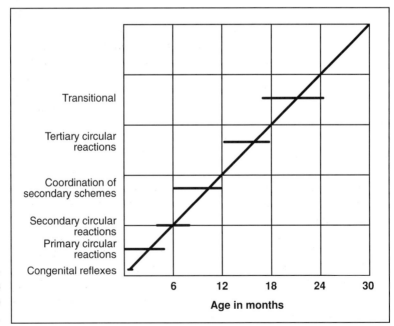

FIG. 3.9.
One infant's development over the sensorimotor period.

next major period. This will be discussed later. In the meantime the graph in Fig. 3.9 — based on the development of one particular child through these periods — will give you some idea of the chronology involved, although it is important to stress that it is not actual *ages* for stage transition that are important in Piaget's theory, so much as the actual development of the coordinations or operatory structures that characterise them (Fig. 3.9).

Again, let us remind ourselves that Piaget called these coordinations *sensorimotor* knowledge. As with rolling out a ball of clay (or with our knowledge of many physical actions, such as cycling, in adulthood) it is, so to speak, "in the muscles". It involves no conscious reflection. After the first year or so, however, a slow process of "representation" of this knowledge begins at a conscious, reflective level. I will take up discussion of this new stage of development later; but it is first necessary to discuss some other crucial aspects of Piaget's model of development.

Equilibration and the mechanisms of development

As we have seen, coordinations of perception and action are at the root of the matter, and I have already used terms like structures and schemas. What these consist of, and how they are constructed "in the mind", however, is another matter. This is the problem that Piaget recognised as the key to the understanding of development — the "how" of development. We need to consider these ideas carefully because, almost uniquely among theorists of cognitive development, Piaget attempted to describe a detailed developmental *process*. In addition, it so often happens that secondary accounts of Piaget's theory offer a description of the "symptoms" of the stages, without seriously considering the mechanism of development and the dynamics underlying the symptoms.

At the root are internal compensations or regulations which need to change in order to cope with external disturbances. By "disturbance" Piaget meant virtually any previously unpredicted effect: for example, an unexpected obstacle in a pathway; an unexpected force of resistance in lifting or moving a familiar object; or any observation not predicted by the current system of coordinations. The disturbances are compensated for by "cancelling" (ignoring or pushing out of the way) or by "neutralising" (creating a reciprocal force), depending on the nature of the "system" of coordinations in question. As Piaget (1975, p.28) put it, "all compensation works in an opposite or reciprocal direction to that of the disturbance ... which means it either cancels (inversion) or neutralises the disturbance (reciprocity)."

For a disturbance to be "unexpected" means that it doesn't conform to a currently represented set of coordinations — that is why it is a disturbance. Generally, we have equilibrium when the coordinations as represented by the Subject (S) correspond exactly with those in the world of Objects (O) as experienced:

$$\text{Coords.S} \longleftarrow \text{Coords.O}$$

Disturbance arises when the equilibrium between these is no longer obeyed, as when a ball of different, stiffer clay presents a resistance greater than what we have been used to. This arises as a new "observable" in the Object (Obs.O) which is duly registered as a disturbance (a "surprise"; something unexpected) by the Subject (Obs.S). Piaget used diagrams like the following to illustrate these relations:

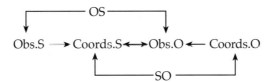

In this diagram SO represents the subject's actions on O (arising from a pre-existing scheme). OS represents the resulting observables impinging on S. The equilibrium is the double-headed arrow. The diagram nicely captures the relations involved in the interaction, while indicating the complexity of most of our actions. You might like to study it for a while to make sure you have grasped the relations involved. A more "flesh and blood" version is indicated in Fig. 3.10.

But this diagram and picture represent only a snapshot from a moment in time. In reality such actions, disturbances, compensations, and so on may be taking place in swift succession. This gives rise to a dynamic process of re-equilibrations through successive states of equilibrium, E1, E2, and so on. *This is what constitutes development according to Piaget:*

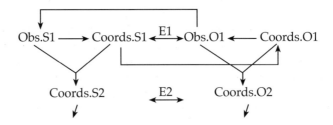

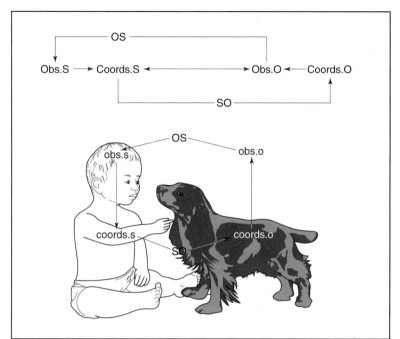

FIG. 3.10.
Dynamic and continuous process of equilibration: action yields novel coordination in the object, observed by the subject, whose coordinations have to be re-equilibrated as a result, leading to compensated actions, and so on.

In other words, the process of development consists of progressive enrichment of equilibrations. This enrichment may take several forms. First, the equilibrations may pertain to a broader range of content — to a wider range of objects from a particular category, for example. Second, equilibrations pertaining to different objects may mutually equilibrate to a more integrated structure — as seen in the concept of object permanence, for example. Conversely, sub-schemes may form to create a more differentiated system (sub-concepts may form), which are, of course, reciprocally accommodated.

All of these involve relations that constitute "operatory structures", in Piagetian terminology. This means that the system now acts on a new, conceptual level, capable of the inventiveness of reflective abstraction. Piaget distinguished this from "figurative" or empirical abstraction — i.e. the mere generalisation of properties (e.g. colour, weight, volume) from direct experience. Reflective (or reflexive or logico-mathematical) abstraction is more than mere generalisation, involving a construction at a higher level, and consists of the "realisation" of properties and relationships not directly given in experience by the *mental* actions or transformations of the operatory structures. Accordingly, two kinds of knowledge develop in Piaget's theory, the figurative and the logico-mathematical, or operative. Whereas the former are compressed "copies" of reality the generativity of the latter allows representations beyond reality, and thus the "anticipation" of novel possibilities, as in maths and theories of science.

To Piaget, then, knowledge is characterised, not as assemblies of facts or experiences (the associationist's "copies" of the world) but of "invariance under transformation". The result is a logic of action which "organizes reality by constructing ... the schemes of the permanent object, space time and causality ... structures of ordering and assembling that constitute a substructure for the future operations of thought" (Piaget & Inhelder, 1969, p.13). These developments alter reality to the child, from a shifting, unpredictable tableau, to a manageable, predictable world — and it is one not given in genes, nor "copied" as shallow associations, but constructed in the form of schemes and their operations.

The semiotic functions.   Development in the sensorimotor period is, as we have seen, a period of progressive emancipation from immediate sensory and perceptual experience by virtue of slow development of schemes, themselves reflecting underlying coordinations of action and experience. But "the sensorimotor mechanisms are pre-representational" (Piaget & Inhelder, 1969, p.52). What does this mean? It means that the coordinations of sensations and action in schemes give rise to behaviour patterns (as in riding a bike in adults) without intervening thought, mental image, or other shadow, template, or whatever, of the process. This allows, of course, that aspects or fragments of a scene (such as a bottle teat, or corner of a blanket) can be effective as "signifiers" of a behaviour pattern, but these are still "part of" the schema, undifferentiated from it. Although even a young infant will take a glimpse of a teat-end to signify the presence of a whole bottle, or assimilate a novel-shaped object to a "grasping" scheme, this is not the same thing as a differentiated sign or symbol.

In the second half of the second year behaviours arise that, according to Piaget, suggest that a differentiated mental representation of an object or event, not currently present, has formed. For example, *deferred* imitation appears, in which a gesture, formerly copied immediately, may begin to be repeated some time later. So that, instead of a direct mapping:

$$A \longrightarrow B \text{ (sensory coordinations into motor coordinations)}$$

We appear to get an intervening representation:

$$A \longrightarrow [R] \longrightarrow B$$

(where R is some internal representation of the sensorimotor pattern as a whole, but one differentiated from it).

Such representation extends the powers of sensorimotor intelligence beyond the here and now, into what can be considered as thought proper according to Piaget (1977, p.72): it "... makes thought possible by providing it with an unlimited field of applications in contrast with the restricted boundaries of sensorimotor development." This representational capacity is called the semiotic function, and is considered to be crucial to subsequent development. It soon becomes apparent in other areas, such as symbol use and symbolic play. Whereas the sensorimotor schemes are built on "signs", or directly perceived attributes of objects, the child can now use symbols (*differentiated* signifiers, either invented or provided by the culture) to call up, manipulate, and transform such schemas in the new representational plane.

The most prominent early expression of this new symbolic ability arises in the context of play. Symbolic play is to be distinguished from mere "exercise play", consisting of repetitious actions, as in the earlier sensorimotor periods. In symbolic play, surrogate objects or events are used to *represent* other objects and events. For example, bricks are used to represent a vehicle, dolls to resurrect a dinner scene, or the self to become an aeroplane, a bird, or a car (all with appropriate sounds and gestures).

Language begins to appear about the same time as deferred imitation and symbolic play. Vocal gestures increase in the period 6–12 months; recognisable phonemes begin to be used around 12 months; the "one-word" sentence, or holophrase, appears around 18 months; and two-word sentences signal the early learning of grammar around 2 years.

Piaget naturally recognised the advantages with which language overlays the sensorimotor intelligence — albeit only as one expression (along with imitation and play) of the general semiotic function. Just as each of these begins to detach thought from action, to which they are tied in the sensorimotor stage, so language enables thought to range over space and time and become another source of representation. In addition, because language is already a social instrument, it "contains a notation for an entire system of cognitive instruments (relationships, classifications, etc.) for use in the service of thought" (Inhelder & Piaget, 1958, p.87).

The inventiveness with which sensorimotor operations culminate is, according to Piaget, the great achievement of sensorimotor development even in 2-year-olds. The gain is one of inventive adaptability to novel situations without the haphazardness of trial-and-error: "sensorimotor schemata that have become sufficiently mobile and amenable to coordinations among themselves give rise to mutual assimilations, spontaneous enough for there to be no further need for actual trial-and-error and rapid enough to give an impression of immediate restructuring" (Piaget, 1972, p.106, cf. Marti, 1996). Accordingly, cognitive functioning becomes freed from the here and now, and far more rapid and creative.

With these developments come a new subjectivity and intentionality not foreseen on previous levels or in any other species.

Pre-operational intelligence and concrete operations

As actions come to be internalised during the development of semiotic functions we would expect thought itself to thus come to show all the same powers of objectivity, reversibility, compensation, predictability, and so on. Numerous observations suggest, however, that this realisation is severely limited in young children, and takes a long time to develop. For example, a 4-year-old who can find his or her way around the house or school, or walk to near localities, has great difficulty in finding the same route on a cardboard model. The child who has long been drinking successfully out of a beaker by tipping it (and thus understanding the coordinations involved in changes in the liquid, at a sensorimotor level) has difficulty drawing such changes accurately (Fig, 3.11).

Thus according to Piaget and Inhelder (1969, p.94), "The first obstacle to operations, then, is the problem of mentally representing what has already been absorbed on the level of action." Indeed, they argue that it is not for another five years or so (when the child is 7 to 8 years old) that these powers are actually developed in thought — and even that is only part of the way towards "fully operational" thought

FIG. 3.11. The failure to fully represent coordinations in the pre-operational child is seen in the tendency to draw liquid in an inclined beaker as in the centre illustration, instead of as in the one on the right.

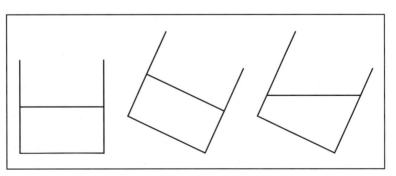

(of which more in a moment). The reasons given for this, and the observations that, Piaget suggested, underpin the idea, have been among the most controversial in Piaget's theory.

The main reason given for this enormous delay is that representational development depends on "constructive processes analogous to those which took place ... on the sensorimotor level" (Piaget & Inhelder, 1969, p.94). You may remember how this involved "the transition from an initial state in which everything is centred on the child's own body and actions to a 'decentred' state in which his own body and actions assume their objective relationships with reference to all the other objects and events registered in the universe" (Piaget & Inhelder, 1969, p.94). At the level of representation in thought these relationships are even more difficult to develop. This is not just because they involve a wider and more complex universe, and operations of greater generality (such as the coordinations in number and classification). They take place in a wider context of social interaction in which alternative viewpoints have to be contended with, and actions often, if not usually, involving *interpersonal* coordinations, not just *intra*-personal ones.

These arguments, however, have depended on the identification of "deficiencies" of thought in the child between 2 and 7 years. And these, in turn, have been based on investigative procedures that have themselves been the targets of much criticism. Let us look at the chief examples as described by Piaget and Inhelder (1969).

Conservation. These are without doubt the most famous of Piaget's experiments. In the typical procedure a child is shown two displays and agrees that they are the same with respect to a particular property (they may be adjusted until such agreement is forthcoming). In the second phase one of the displays is rearranged with respect to the given property, and the child is asked whether they are still the same, or different. Some examples are shown in Fig. 3.12.

Note that mature conservation requires the understanding that the correct reply is "logically" — i.e. *necessarily* — correct, and not merely true in an empirical sense (Smith, 1993). Prior to ages 6–7 years, children's perception appears to be "captured" by the separate dimensions, usually focusing on one specific variable (e.g. the height of the liquid irrespective of the width). In other words, there is still centration or egocentrism with respect to particular variables. After the development of conservation, the coordinations and mutual transformations of these variables appear to be represented as a dynamic interrelations, not just successive states. This implies *de*centration, the understanding of reversibility/inversion (the declaration that a trans-

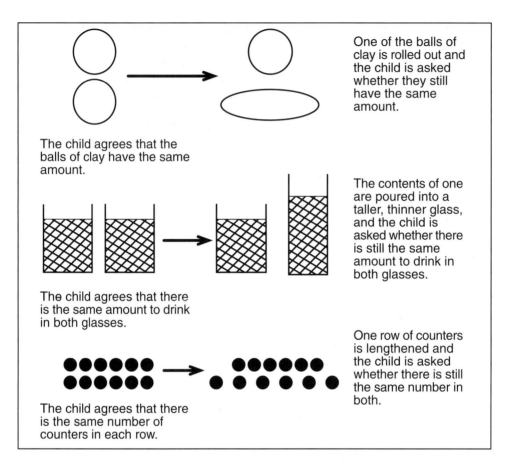

One of the balls of clay is rolled out and the child is asked whether they still have the same amount.

The child agrees that the balls of clay have the same amount.

The contents of one are poured into a taller, thinner glass, and the child is asked whether there is still the same amount to drink in both glasses.

The child agrees that there is the same amount to drink in both glasses.

One row of counters is lengthened and the child is asked whether there is still the same number in both.

The child agrees that there is the same number of counters in each row.

FIG. 3.12.
Typical conservation tasks.

formed state can return to its original state), and reciprocity / compensation (changes in one variable are compensated by changes in others). This representation in turn allows continuous predictability. As one child put it, "I fill it up in my mind, and I see where it comes" (Chapman, 1988, p,155). Thus the changing *perceptual* tableau is tied together by an invariant *conceptual* structure.

This is why Piaget claimed that conservation is the key signal of a maturing operational structure at the representational level. As the advent of other operatory structures at this time signals the advent of logical thinking proper, and sets the foundations for its full development later, it is worth spending a little time looking at these.

Seriation. When children under 7 years are asked to place in order 10 objects whose differences in length are so small that they must be compared two at a time, they only manage orderings of small groups, of two or three, and no coordination into a complete series. At some later stage they may attain this by trial and error arrangements until the final series is achieved. Only around 7 years of age is a *systematic* method for finding the smallest, and then the next smallest, and so on, displayed. This suggests development of an "operatory structure" because it reflects a coordination (reversibility) such that any object can be simultaneously small in relation to one object, but larger in relation to others. Again it implies the understanding of a logical necessity.

These same operatory coordinations are demonstrated in another way, according to Piaget — namely the capacity for transitivity in thought. The child with such a structure can reason that if an object A is smaller than B, and B is smaller than another object C, then A is also smaller than C. According to Piaget, "preoperatory subjects" are incapable of doing this. Again, you should be able to see how this involves the lack of coordination in representation.

Classification. When preschool children are presented with a variety of objects and asked to "put things that are alike together", they tend to group on the basis of a single dimension such as shape or colour, and arrange the subsets to form a figure like a square or circle. Inhelder and Piaget (1958) called these "figural groupings". Later, between 5 and 6 years, they will form seemingly rational groups and subgroups, but there still appear to be lacunae in the child's thought.

In a famous study the child is shown a row of flowers consisting of two types — red and white (Fig. 3.13). The child is asked "are there more red flowers or more flowers?" Usually the child can only say that there are more red flowers or that they are both the same. As Piaget and Inhelder (1969, p.103) explain, there is a failure in coordination of the class with its sub-classes, or the ability to think of the whole and its parts at the same time: the child "is unable to respond according to the inclusion A<B, because if he thinks of the part A, the whole ceases to to be conserved as a unit." Only at about age 8 does "classification", and its implication for logical necessity, arise as an operatory structure —

red flowers   white flowers

FIG. 3.13.
Classification: "Are there more red flowers or more flowers?"

and again, in Piaget's eyes, as a further illustration of coordinations in representation.

Number. Number, too, is treated by Piaget as an operatory structure dependent on coordinations in representation, and a particularly strong illustration of the vitality of logical necessity in mature operations. The absence of coordinations at first is shown in the preschool child's failure to conserve spatial arrays of elements. Attention is arrested by perceptually prominent variables, such as the length of the row, as was illustrated in Fig. 3.12 on conservation of number. Number concept begins to develop when the child begins to ignore perceptually prominent qualities of the array, and even the class of the elements, and concentrates instead on the one-to-one equivalence of arrays.

According to Piaget, this really consists of a synthesis (or inter-coordination) of the coordinations in seriation and classification. First, the number concept involves sets in class-inclusion coordinations (i.e. 2 is included in 3, which is included in 4, and so on). The final, or *cardinal*, number in a set has a necessity about it, which transcends mere perception, order of counting, and so on. Second, the sets are distinguished from one another by representing their elements serially in space or time: 3 is greater than 2, which is greater than 1, so 3 is greater than 1 — again, a logical necessity. It is for these reasons that, according to Piaget, the number concept appears in development *together with* classification and seriation, and never before. But every child needs to understand these logical necessities before even simple counting can be properly understood (Nunes & Bryant, 1996).

Space, time, and causality. The operatory structures just described relate to thinking about objects and materials. But the child also develops ideas about other, non-object, phenomena such as the nature of space, of time, and causality. These, too, are based on operatory structures involving the development of coordinations in representation, according to Piaget. For example, extension in space as in measuring a line consists of coordinating segments of the line, as in class inclusion, and also of seriation — i.e. another synthesis of coordinations, but different from that in number. Other spatial structures result from coordination of viewpoints, resulting in the ability to decentre from one's personal viewpoint, and even to use joint-coordination systems of reference as in map grids. These structures are all vital in the logical management of space.

That the preschool child has a poor conception of time is shown in a number of ways. Thus the speed and time of arrival of a vehicle at a terminus are rarely fully coordinated at this age — the child cannot predict one from the other. Later, the child begins to "see" that if one vehicle overtakes another on the same trajectory it arrives at the terminus sooner. Duration and distance then become coordinated more precisely. According to Piaget, this again depends on the inter-coordination of operations (and *their* coordinations); in other words.

1. Seriation (now applied to events rather than objects).
2. Class inclusion (now of intervals rather than objects).
3. A segmentation of the tempo of events analogical to that in spatial metrics (see earlier).

Whereas at first these are independent systems, they come together to constitute time as an objective relation.

Preschool children also have a "precausal" notion of events, often relying on teleological, "animistic," or anthropomorphic explanations of events, in which all events are assimilated to the child's existing action schemes. Thus the sun may be conceived as a ball that someone threw in the sky, and the moon as following us around (Piaget & Inhelder, 1969, p.110). A "rational" concept of causality emerges as a result of "general coordination of action", as distinct from the assimilation of events to egocentric action schemes.

In one experiment illustrating this, Piaget and Inhelder (1969) designed a box containing 10 white beads and 10 black beads in separate shallow compartments. When the box is rocked with the lid closed, children are asked to predict what will happen to the black and white beads, which will obviously mix in the rocking. Four- to 6-year-olds argue that the beads will return to their proper places. Only after around 8 years is it recognised that this is a highly improbable event.

Social behaviour. The emergence from a sensorimotor into a representational period is not simply an "internal" cognitive development, but one that is manifest in the child's social behaviour. Contrary to many impressions given in recent years, Piaget was well aware of the connections between cognition and social-emotional behaviour (Smith, 1996a), even if he concentrated his efforts on elucidating the former.

According to Piaget, it is in fact the advent of operatory structures that allows lasting sympathies and antipathies with other people. They also furnish a new sense of self, with assertions of independence and individuality: "a complex and contradictory situation in which the self wants to be at the same time free of, and esteemed by, others" (Piaget & Inhelder, 1969, p.115). Many develop-ments in social behaviour reflect the construction of operatory struc-tures, according to Piaget.

Before 7 years of age the lack of such structures is reflected in social exchanges that are "egocentric" (i.e dominated by perception), with experiences assimilated to the child's own action schemes. For example, in a game like marbles a preschool child will behave according to his or her own view of the game, without much appar-ent concern for the rules of the game and the behaviour of others following them. True cooperation is consequently absent. Likewise, although a preschool child has learned the "rules" of speech, there is not yet true socialised language, but only sequences of "collective monologues" in which children talk, but mainly to and for them-selves. Accordingly, the preschool child has systematic difficulty in taking the point of view of another, and thus in getting another child to do something by means of language.

Only after around 7 years of age does the child begin to coordinate the behaviours, feelings etc. of others into operatory structures and overcome such representational deficiencies. A similar progression is observed, according to Piaget, in moral behaviour, from justification of actions in terms of rules or laws to a more rational justification in terms of mutuality and intentions, rather than blind obedience. This reflects, according to Piaget, the development of a functional unity binding cognitive, social, emotional, and moral behaviour.

Logic as the criterion of development

The concrete operational structures furnish the beginnings of "logical" thought. It is, therefore important to consider how Piaget attempted to accommodate his theory within this broader umbrella of verifiability of knowledge that we call "logic". What it means has, in fact, created continual debate.

There is much to recommend logic as a target and criterion of devel-opment. As Piaget (1973, p.28 — see Tomlinson-Keasey, 1982, p.134) explains, logic is "at present perhaps the most exact discipline in terms of the rigour of its demonstrations". In keeping with his early intuitions about part–whole coordinations, Piaget started to inquire in the 1930s whether the concrete operations could be described in terms of the mathematical theory of groups. In his work on *Structuralism* (1971, pp.18–21) he describes this theory as having:

> conquered the whole of nineteenth century mathematics
> ... Groups are today the foundation of algebra. Their

range and fruitfulness are extraordinary. We run into it in practically every area of mathematics and logic. It is already being used in an important way in physics, and very likely the day will come when it acquires a central role in biology as well. Since groups may be viewed as a kind of prototype of structures in general ... we must look to them to ground our hope for the future of structuralism ... It is because the group concept combines transformation and conservation that it has become the basic constructivist tool.

A mathematical group (as in arithmetical operations) is a system composed of elements and operations which create certain properties such as combination (addition), inversion (addition versus subtraction), and associativity (correspondence irrespective of order of operation). In the "group of displacements", mentioned earlier, the operations are real actions with all the formal properties of groups. Piaget argued that the concrete operations also have this group structure, except now in the form of *interiorised actions*. They are *mental* operations, with all the inventiveness already mentioned. In the number system the additive operation is an interiorised action in which its inverse is understood simultaneously. "A grouping is a structure, at once mobile and closed, linking operations to each other according to a principle of reversible composition" (Piaget, 1941, p.218; quoted by Chapman, 1988, p.146). And the over-arching structure (or *structure d'ensemble*) is mutually coordinated.

In several subsequent works Piaget offered formal descriptions of a number of groupings among concrete operations (because they still lack certain group properties, he sometimes referred to the structures of this stage as "groupoids", or "*groupements*"). For example the "simple addition of classes" (class inclusion) forms a superordinate class from two subclasses having a common property defining the class (A1 + A2 = B), in an operation that can be inverted, and so on. The grouping called "multiplication of classes" stems from cross-classification of two class-inclusions: e.g. B1=A1+A2; B2=A3+A4, which yields B1xB2=A1A3+A1A4+A2A3+A2A4. Thus arise new, "logical", possibilities.

In fact, Piaget used different models of logic at different times to serve different purposes (see Piaget & Garcia, 1991; Piaget, Henriques, & Ascher, 1992). But just how successful he was in convincing others about logic being the most significant outcome of cognitive development is a question I shall return to later.

The propositional (formal) operations

According to Piaget, the child with sensorimotor intelligence can do things with objects, and the concrete operational child can *think* about doing those things. But the latter cannot think about propositions and relations detached from particular objects and events. This ability requires another period of development. In the period from 7 years or so, up to adolescence, operatory structures develop from coordinations involving only concrete objects and events to include more general coordinations. The result is a "final, fundamental decentering" (Piaget & Inhelder, 1969, p.130). The child is then freed from the here and now to be able to entertain the possible and the hypothetical, as in scientific reasoning.

In Piaget's theory, this "liberation of thought from content" involves further "coordinations of coordinations". The most significant of these is a combination of the two most distinct groupings of concrete operations, namely reversibility by inversion and reversibility by reciprocity. These now become combined into a single powerful system (not a mere juxtaposition, but an "operatory fusion"), allowing "operations on operations" or *propositional* operations which can include inversions and reciprocities together. Again, this occurs through the mechanisms of disturbance and re-equilibration.

The new "combinatorial system" permits all relations and classes among elements to be entertained, not only those occurring in reality, and thus development from a more simple logic to a "formal propositional logic". In their book *The growth of logical thinking*, Inhelder and Piaget (1958) describe 15 investigations that demonstrate this propositional logic at work.

Perhaps the best known of these is the coloured liquids task. In this task, children of various ages were presented with four flasks of colourless, odourless liquids, and also two beakers and a small bottle of colourless liquid with a dropper. It was demonstrated to the children that mixing two of the liquids from the flasks in a beaker, and then adding a few drops from the small bottle produces a bright yellow colour. Adding liquid from a third flask left it unchanged, whereas adding liquid from the fourth made the colour disappear. The flasks were then randomly rearranged, and the children asked to try to reproduce the yellow colour. The younger children (under 11 years) tended to mix liquids in a haphazard manner, whereas those over 11 years tended to do so more systematically, taking two by two as if by a mental "matrix", and thus reaching a solution more efficiently.

This reflects more flexible thinking in which form is liberated from content. Relations and combinations not actually present in the concrete, are entertained. Such flexibility of representation furnishes a richer logic than is present in the concrete operations "by considering this reality no longer in its limited concrete aspects but in terms of some or all of the possible combinations" (Inhelder & Piaget, 1958, p.133).

The synthesis of the two forms of reversibility, N (reversibility by inversion) and R (reversibility by reciprocity) forms the so-called INRC group. Piaget and Inhelder (1969) give the following example of how a child with this combinatorial structure will make sense of experience. A child between 12 and 15 years old notices a car stopping and starting and a lightbulb coming on and off at the same time. Various lines of logical reasoning or hypotheses are now possible which were not possible before. One of these is that the light *causes* the stopping, which is confirmed by looking for occasions in which the bulb lights up without the car stopping (i.e. the inverse case). Another hypothesis is that the light coming on is *caused by* the stopping (i.e. the reciprocal case). This hypothesis is confirmed by looking for occasions in which the car stops *without* the light going on (an inverse of the reciprocal which is also a correlative of the first, direct case). Thus, as those authors put it:

> without knowing any logical formulae, or the mathematical criteria for a mathematical "group"... the preadolescent of twelve to fifteen is capable of manipulating transformations according to the four possibilities; I (identical transformation), N (inverse transformation), R (reciprocal transformation), and C (correlative transformation).

Another group developing over this period is the set of so-called binary operations. For example, in propositional logic formulation, a proposition can be represented as p (it is a swan) and its negative as -p (it is not a swan). Another proposition can be represented as q (it is white) and its negative as -q (it is not white). Children in the concrete operational stage can combine these in the four possible ways:

> it is a swan and it is white
> it is not a swan and it is white
> it is a swan and it is not white
> it is not a swan and it is not white.

But it is only after the development of the new combinatorial system that these can be "inter-combined" in representations that go beyond their limited, concrete manifestations: e.g. "it is a swan and it is white" implies "it is not a swan and it is not white"; or "it is a swan and it is not white" inverts with "it is not a swan and it is white" — operations to which Piaget gave names like "implication", "inverse of implication", and so on. In this way, Piaget attempted to describe the origins of propositional logic in the formal operatory structures by tabulating truth values in terms of class unions and intersections, thus arriving at the 16 binary operations, and extensions of them.

All this may sound like logical games but, according to Piaget, they describe what goes on in the logic of hypothesis-construction and hypothesis-testing, and thus scientific practice. As an inter-related set or group "they are necessary for a dissociation of factors ... and therefore the exclusion of false hypotheses" (Piaget & Inhelder, 1969, p.135).

Other formal operatory structures or schemes develop from age 11 onwards, such as the concept of proportionality, that of "double systems of reference", and notions of probability. These all help furnish what Piaget called the "experimental spirit", manifest in the way that between 11 and 15 years children increasingly induce general laws to explain the functioning of situations, and use hypothetico-deductive thought to test them. They also come to appreciate crucial aspects of experimental design, such as keeping variables constant while testing for the effects of others. According to Piaget (1974/1976, pp.352–353, quoted by Brown, Metz, & Campione, 1996), the child,

> ... thereby becomes capable of varying the factors in his experiments and of envisaging the various models that might explain a phenomenon, and of checking the latter through actual experimentation.

This, then — however truncated it may be — brings us to the end of what is usually thought of, and still taught, as "Piaget's theory". It is not the end of the story, though. Remarkably, even near the end of his life, Piaget was trying to keep ahead of critics. In books only recently published in the English language, what has come to be called "Piaget's New Theory", has created a wave of excitement. The implications of what are radically new formalisations are still being digested with some astonishment. Before going on to describe it, however, I think it is appropriate to consider some of the kinds of theoretical development, as well as other criticisms about Piaget's "standard" theory, to which Piaget's *new* theory was, at least in part, a substantial response.

Cognition in context

A number of theorists, though wishing to adhere to the central tenets of constructivism, have also tried to overcome what they have seen as weaknesses in it by examining the role of the contexts in which problems appear, and the background knowledge that children bring to them. As mentioned earlier, by the 1970s a number of investigations were beginning to cast doubt on the assumptions, implicit or explicit in many models, that there are universal laws of thought or logic that operate independently of context and content, and that it is the task of the psychologist simply to discover and describe them. That search had proved to be consistently frustrating. As Wason and Johnson-Laird (1972, p.156) noted after one series of studies, "Only gradually did we realise that there was no existing formal calculus which correctly modelled our subjects' inferences" and that "Human reasoning cannot be described by context independent formal rules."

Similar studies have been targeted against the perceived Piagetian doctrine that younger children are "illogical". Studies reviewed by Donaldson (1978) demonstrated that, when the task and its context are made clear to children, they exhibit logical thought and understanding well before the ages that Piaget had suggested as a lower limit. Take, for example, the typical conservation tasks. McGarrigle and Donaldson (1975) studied 4- and 5-year olds on the tasks under two conditions. The standard condition followed that of Piaget, the rearrangement of materials, such as the row of buttons, being done openly and deliberately by the experimenter in the usual way. Only 16% of children gave "conserving" responses to the question "do they (the rows) still have the same amount?" In the modified condition a toy bear (manipulated by the experimenter) "escaped" from its box and "accidentally" lengthened one of the rows while rushing around the room. Now, on being asked whether both rows contained the same amount, 63% of children gave conserving answers. It seems that, given a sensible rationale for the question (the "accidental" rearrangement), children were able to make logical responses after all.

Although Donaldson's studies have been questioned on methodological grounds (e.g. Eames, Shorrocks, & Tomlinson, 1992), similar questions have been raised in other studies. Light, Buckingham, and Robbins (1979) had pairs of children "racing" to fill a grid with pasta shells, initial equality of quantity being ensured by measuring into similar beakers at the outset. This equality the children agreed to. Then the investigator "noticed" that one of the beakers was chipped and safety demanded transfer of contents to another, larger, one (the only alternative available). The shells were duly poured from one to the other. After questioning, many more children agreed that the quantities were still the same, than had done in the pre-test with the standard procedure.

Light et al. concluded that context-free conservation tasks are not good ways of finding out what a child's cognitive level is. Others have concluded that, because children normally think, act, and communicate in a specific context, familiarity of context is an important factor in investigations. Elliot and Donaldson (1982) argue that errors in the tasks are misinterpretations of the questions, and not signs of the state of an underlying "cognitive structure". More importantly, they conclude that "it is essential to have a highly interactive model of the way in which a pre-school child approaches an experimental test of his comprehension." (Elliot & Donaldson, 1982, p.165). Such an "interactive model" has been the broad aim of a number of studies since.

It has also been shown that children's performances on analogical reasoning problems *generally* improve when they tap more *generally held* understandings. For example, nearly all preschool children understand the transformations involved in melting or cutting, and readily complete analogies involving them. If *A* is a piece of chocolate which, in *B*, has melted, and *C* is a snowman, then they have no problem in identifying the melted snowman from alternatives, as *D* (for review see Goswami, 1996). Richardson and Webster (1996b) compared performances of 10-year-olds on contextualised versions of analogies problems with their performance on the standard versions (actually taken from an IQ test — see Fig. 3.14). Performance on the former was considerably improved.

Ceci & Roazzi (1994) report a study in which children had to predict movements on a computer screen of three geometric shapes, actually dictated by an underlying complex rule imposed by the investigators. Even after 750 trials, subjects were still predicting at just above chance. But performance dramatically improved when the shapes were substituted with animals (bees, birds, and butterflies) and incorporated into a game in which they had to be caught in a net, although exactly the same underlying rules of movement remained. In this context children were able to bring their background knowledge to bear on the problem, induce the underlying rules, and *deduce* accurate predictions from them.

Keil (1988) showed how performance on reasoning tasks can be dramatically improved if relations in background knowledge can be metaphorically mapped onto those in the task. Carey (1988) suggests the role of background knowledge in differential performance on class-inclusion tasks, and reviews studies indicating how children's scientific reasoning depends on their degree of knowledge of the domain in

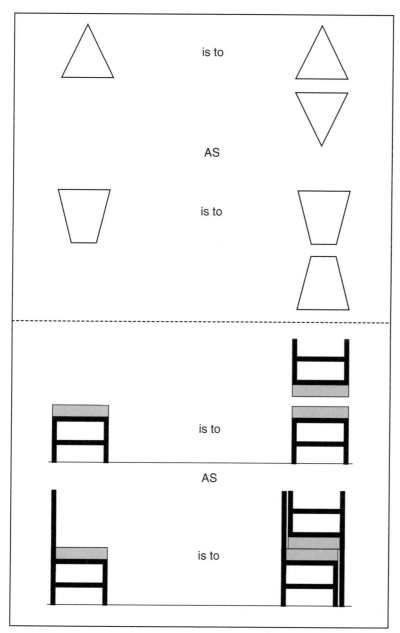

FIG. 3.14. When children are given a "contextualised" version (bottom) of an analogies task (top) their performance is much improved (NB the correct element in the bottom right in each case has to be selected from an array of alternatives not shown here).

question — a dependence that would, of course, be expected among scientists in general. Even in simple categorisation tasks, many studies have now shown how differences in background knowledge produce large differences in classification among the same elements (see Wattenmaker, 1996, for review).

The issue is seen acutely in debates around what IQ tests measure. Although test items presented in verbal format, and often requiring little more than general knowledge, are obviously tied to a specific culture, and, in that sense, "culture-biased", a number of well-known items and tests are based on *non*-verbal items.

Example of such items are the abstract analogies, already illustrated in Fig. 3.14. The most famous of them, however, is undoubtedly the Raven's Matrices test made up of so-called matrix items, like that shown in Fig. 3.15. It has often been claimed that such items are "culture-free", tap "real" intelligence, and thus that scores and individual and group differences in them must be valid indicators of levels of cognition. According to Carpenter, Just, and Shell (1990, p.404) the Raven's is thought to test "the ability to reason and solve problems involving new information, without relying extensively on an explicit base of declarative knowledge derived from either schooling or previous experience."

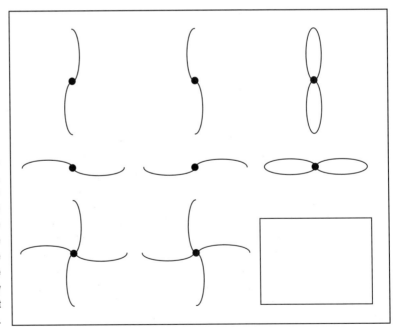

FIG. 3.15. A typical matrix item, this one showing an "addition of two figures" rule (the correct entry for the blank space in the bottom right has to be selected from an array of six alternatives not shown here).

Yet it is possible that solving a Raven's matrix may require background knowledge, and understanding of context, that is at least as culturally tied as verbal items. First of all, the items are administered in a socially fraught "test" situation, itself a specific cultural device. But so is the very layout of items. They are presented as black and white figures, flat out on paper, with the "pick-up" of information arranged from top left to bottom right. And there may be further dependency on background knowledge. Carpenter et al. (1990) describe the contents of the items in terms of "rules" of transformation — for example, where features are simply added or subtracted along the rows, this is "figure addition or subtraction"; or a feature may be subtracted from one element and given to another, which is "quantitative pairwise progression"; and so on. These are taken to require "pure" cognition because they have to be figured out from the item alone.

Yet a moment's reflection shows such "rules" are actually information-handling tools for storing and extracting information from text, from tables of figures, or accounts, timetables, and so on, all of which are more prominent in some cultures and subcultures than others. Indeed, when Richardson (1991) presented 10-year-olds with a contextualised version of Raven's Matrices, requiring exactly the same logical processing, but couched in meaningful social scenarios (Fig. 3.16) performances were dramatically improved, and there was no relationship between performance on one kind of item and performance on the other.

Here, I am touching on models of *socio*-cognition which I will be examining in Chapter 4. But generally, in all the cases just mentioned (as in real-life situations) children appear to be using their knowledge resources in order to map known environmental structures onto any situation in which information is incomplete, and generating predictions accordingly. As Butterworth (1992, p.8) puts it, "everyday reasoning is generally based on types of culturally-specific knowledge, whose representation is evoked by the appropriate context." A crude example may be that of how knowledge of whether we should be driving on the left- or right-hand side of the road maps out a variety of perceptual variables, expectations of traffic movements, personal motor commands, and so on, in specific ways. A rather critical form of reasoning would be severely limited in the absence of such knowledge. But this would not be an indication of an individual's general "level" of reasoning ability. In recent years, indeed, there has been increasing stress on the structure of social relationships and its correspondence with the structure of a task — what has been called "social marking"

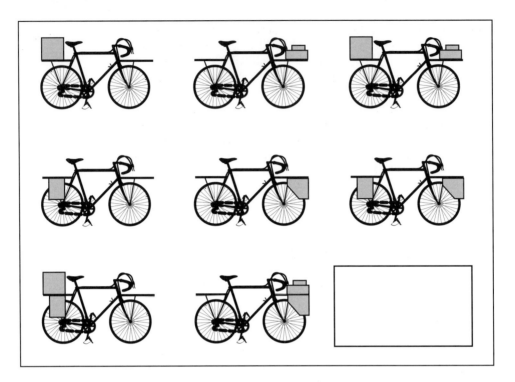

FIG. 3.16.
A "sociocognitive"
version of the matrix
item in Fig. 3.15. — as the key facilitator in reasoning (De Paolis, Doise, & Mugny, 1987; Girotto, Light, & Colbourn, 1988).

Some of this work has involved the Wason Selection Task. In this task subjects are presented with four cards with letters or numbers printed on them like this:

E K 4 7

Then they are presented with a rule connecting them: "If a card has a vowel on one side, then it has an even number on the other side" (Johnson-Laird, 1983; Wason & Johnson-Laird, 1972). The task is to state which cards it will be necessary to turn over to decide whether the rule is being obeyed. Typically, most subjects will suggest the importance of turning over the E; but only around 12% appreciate the need to turn over the 7 (the only other card that can falsify the rule).

An alternative version of the task involves identifiable objects and something like a real context, e.g.:

Manchester   Sheffield   Train   Car

with the rule "Every time I go to Manchester I travel by train." Although the problem has exactly the same logical structure as the first version, over 60% of subjects now appreciated the need to turn over the card with Car on it (if the card had Manchester on it, that would negate the rule)(Johnson-Laird, 1983).

A number of other studies have shown similar effects (Ceci & Roazzi, 1994), in each case performance being boosted by recruitment of a familiar contextual structure. Thus it has been argued that people and children reason on the basis of "pragmatic reasoning schemes" induced from experience in context, rather than domain-independent abstract rules or logic (Cheng & Holyoak, 1985). Instead of strictly "mental" rules, inferences and deductions arise from social knowledge. As Holyoak and Cheng (1995, p.289) point out:

> For a person acting within a social context, the evaluation of actions is guided in part by a complex web of contract-like regulations. Some of these regulations are codified as laws, imposed by the authority of the state or religion; others are based on looser regulations that arise from expectations about behaviors appropriate for members of particular social groups (for example, a scout troop, an urban gang or a family), from informal agreements between individuals, or from self-imposed codes of conduct.

In a number of studies they show how premises that evoke pragmatic schemes, such as permissions and obligation, significantly facilitate problem solving.

In a more general comment on such effects, Bruner (1986) points out how many people err in the following problem:

> All As are Bs
> Are all Bs As?

But few fail when the same problem structure is couched in a familar context:

> All humans are mammals
> Are all mammals humans

Of course, it is possible to abstract mental "rules" from myriad contexts of instantiation, conventionalise a form of expression about them, talk about them, or even attempt to contrive equally abstract problems out of them. But it is children's ability to use them in real contexts that is important for development, and ultimately for understanding of the abstract, logical content itself. This is why some theorists have suggested that it is absurd to present children with tasks like abstract analogies which have no obvious deep structure in goal or purpose (see Brown et al., 1996). There is little doubt that this matter will continue to be the subject of debate, with commentators like Smith (1993), for instance, arguing that it is the understanding of logical *necessity* — as Piaget insisted — rather than specific practical "success", that is the hallmark of reasoning, and thus of cognitive development.

Other criticisms of Piaget's theory

Piaget's theory is itself an "operatory structure" of very great beauty, combining many parts in nested equilibrium. It may, indeed, be the case that no scientific theory has *ever been* so complex (which is, perhaps, not surprising given the topic), matching the greatest theories such as that of Charles Darwin in the natural sciences, and that of Freud in personality theory. It has also been very misunderstood: I have even heard it described by experienced psychology tutors as a "maturationist" theory, and Bickhard (1997) mentions attempts to interpret it within an empiricist framework, leading to such bad distortions that Piaget was attributed with views he had never held. In addition, there is remarkable imperviousness to the idea of emergent properties of self-organising systems (a point I will return to in Chapter 5). Sometimes it seems almost churlish to criticise such a monumental construction. Yet such criticism is the basis of the growth of all knowledge. So I will present the major areas of criticism in turn.

The "logical" mind

As already mentioned, Piaget was interested in *necessary* knowledge, and attempted to account for its development by equating structures of the mind with various mathematical and logical structures. He used different mathematical and logical schemes at different times, and with different problems, and, when they failed to "work" adequately, moved to others. For example, the symbolic (propositional) logic was long used as a "description of the formal structures that mark the completion of the operatory development of intelligence" (Inhelder & Piaget, 1958, p.143). But in the end that form of description appears to have been disappointing. On the one hand, errors and limitations in Piaget's rendering of the logical content of formal operatory structures have been pointed out several times, but I won't go into these here (see Grize,

1987). On the other hand, it appears that Piaget himself became dissatisfied with that rendering, and had already embarked on a major reformulation which his death cut short (Piaget, et al., 1992; cf. Beilin, 1992 — see "Piaget's new theory", later).

Criticism in a similar vein has arisen from studies of cognition in context, or "situated cognition", as just discussed. These have suggested that even mature cognition is far from being logical in any detached sense, but rather bound up with the structure of the current task and background knowledge bearing upon it. This leads to a rather different view of the developing mind from that proposed by Piaget. As Thelen (1995, p.73) explains, many contemporary developmentalists differ from Piaget, "... not in his account of the seamless connections between action and thought, but in the very nature of the mind that is the product of this developmental process."

The nature of operatory structures

Similar criticisms apply to the ambiguity and vagueness in Piaget's use of the term "structure". As Chapman (1988, p.131) notes, "The point of calling attention to the group-like character of such psychological structures is simply to provide a means of describing the formal properties of the total system in which the respective operations function." Be that as it may, there is little doubt that Piaget saw such group-like structures as having a real existence, "causally active" in "living organisations", "immanent" in living things, and "the true psychological units of logical and mathematical thought".

What we most need, in any adequate model of cognition and its development, is an accurate description of the form of representation of the internalised actions, coordinations, and so on, *in the mind*. As Chapman (1988, pp.357–8) notes,

> The question is how the formal properties of the structures described by the observer are mapped onto the functional properties of the structures active in the mind of the subject...the manner in which formal structures are reflected on the functional level is not clear from the beginning. The formal analysis is only the first step; the second step is to clarify the nature of the mapping between form and function.

So as Mandler (1992, p.274) complains about Piaget's theory, "it does not specify the format of the concepts ... One cannot merely say that a sensorimotor scheme has been transformed into a concept; one needs to specify both its details and how it is represented." As Bickhard (1997) points out, experience and action are temporally based and it isn't clear how Piaget's atemporal structures give rise to dynamic forms of action.

However, it is only fair to point out that the nature of representational content, as we have seen in previous chapters, has long been, and remains, the central problem in cognitive psychology. At the end of the day, it has to be remembered that, even given the voluminous nature of his work, Piaget thought his efforts to be only a start — a preliminary description and classification of cognitive forms, like the "embryologist or paleontologist who seeks to identify successive forms in a process of morphogenesis" (Chapman, 1988, p.281). The substantive content of those forms, and the nature of their transformation comes after that.

Facts of development

Empirically, although many of the crucial Piagetian observations have been replicated many times, other predictions arising from the model of stages, or the supposed abilities of children within particular stages, have not been met. In one series of studies, for example, a search was made through the protocols of adolescents solving logical tasks to see if they used the 16 binary operations. In fact only five could be found (Weitz et al., 1973; see Tomlinson-Keasey, 1992). Experimental pedagogy (Brown et al., 1996, p.158) has shown that scientific thinking, even among young schoolchildren, "far surpasses that which would be expected on the basis of Piaget's developmental model."

Chapman (1988) discusses the large number of such "asynchronies" that have appeared in the literature. The first was reported by Piaget himself, namely the *décalage* of operatory structures across domains of content, as in the attainment of conservation of quantity, weight, and volume at markedly different ages. A second is that, whereas Piaget's theory suggests that, within any given content, characteristic concrete operations (e.g. conservation, transitivity) should appear at the same time, this has been found not to be the case. Finally, according to Piaget's theory of number arising from the "fusion" of the operatory structures of series and class inclusion, the latter should appear before the former, but, again, there is evidence to suggest that serial relations appear first, then number, then classes.

Most recent attention has been drawn to experiments "showing" that concrete operational tasks can be solved by preschool children, when certain "performance factors", such as memory of the premises, are removed. These doubts first set in around transitive inference tasks. In such problems it is shown, for example, that a blue rod is longer than a green rod, and the green rod is longer than a yellow rod, and children have to answer a question about whether the blue rod is longer than the yellow rod. Such inferences cannot be made by preschool children according to Piaget, because they lack the necessary operatory structures. However, by first "drilling" preschool children on the premises of the task, Bryant and Trabasso (1971) boosted their performance, thus suggesting that it is children's *memory* rather than their operatory structures that is deficient.

In addition, many investigators working with infants have reported apparent mental abilities well in advance of the ages when Piaget said they would emerge. For example, Freeman, Lloyd, and Sinha (1980) showed that 9-month-old infants are more likely to search for an object hidden in an upright container than when it is hidden under an inverted container or behind a screen. Mandler (whose work I mentioned earlier), concludes (1992, p.276) that, "I take it as demonstrated that conceptualization above and beyond perceptual and/or motor schemas occurs by 8 months and perhaps earlier." In consequence she argues that conceptual development develops in parallel with sensorimotor development rather than following relatively late.

The problem, here, is the possibility that the children are solving the "simplified" task through a structurally simplified form of reasoning. As Chapman (1988, p.354) notes, there is a lack of agreed-upon criteria for ensuring that we are comparing like with like: much of this work "has been carried out in ignorance of [Piaget's] work on preoperational structures ... that theoretically could allow preoperational children to generate correct answers under certain task conditions". I discuss such possibilities further later. Much of the doubt has been about whether children who get the "right" answer actually understand its logical necessity, the latter being the true criterion of development in Piaget's terms.

This problem of interpretation is shown strikingly in the domain of number. Although it is possible to get even preschool children to count in order to compare two sets of items, experiments have shown that the two are not connected logically, in that straight judgements of the equivalence, or otherwise, of set sizes are often made independently of the results of counting (e.g. Cowan, 1987; Cowan, Foster, & Al-Zubaidi, 1993). This suggests that children may use the cultural tool of counting without understanding its logical significance. As Nunes and Bryant (1996, p.41) put it, "This sort of result was the reason for Piaget's emphasis on the need to consider children's understandings of the invariants of number in describing their mathematical reasoning and not only their knowledge of culturally transmitted number conventions" (see also Smith, 1997).

Role of context

In consequence of studies of "cognition in context", like those illustrated earlier, a virtual barrage of criticisms in the 1980s denigrated Piaget's theory for being individualistic, asocial, and ahistorical (see contributions in Light, Sheldon, & Woodhead, 1991). Much was summarised in Bruner's caricaturisation (1985, p.25) of Piaget's "lone child" who "struggles single-handed to strike some equilibrium between assimilating the world to himself or himself to the world".

However, there has been much retort to these depictions. Some of them point to Piaget's work on *The moral judgement of the child,* and a series of *Sociological essays* published in the 1950s. These describe Piaget's stress on social context as the medium of intellectual exchange for development, and his efforts to formalise *social exchange* in terms of logical groupings. In those works (and elsewhere) Piaget uses concepts like the "coordination of viewpoint" and "sharing of thought". As Chapman, 1989, p.186 points out, "[T]he coordination of action between individuals (cooperation) has the same formal properties as the grouping of operations within the individual."

As Chapman (1988, p.180) suggests, these notions make it clear that the same form of groupings could be found at the level of social organisation as at the individual level; that individual cognition is imbued with social meaning; and that "Piaget's theory is in fact more thoroughly social in character than many other theories of social development." In addition, Piaget was critical of other theorists' claims that children simply acquire knowledge of their social environment, without describing how it is done. Alongside social forms there must be some internal mechanism for assimilating them: the two are sides of the same coin, he said.

Methodology

The mainstay of Piaget's methodology was the "clinical method", drawn partly from the clinical interview in psychiatry. He discusses its characteristics and benefits at length in *The child's conception of the world* (1926/1972). First he noted the disadvantages of orthodox testing, in that stereotyped questions ignore the role of current context, and may obscure answers based on the form of the question from ones based on genuine thinking. On the other hand, direct observation may not reveal thoughts, and distinguish real beliefs from play, which some form of counter-questioning may help us to do (Piaget, 1926, p.35):

The clinical examination is thus experimental in the sense that the practitioner sets himself a problem, makes hypotheses, adapts the conditions to them and finally controls each hypothesis by testing it against the reactions he stimulates in conversation. But the clinical examination also depends on direct observation, in the sense that the good practitioner lets himself be led, though always in control, and takes account of the whole mental context ...

To the methodological purist such confounding of the observational (inductive) and experimental (hypothetico-deductive); of "control" while "letting himself be led"; of deciding what to control "adaptively" in the act of testing the hypothesis; and the lack of prior systematicity in questions asked, and so on, would be a nightmare.

A large number of criticisms in recent years have argued that the tasks as conducted by Piaget are "unreal" and mislead both the child and the interpretations of the investigator. When, in contrast, the tasks are couched in order to make "human sense", children are not only more successful, but also achieve them at a younger age (Donaldson, 1978). This body of evidence has partly struck at Piaget's theory of stages (either in total, or at the ages Piaget described) and partly at the Piagetian ideas of "what is developing". Again these studies are taken up in the next chapter.

Piaget and language

As mentioned earlier, Piaget saw language as an *expression* of cognitive development rather than a mediator of it — as one more variety of symbolic functioning: "children assimilate the language they hear to their own semantic structures which are a function of their level of development" (Inhelder & Piaget, 1969, p.3). Inhelder and Piaget rejected the idea that language is the actual basis of logical thought and its development.

To support this rebuttal Piaget and his colleagues pointed to certain empirical evidence. In terms of evolution and of development, human intelligence is prior to language, and the latter's structural principles must depend on the former rather than vice versa. Empirically, before they can talk, in the pre-verbal sensorimotor period, children are already organisers, inventors, and discoverers, exhibiting operations with structures and processes that are isomorphic with later operations of thought. The child is already a kind of logician, physicist, and psychologist. According to Sinclair (1982, p.169):

Thinking, in the sense of operations and concepts that make it possible to absorb information to fit into a meaningful framework and go beyond it towards new discoveries and inventions, has its roots in activity, not in language. The fundamental structures and mechanisms of thought are prefigured in the infant's behaviour well before the appearance of language.

In addition, Piaget and his colleagues pointed out that deaf-mutes, although devoid of language, develop functional logical thought (though with some delay). And they did experiments in which conservers and non-conservers were shown pairs of objects in which the members of each pair varied in, for example, size (one member being longer than the other) or number (one member having five marbles, the other only two). Then the subjects saw these separate members of the pairs given to two separate people. They had to describe, verbally, what had happened.

What was observed was that the non-conservers ("pre-logical") used absolute terms or scalars: "this man has a big one, that man a small one" (Piaget & Inhelder, 1969, p.89). Conservers, on the other hand, used relational terms or "vectors": "this man has a bigger one than the other man." The latter reflects coordination in thought, which language "follows" rather than precedes. In addition they found that non-conservers can be trained to use vector expressions, but only with great difficulty, and with little effect on logical thinking as such. As Piaget and Inhelder (1969, p.90) put it, "These data ... indicate that language does not constitute the source of logical thought but is, on the contrary, structured by it."

As we shall see in Chapter 4, however, a number of more recent theorists have argued that the infant's actions are themselves embedded in social structures and processes, which are also the basis of communication and language learning. In such models language and thought originate, not separately, but *together*, from a common informational and conceptual base.

Piaget's new theory

This has to be something of an annexe to the foregoing — and in many ways an incomplete and unsatisfactory one — because Piaget's most recent formalisation is still being unpacked and evaluated. But I hope it is an account you will be able to relate to the one given earlier on the "standard" theory, and criticisms of it.

As already mentioned, Piaget attempted to use what mathematical tools were available at the time to formalise his theory. Thus, much of his description in the 1930s and 40s relied on the mathematical theory of groups. From around the 1970s, however, Piaget started to resort to a fairly new mathematical theory, known as the "theory of categories", together with something called the "concept of morphisms". The fruits of these efforts, amounting to a radical reformulation of the standard theory, have only relatively recently been published in English (Piaget, Henriques, & Ascher, 1992) and are causing quite a stir.

As Bickhard (1997, p.239) explains, although under constant attack in the last 20 years, Piaget continued to develop his model in new and more powerful ways:

> This last phase of Piaget's theorising, however, has been mostly ignored through the 1980s and into the 90s because of the assumption that Piaget had already been refuted. Much of this work has only slowly been translated into English, and at times translated against the resistance of those who claimed it was of no contemporary importance.

Yet, as Barrouillet and Poirier (1997, p.216) note, "This approach modifies in a major way the operatory theory." It has been described as "Piaget's new theory" (Beilin, 1992), with suggestions (Acredolo, 1997, p.235) that "we are long overdue in making the new theory the Piagetian theory we introduce to our undergraduate and graduate psychology and human development students."

To understand the roots of the approach it is perhaps best to look at some empirical results that were difficult to explain by the "standard" theory (see Barrouillet & Poirier, 1997). For example, children were given the kind of class-inclusion problem shown in Fig. 3.13, but made up of apples and strawberries, and thus fruits. After success with the standard question (are there more apples or more fruits?), the children were asked if there was any way we could get *more* apples than fruits. Even an 8-year-old would suggest simply adding more apples (C. Voelin's experiments described by Barrouillet & Poirier, 1997).

In another modification, after a child's initial success in the class inclusion task, the whole array was hidden behind a screen (Markman, 1978). The child was then informed that some fruits were being taken away, and asked if there would now be more apples or more fruits. Most 7–8-year-olds replied that they didn't know because they couldn't see what was happening — i.e. they could reason on the basis of visible states but not on the basis of (stated but unseen) transformations.

In other work it became clear that difficulty with the standard class-inclusion task seemed to vary with content — e.g. bees and flies instead of apples and strawberries. And "mixing" the subclasses in the array, instead of presenting them as sub-divisions, seemed strangely to ease the task. Many other studies of this sort (reviewed in Barrouillet & Poirier, 1997) found that, success on the standard task notwithstanding, the "logical" answers were only forthcoming in 9–10-year-olds.

Such results call into doubt Piaget's original account of operatory structures based on coordination of classes *per se*. They make clear that success on conservation, seriation, and class-inclusion tasks alone does *not* guarantee the understanding of logical necessity, and so the final attainment of concrete operations. Thus realising that operatory structures based on coordinations of actions will not suffice, and following a remarkable set of experiments conducted in the 1970s and early 80s (described in Piaget et al., 1992), Piaget turned to his formulation based on the new ideas of correspondences, morphisms, categories, and transformations. Let us, then, try to unpick these formidable-sounding terms.

A correspondence is any aspect whereby objects, variables, actions, and so on, can be compared: for example, an ordered relationship between one set of objects or states and another, such as the level of water in vessels and the volumes of water, or successive states in the rotation of an object in space. The particular form of the correspondence is called a morphism; and it is one that can be found across different contents, or imposed upon them. For example, the ordering of objects according to number; or the relationship we call Mother, across different sets of individuals: "morphisms are, by definition, instruments for transferring invariant forms" (Henriques, 1992, p.189). Finally, the existence of that morphism across other kinds of objects or relationships is called a category (which thus has little to do with the everyday notion of category — Papert, 1992). Development is then said to pass from an intramorphic stage, to an intermorphic stage, and finally to a transmorphic stage.

One experiment said to demonstrate this used the kind of apparatus shown in Fig. 3.17. This consists of discs of different radii concentrically positioned on an axle supported on a stand. The discs each have a hook at the top to which weights of different sizes can be attached, and which will thus tend to rotate the discs in one direction or the other when the stop peg is removed. The child is asked to attach weights to two or more discs such that no rotation takes place (there is equilibrium).

The first observation was that even children as old as $9^1/_2$ years, who performed adequately on the standard conservation tasks, attempted

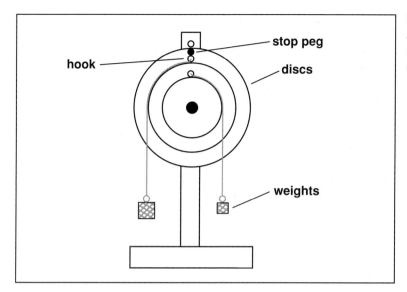

FIG. 3.17.
Apparatus for testing
reasoning by
morphisms.

only to equalise weights. That is they reasoned only on the basis of the simple correspondence:

$$\text{magnitude of weight} \longleftrightarrow \text{size of effect.}$$

This is known as intramorphic reasoning because the children are making predictions on the basis of covariation within that correspondence. Children of around 11 or 12 years also used a second correspondence, size of disc:

$$\text{size of disc} \longleftrightarrow \text{size of effect.}$$

For example, one 12-year-old noted that "on the big wheels the weights have more force" (Piaget et al., 1992, p.159) — and, by using a combination of the two morphisms, arrived at an equilibrium, but couldn't explain why. So that reasoning, by using the two morphisms in conjunction, had become intermorphic, but still by an *additive* process of summing the independent effects. Thus, one child recognised that "It depends on the point where the weight is hung and on the size" and reckoned that this is so because "the difference between the weights...is the same as between the discs" (1992, p.160). Another suggested that "for each unit of displacement [across discs] you have to add a unit of weight." (1992, p.161).

The problem with these children is that they have no appreciation of the *interdependence* of these two correspondences (the effect of size of weight on the force depends on the size of the disc — i.e. an interactive or multiplicative relation). They seem to reason only on the basis of the observable relations (correspondences), and not the abstract, "invisible", one. As Barrouillet and Poirier (1997, p.230) put it, "The intrinsic limitation of these levels is that children can only anticipate relations between known states without being able to reason on undetermined states." The latter requires more than what is directly observable — thus more than comparison of mere states. A *transition* is hinted at in observations where, for example, one child says "the heavier weight changes more" across discs, or "the difference in the big weight's influence is greater than the little one's" or recognises that "the relationship isn't the same" (Piaget et al., 1992, p.161). However, these intermediate subjects, with implicit recognition of an interaction, are still explicitly additive in their attempts to equilibrate and in their explanations.

According to Piaget and colleagues, completion of the transition requires the construction of a new, *trans*morphic correspondence (i.e. between the two key correspondences just described), yielding a new morphism. How does this crucial development come about? As just suggested, it isn't directly observable (like the other correspondences), so has to be constructed; and *this* can only happen by the individual operating on the originals. "In order to compose intermorphic correspondences with one another, the subject sets himself 'to operate' on these morphisms [by] a generalization of the ... prior morphisms" (Piaget et al., 1992, p.216).

But this requires thinking in terms of the transformations in those prior morphisms, and not just the observed states. That is, it means bringing the tacit *transformations* in the first two correspondences — "weight effect" and "disc effect" — into a new correspondence of tranformations: i.e. by "subordinating observed correspondences to operatory systems based on transformations" (Barouillet & Poirier 1997, p.223). When this is done it is "seen" that the transformation due to weight size and the transformation due to disc size are coordinated with each other. This new correspondence then offers a more general, "freer" composition in which successful prediction *and* a sense of necessity are bound up. The transmorphic level — the coordination of transformations rather than states — is on a new plane, rather like theory-change in science. The mechanism of construction of this new plane is a point I return to later.

Now let us consider another example, that of the standard class-inclusion or classification problem. Reasoning in the standard task (are

there more apples or more fruits?) involves a number of correspondences: a correspondence between the number of objects with
something in common and their extension in a group — i.e. apples and
their ordered number and strawberries and their ordered number
(correspondences 1 and 2 in Fig. 3.18). There is also a third, reciprocal,
correspondence, in that the array of the class of "fruits" can be mapped
into five apples and three strawberries (correspondence 3 in Fig. 3.18.).
Note that these are "empirical" correspondences, because they are
directly observable.

Young children can reason at this *intramorphic* level by having such
simple correspondences — e.g. they can count the numbers of apples
or strawberries and compare them. They fail the class-inclusion task,
however, because these correspondences are not coordinated; i.e. they
cannot compare *apples* and fruits because this is not a simple empirical
correspondence. The *intermorphic* level — and with it success on the
task — is reached when these correspondences are coordinated, and the
numbers of objects in a class and any one of its sub-classes can be
compared.

However, although successful in the standard task, the modified
task described earlier (when subjects are simply informed about manipulations being carried out behind a screen) shows that development is
still incomplete: reasoning is empirical, about states, and cannot deal
with (unseen) transformations. According to Piaget et al., (1992, p.216):
"it is only a matter of putting correspondences themselves into correspondence and, therefore ... involves nothing beyond the construction
of a single mechanism of comparison."

FIG. 3.18.
Correspondences in
the typical
class-inclusion
problem.

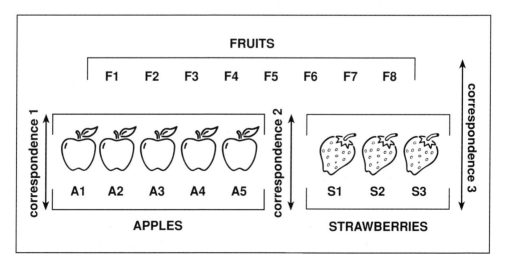

The new morphism again involves a generalisation from the "exogenous" correspondences to a more abstract correspondence based on transformations. These transformations are certainly present in the original morphisms. For example, the child already realises, on the basis of correspondence 1 (Fig. 3.18.) that adding more apples to the original group — i.e. a tranformation — will produce a larger group. And, of course, a similar transformation takes place simultaneously with fruit. Development is a question of bringing these transformations into correspondence in the "totality of hierarchical levels" (Barrouillet & Poirier, 1997, p.223) — one which now surpasses merely empirical correspondences. This full coordination of morphisms is not attained until the age of 10–11 years (always bearing in mind that age is only a useful reference point, and not a determining factor in itself). *How* it happens is, again, a point I return to later.

So how is the new formulation of development superior to the old one of operatory structures based simply on coordinations of actions? The advantages are several. First, by admitting the importance of empirical correspondences as the grist of construction, it restores a balance between figurative and operatory representation, recognising an "organic" connection between them, and admitting a new kind of "logic of meaning". This explains the role of semantic content in tasks: for example, the previously puzzling finding that the *content* of class-inclusion tasks seems to affect performance. By the same token, *décalages*, always puzzling in the standard theory, are also explained. Indeed, some measure of domain-specificity is now possible, or even expected. The empirical problems arising from the various modified tasks, described earlier, are now explained and encompassed within a new developmental picture. The new formulation also rationalises the earlier preoccupation with operatory stages. The intra-, inter-, and transmorphic levels are not seen as discrete developmental stages, as coordinations of purely operatory structures, but as ones emerging by generalisation from exogenous sources. Finally, and perhaps most importantly, logical necessity is given a "deeper" rationale. As Barouillet and Poirier (1997, p.224) point out, "In effect, children operate directly on the transformations which formed the contents of earlier morphisms. They identify the reasons for the observation made possible by the intermorphic comparisons."

Of course, the new formulation leaves unclear the cognitive mechanisms of development of the transmorphic level. Piaget spoke of "generalisation", "operatory generalisation" or reflective abstraction, "teasing out" the nature of changes at the intra- and intermorphic levels, and bringing them into transformational correspondence at the transmorphic level. But we are left a little in the dark about where these mechanisms come from. What is the source of their functions? Piaget et al., (1992, p.216): "In order to compose intermorphic correspondences with one another, the subject sets himself 'to operate' on these morphisms [by] a generalization of the ... prior morphisms." But this implicitly suggests a separate, independent consciousness at work. Where does it come from? The temptation to fall back on some innate executive control structure, as do Barrouillet and Poirier (1997), following Case (1985, 1992), is, perhaps, understandable, although this is a "solution" that would seem deeply ironic to Piaget.

Finally, there may be a still deeper, and still more ironic, flaw in the new formulation. Piaget was strongly against the "copy" theory of cognitive development intrinsic to raw empiricism. Although the new formulation accords a new status to the grist of experience, and weakens an abstract "logicism", it seems to do so by just such a copying mechanism, or at least "figurative" representation as more or less direct impression. Bickhard (1997) calls this "encodingism", and describes it as a serious error in the new formulation. The reality is, of course, that even empirical correspondences are not directly available, but have to be constructed from raw sensory data: the new formulation does not explain how that happens (see Chapter 5 for further comments on this).

It remains to be seen whether the current analyses can clarify these possible problems, and whether Piaget's pure constructivism will have to be further attenuated (some might say corrupted!) by more nativism, or even empiricism. But let me return, now, to my general theme by considering some applied aspects of constructivism, and then of criticisms of constructivism in general.

Practical applications of constructivism

Generally, constructivist ideas have been appealing wherever it is necessary to account for "emergent" properties in which, as it were, the outcome is greater than the sum of parts, or when, as Bruner (1986) put it, we go "beyond the information given". Gestalt theory (although often vague in terms of process description) has been popular as a description of emergent effects, whether in perception, in creative problem solving, or the understanding of social events. This remains so today. For example, Gestalt principles such as "good figure" and "proximity" are invoked in the design of instructional graphs and maps (Winn, 1990, p.557): "It is clear...that the careful manipulation of these factors by designers will certainly affect the preattentive configuration of parts into components in graphics."

There has long been a widespread feeling that general schema theory has strong implications for education. One of these is the demonstrated and widely acknowledged point that the knowledge structures that a child currently has will influence both the level of current problem solving *and* the ease with which he or she may acquire additional knowledge in the same domain. This relationship, in turn, has implications for how that additional knowledge should be taught or presented for learning. Glaser (1984, p.10) states:

> The notion of schemata as theories that are a basis of learning suggests several important pedagogical principles. First, one must understand an individual's current state of knowledge in a domain related to the subject matter to be learned ... Second, a "pedagogical theory" can be specified by the teacher that is different from, but close to, the theory held by the learner. Then third ... students can test, evaluate and modify their current theory so that some resolution between the two is arrived at.

This view, of course, puts the teacher in a rather different role from that found in the traditional classroom: "The method requires that a teacher be continually vigilant and keep in mind the particulars of each student's thinking" (Glaser, 1984, p.10). In a general sense, such theorising is also reflected in modern computer-guided instruction, which is more interactive, taking more account of different levels of previous knowledge, and current informational needs, compared with the impersonal, associationist programs of the 1960s (see Chapter 2).

As is well known, Piaget's theory was invoked to support a "child-centred" movement in education in a number of countries. In Britain it was taken as a framework for the Plowden Report, *Children and their primary schools* (HMSO, 1967). A common interpretation of Piaget's theory has been that knowledge cannot be transmitted from one person to another (or from teacher to child) as a "given". According to Piaget (1988, p.14), a child is receptive to ideas "only if he is capable of assimilating them, and he can do this only if he already possesses the adequate instruments or structures". Hence Piaget's insistence that figurative knowledge (consisting more or less of "copies" of external reality) can be taught, but logico-mathmatical knowledge has to be constructed. Elliot and Donaldson (1982, p.158) state that:

> Piaget is concerned to maintain that the development of the kind of knowing which lies at the heart of human

intelligence — the kind that crucially distinguishes a mature from an immature mind — is something which each of us must construct for himself.

Furthermore, the stage-like nature of development means that the child is intrinsically limited in attempts to learn (or develop) new structures, or forms of reasoning, far beyond the level he or she is currently at.

However, it has often been pointed out that the child-centred framework for education was not an accurate reflection of Piaget's theory, and that its implementations in any case were patchy, piecemeal, and occasionally even distortions of the theory. One reason for this may lie in the paradoxical fact that Piaget himself showed little interest in schooling, and what he had to say about the implications of his work for it was not encouraging (Davis, 1991; Ginsburg, 1988).

Because of this, Piaget's theory offers only very general guidelines for educational practice. In consequence, notions about the child being allowed to learn for him- or herself, with a minimum of intervention, and maximum opportunity for "activity for its own sake", are simplistic distortions of the theory, and, indeed, have more in common with nativist models (see Chapter 1). Likewise, suggestions that Piaget's theory offered a far too pessimistic view of the role of the teacher, and of the educability of the individual (see next section; and also Chapter 4) have been criticised as gross misreadings of the theory (e.g. Smith, 1993).

Criticisms of constructivism in general

Theoretical content in constructivist models has been diverse, but there are common themes. First, in their most pure forms, there are no innate concepts "ready made", as it were, to equip us to deal with sense experience, and thus the source of our "true" knowledge. Nor are our knowledge and thoughts "made up" from sensory experience alone. Rather we are born with perceptual or conceptual primitives of some sort, and these actively build from sense experience new schemes that are the basis of knowledge and thought, but whose form and function are not determined or constrained by those primitives. This contrasts with the position of even "weaker" nativists whose constraints on development still have such a determining role (in the most recent theories they have evolved by virtue of their adaptedness to some more or less specific aspects of environmental structure) so that some correlation between genetic structure and developmental outcome persists throughout.

The specification of these primitives, the nature of the products, and how they function, is where theories vary. Most criticisms of constructivism have been about the vagueness of "what is in the system": what is constructed, from what starting points, *how* it is constructed, and how the result does its work *when* it has been constructed. Although the general idea of a "scheme" is widespread, what form it takes and how it functions is often more a matter of hunch than clear demonstration.

All models, however, tend to suffer from the same vagueness. For example, Mandler (1992, pp.276–277) says that:

> It is not necessary to posit innate knowledge ... to account for the early appearance of concepts. We need only to grant that infants are born with a capacity to abstract certain kinds of information from the perceptual displays they process, and to redescribe them into conceptual form.

But we are not given much indication of what that information is, nor what the capacity to abstract it is, nor how it works. Mandler says that the redescribed concepts take the form of "image schemas" which are of "analog form". But how is an image schema different from just an image; and how can its new form be literally analog when it is recoded in a new language, that of nerve impulses? In addition, the notion of redescription in Mandler's model suggests another independent process which is not itself described.

It is hardly surprising that, given such vagueness, critics such as Chomsky (e.g. 1980, p.37) find constructivist theories hopeless in explaining the complex structures of knowledge and cognition:

> The expectations that constructions of sensory-motor intelligence determine the character of a mental organ such as language seems to me to be hardly more plausible than a proposal that the fundamental properties of the eye or the visual cortex or the heart develop on that basis.

In sum, whereas it is relatively easy to envisage the functional counterpart of "associations", or of "genetically coded neural programs" (as in bird song, instinctive behaviours, and so on), envisaging functional counterparts of structures like schemas is exceedingly difficult. This remains the great challenge for constructivist theorists.

Sociocognitive models 4

Introduction

In the previous chapter I touched on models that have stressed the relationship between cognitive development and *contexts* of cognition. That description was mainly of physical contexts, as interpreted in a broadly constructivist framework, although I also touched on social contexts. Here I want to offer a much broader description of the many models that have attempted to describe and explain human cognition and development in social context in a fuller sense. The fact that humans exist in social conglomerates has challenged psychologists to describe and characterise relationships between the individual and the social world, and to specify their implications for cognitive development. Does the child think purely for him or herself, or as part of a social conglomerate? Is the child's developing knowledge and reasoning purely personal, or are they patterns shared with others? What are the implications of either of these presuppositions for the understanding of the developing mind?

These questions have been debated since at least the Ancient Greeks. But, as Dumont (1965) pointed out, since the 17th century psychological theory has been dominated by the idea of the autonomous individual as the centre of knowledge and cognition. As Wertsch and Sammarco (1985, p.276) put it, one of the most fundamental assumptions of Western psychology has been "that the boundaries of the individual provide the proper framework within which psychological processes can be adequately analysed". Perhaps not surprisingly, however, within this broad presupposition, it isn't difficult to see how the sets of assumptions identified so far throughout this book have figured, so that "social" models can be described as offshoots of the three categories of models already described in Chapters 1 to 3. Accordingly we can call them "social nativist"; "social associationist"; and "social constructivist". Again, I make no attempt to offer an exhaustive survey, but only illustrations sufficient to identify these key assumptions and typical contents.

Social nativism

The idea that we think and reason "together", as social conglomerates, has frequently been attributed to "innate" knowledge, or cognitive programs, tendencies, or predispositions. As with nativist models of cognition in general, the development of children's social cognition is then seen, in large part, as consisting merely of the maturation of such genetically determined forms.

As mentioned in Chapter 1, studies within the "smart infant" framework have stressed that young infants and neonates display as much knowledge of, and cognitions about, other people as they do physical objects and events. For many theorists, the most striking studies in this regard have been those of Trevarthen and his colleagues (e.g. Trevarthen, 1977, 1979a,b). Those investigators carried out detailed analyses of video recordings of young infants interacting with their mothers (Fig. 4.1). They found that participation in a number of forms of social expression alternates between partners, with brief periods of

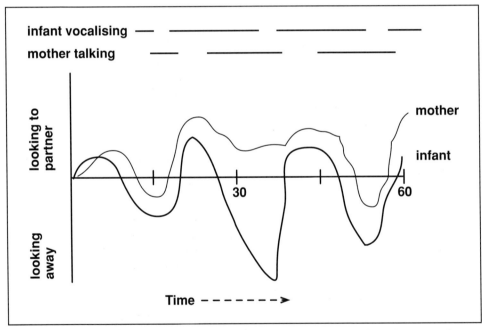

FIG. 4.1.   Hypothetical graphical representation of typical mother–child interaction condensed from various sources (see Brazelton & Cramer, 1991; Trevarthen, 1977). Curves show general level of activity (including arm waving, jiggling, smiles, touching, reaching, and so on) during periods of facing and looking away. Lines above show periods of vocalisation. Time is in seconds.

overlap, in a dialogue-like pattern. Trevarthen (1977, p.239) said that he became convinced that "an exceedingly complex innate mechanism foreshadowing the cooperative intelligence of adults, and more general than the mechanism of language, was already functioning in early infancy."

A host of observational studies that followed in the 1970s and 1980s revealed that within a few months infants are displaying acute social sensitivities in all the complex games and routines (such as "peek-a-boo") that they get involved in with parents or caregivers. Trevarthen (1979) called this phenomenon *primary intersubjectivity*. It becomes even more complex when games with objects start to appear at around 2 months — and what Trevarthen (1979a) called *secondary intersubjectivity* develops. There is little dispute about the veracity of such findings: it is how we theorise or model, and thus explain, them that is crucial.

As with cognition in general, many models have attributed the contents of such intersubjectivity to information in the genes. Trevarthen (1983, p.145) concluded that "innate interpersonal abilities regulate and drive forward the growth of cooperative awareness." Schaffer (1991, p.8) says that the newborn:

> ... comes into the world with certain predispositions — certain tendencies, that is, to selectively attend to particular kinds of stimuli and to structure its responses in certain ways. What is especially striking is the way in which both perceptual and response tendencies are pre-adapted to mediate the infant's interaction with the social environment.

As a perceptual tendency, Schaffer (1991, p.9) instances infants' sensitivity to human faces, and to the particular acoustic distinctions prevalent in human speech. These tendencies have been interpreted from the habituation and/or preferential-looking techniques described in Chapter 1. Such preferences are those "that are biologically of greatest importance to them", so that "infants arrive in the world especially attuned to the kind of stimulation provided by other people."

As a response tendency Schaffer instances the "burst–pause" pattern in infant feeding described by Kaye (1977) and others. Kaye reported that, when feeding from breast or bottle, infants tend to suck in sequences of "bursts", each lasting a few seconds, with short pauses in between (Fig. 4.2). Such a feeding pattern has not usually been observed in other mammals. During the pauses, mothers tended to stroke, jiggle, or talk to their babies, whereas they were otherwise quiet. Schaffer (1991, p.10) argues that this pattern gets babies used to

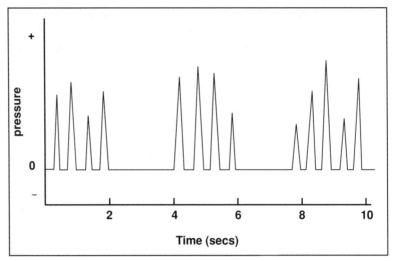

FIG. 4.2.
Typical baby sucking
rhythm (diagram of
typical trace collected
using a dummy-teat
with pressure sensors
connected to a
computer).

the typical interaction patterns of social intercourse, and that it is an innate one: "social preadaptation determines the nature of the infant's initial encounters with other people."

The idea that sociocognitive development is constrained by foundations laid down genetically and present at birth has continued to be a very popular one in recent years. As noted in Chapter 1, Meltzoff and colleagues have argued that early imitative abilities in infants serve a social and communicative function (Meltzoff & Moore, 1992, p.127). "Armed with an innate capacity for intermodal representation and imitation, the human newborn is provided with a firm foundation and powerful tools for subsequent cognitive and social development." Indeed, Johnson and Morton (1991) argue that attentional biases towards other people in infancy are due to a basic neural mechanism which they label CONSPEC. Gardner (1984), Karmiloff-Smith (1992), and others see social development (or "person" knowledge) as one of the areas in which some basic, but necessary, innate constraints operate. As Sperber (1986, p.1308) states: "the construction of abilities from within, or the internalisation of culturally constituted abilities, can only take place on some well-developed innate foundation."

As with cognitive nativism in general, there have been many attempts to find an evolutionary adaptationist/selectionist rationale for such models. As Cosmides and Tooby (1994, p.88) put it, the "statistically recurrent conditions encountered during hominid evolutionary history" equipped humans with a diverse range of adaptations for dealing with other people as well as the physical world: "... from solicitation of assistance from one's mate, to language acquisition...to coalition formation and cooperation, to the deduction of intentions from facial expressions, to avoiding incest, to allocating effort between activities, to the interpretation of threats, to mate selection ...", and so on.

A relatively recent version of social-nativism is that known as "theory-of-mind" (or TOM) theory. This idea suggests that an apparent leap forward among 3–4-year-olds in their understanding of the intentions of other people, requires that they form such a theory-of-mind. The idea is based on success or failure in two or three simple tasks — known as "appearance–reality" and "false-belief" tasks — and is well illustrated by describing those tasks.

In the first of these a child, may, for example, be asked to predict what is in a Smarties box, and then is shown that it actually contains pencils (Sullivan & Winner, 1993). The child is asked to confirm that the box actually contains pencils. Then the child will be asked what he or she "thought" was in the box, and finally what he or she thinks another child will think there is in the box. An average 3-year-old will answer "pencils" to the second and third questions as well as the first. It's as if the child cannot switch his or her mind from the overwhelming current perception of pencils to the point of view of the other's (or even his or her own original) belief. A typical 4-year-old can acknowledge that he or she originally thought there were Smarties in the box, and make the inference that *another* child will also think there are Smarties in the box.

A second false-belief task (Lewis, 1995) demonstrates something similar. The child first sees a ball being put in a basket by one figure (a doll, "Sally"), who then moves from the scene. Then the ball is removed and put into a box by another figure, whose actions are unseen by Sally. Sally then reappears on the scene and the child is asked where she will look for her ball. Again, the average 3-year-old fails the false-belief question by suggesting that Sally will straight away look in the box. Proper mental coordination between initial and current locations, on the one hand, and between these and Sally's belief, on the other, all seem to be overwhelmed by perception of the ball's current location. This is not the case with a slightly older child, who quite comfortably responds to the false-belief question correctly, as if being aware of the other's (the doll's) "mind".

Note that the essential requirement for success in each of these tasks is that the child maintain conflicting representations regarding the location of an object *and* what another person will believe about its location (Frye, 1993). The TOM idea is that children in this age group develop, through a process of biological maturation, a specialised theory-of-mind module, which "tunes" them in to the points of view of other people. Sometimes the process is described as a rapid maturation of a neurocognitive "module", quite suddenly expanding cognitive capacities into the appreciation of others' beliefs and false beliefs. Leslie (1992, p.20, quoted by Elman et al., 1996, p.368) argues that:

> the normal and rapid development of theory-of-mind knowledge depends on a specialised mechanism that allows the brain to attend to invisible mental states ... The mechanism is initially innate and in some sense, a specific part of the brain.

Brothers and Ring (1992) have indeed argued that all social information — the processing of faces, voices, and certain movements — is dealt with by a specialised "social module" which matures rapidly under genetic control in early childhood. Karmiloff-Smith et al. (1995, p.203) have modified this idea by suggesting that:

> in normal development there are distinct, domain-specific, skeletal predispositions for discriminating stimuli relevant to language, face processing and theory-of-mind ... With the massive early experience of superimposed inputs (i.e. face, voice and human interactions) ... these predispositions gradually take over privileged circuits in the brain that become increasingly specialised and progressively interconnected ... [This] gives rise to the emergence of separate, modular-like organization for each subdomain relevant to theory-of-mind ... [which] with time give rise to an emergent superordinate modular-like organization for the pragmatics of social interaction along the lines of the Brothers–Ring hypothesis.

Other theorists have stressed the "innate" differences that are seen to explain divisions of labour in a society, explaining why sub-groups tend to think in certain ways, and develop certain kinds of knowledge, compared with others. Perhaps the most prominent kind of social nativism, indeed, concerns sex or gender differences in cognition. Such models argue that sex differences in performance on, for example, certain spatial reasoning tasks, on which males tend to do better than females, reflect sex-linked genetic differences arising by natural selection among our forebears — in males, for better navigation, hunting, and gathering skills (Silverman & Eals, 1992), and in females for more domestic and supportive roles. It has been suggested that a similar evolutionary story explains differences between males and females in mathematical achievement in schools (Benbow & Lubinski, 1993; see Geary, 1996, and peer-commentary therein).

Rather more extreme have been conclusions that more general social and cultural properties of humans — the structure of institutions, economies, and relationships — are the products of what has been coded in the genes through the hand of natural selection. Such ideas have formed into a new discipline over the last 20 years or so called sociobiology (e.g. Wilson, 1975). According to a typical sociobiological thesis, variable perceptions and cognitions are related to variable genotypes, and have evolved within a culture because of a need for divisions of labour and expertise; these divisions may also extend across cultures (Lumsden & Wilson, 1981). According to such an evolutionary model, children just mature into the role that their genetic lot has decided for them — an ideal social-Platonism.

Even more dangerous, of course, is the way that the very same social-Platonism has repeatedly created a scientific racism in which evolutionary or adaptive stories have been imaginatively constructed to "explain" a ladder of racial superiority. Such accounts seem to recur in developmental psychology with remarkable frequency, usually involving IQ as a supposed measure of cognitive ability. In the 1970s, the American psychologist Arthur Jensen suggested that differences in IQ scores between American Blacks and Whites are a reflection of fundamental differences in cognitive ability determined in the genes: Blacks being condemned mostly to the level of relatively simple "associative" thinking, Whites having the added advantage of "conceptual" thinking (Jensen, 1969). On those grounds, at least one scientist advocated a eugenics scheme of voluntary sterilisation, with a cash incentive —$1000 for each point the IQ of the individual concerned fell below that of the mean score of 100 (Shockley, 1972)!

The heated debate that followed has recently recurred, following the publication of Herrnstein and Murray's *The bell curve* (1994) and J.P. Rushton's (1995) *Race, evolution and behavior*. Again we find evolutionary arguments and IQ scores being used to assert permanent "racial" differences in "intelligence" with genes putting constraints on the qualities and levels of intelligence that children can attain (for review see Howe, 1997). These are "logical" expressions of social nativist assumptions.

Criticisms of social nativism

The models briefly mentioned here are all subject to the criticisms of nativism in general that were enumerated in Chapter 2. The main complaint is the vagueness of "what is innate", and thus the descriptive evasiveness entailed in attributing "whatever it is" to the genes. The use of terms like innate "social predispositions", "social tendencies", "social pre-adaptations", and so on, illustrates this problem. And the models rely on a possibly contradictory (Darwinian) model of evolution. Just as information for adaptation laid down in genes is dysfunctional in rapidly changeable *physical* environments, so this must be even more the case with human *social* environments.

These problems are illustrated in controversies surrounding the TOM model in recent years. One aspect concerns "what" is developing. As Frye (1993, p.156) notes, "The contents of children's first theories of mind are not obvious. We do not know what terms they think in when they try to solve theory-of-mind problems." Of course it could be argued that just *such* description ought to be the first priority, before more general models of its origins are constructed. However, there are also arguments about age of onset of TOM. Leslie (1987) argues that the onset of pretend play at around 18 months is its first manifestation. Also, as Frye (1993, p.159) notes (and as described briefly earlier) the intricacy of the interactions of very young infants with their caretakers indicates how "Children show numerous signs of being aware of others' means and goals before the end of infancy ... it extends to almost every social situation where the infant coordinates actions with another." Finally, Lewis and colleagues have shown that performance on false-belief tasks is dependent on such factors as ability to construct a meaningful context from the situation, and family experiences such as numbers of siblings (Lewis et al., 1996).

As already mentioned, social-nativist theories have frequently been controversial. As regards sex differences, for example, it has been countered that the differences in mental ability (such as spatial ability) are *gender* differences (see later under social-constructivism), not sex differences as such. The "racial" thesis has been easily rebuffed by the empirical fact that human "races" don't actually exist in any meaningful biological sense – i.e. as distinct genetic "types". Genetic analyses show that any two humans taken at random, from anywhere in the world, will share as many as 98% of their genes (Lewontin, 1974), and those that vary are not adaptively distinct, which is how biological races are usually defined. This is partly due to the fact that humans, having seemingly originated from a very restricted stock, have also been spectacular migrators and mixers. The "sociobiology" thesis has likewise been attacked by large numbers of critics (e.g. Kitcher, 1985; Rose, Kamin, & Lewontin, 1984) on the basis of misleading evolutionary reasoning, such as extrapolation from simpler organisms (such as ants, bees, and fish) to humans, and the failure to recognise the hierarchical system of regulations governing the expression of genes in complex characters adaptive to changeable environments.

Social associationism

Associationists have not overlooked the fact that humans exist in social context. Indeed, the basic principles of associationism generalise quite readily to social cognition. The associationists of the 18th and 19th centuries stressed the need to form good habits in school and society generally, using repetition and social rewards and punishments. For the 20th-century behaviourist the social environment is just like any other in presenting contingencies of reinforcement — but speculation about the mental or cognitive bases of it should just as equally be banished. Indeed, Skinner's novel, *Walden Two*, in which appropriate social development was the result of suitable schedules of reinforcement, was largely a manifesto for social associationism. Like Skinner, others have pointed out how social reinforcers such as smiles, verbal praise, a pat on the back, and so on, may be effective reinforcers (see Reykowski, 1982).

A study cited by Miller (1993, p.189) illustrates social-associationist modelling in practice:

> Harris, Wolf & Baer (1967) observed an extremely withdrawn child who spent 80 percent of the time at nursery school in solitary activities. Their observations revealed that the teachers had unintentionally reinforced this behavior by talking to him and comforting him when he was alone. The child was ignored by teachers when he played with others. The program of operant conditioning reversed the above contingencies. The boy received teachers' attention when he joined a group and was ignored when he withdrew. He soon spent 60 percent of his time playing with other children.

Some, such as Mowrer (1960), coined the term "secondary reinforcer" to describe the way that an event frequently associated with a primary reinforcer acquired the same powers of reinforcement.

This has been taken to explain how humans are motivated by the pursuit of money, status and esteem. As Rachlin (1970, p.12) explains:

> Secondary reinforcement bridges the gap between laboratory procedures and complex human and animal behavior ... A newborn baby's rewards are easy to enumerate: milk, a change of diapers and a certain amount of fondling by its parents. As the baby grows up the list of things he will work to produce may be enlarged to include praise, money, fame, achievement, and so forth. A dollar bill may not be as rewarding to a baby as a shiny dime. As he grows older, though, the dirty green piece of paper may become relatively sought after. It is reasonable to explain this change as a case of secondary reinforcement — the dollar has become linked to other reinforcers.

And as Skinner (1972, p.136) put it:

> Food, sex, music, and all other values are reinforcers ... We must arrange effective contingencies of reinforcement. In doing so we supplement the sanctions of Adam Smith. In doing so we can do better than the Utopian reformers and move closer to a world in which we can be productive and happy.

Development by imitation of role models, "observational learning", and other principles of socialisation, have also constituted broad associationist models, although, again, there has been little regard for actual cognitive aspects of the processes. On the other hand, Bandura (1989) has augmented his early "social learning theory" with an important role for cognitive regulations in the individual's reactive self-control and guidance of his or her behaviour. He now calls his theory "social cognitive theory" and describes social learning as "knowledge acquisition through cognitive processing of information" (1986, p.xii), rejecting what he calls the "cognitive bypass operation" (cf. Miller, 1993, p.186).

An important aspect of Bandura's theory is the self-knowledge that children gain about themselves, *by* interaction with others. This includes perceptions of their competence in each of the various domains with which they have to deal. There may be a deep disjunction between what children can do and what they think they can do, and a number of studies have shown how this directly affects their behaviour.

Thus, children of similar ability, but with different levels of self-efficacy belief, perform markedly differently on the same tasks. Children with high self-efficacy belief attribute any failure to lack of effort; those with low self-efficacy attribute it to their poor ability (for review see Bandura, Barbaranelli, Caprara, & Pastorelli, 1996).

Criticisms of social associationism

The main issue surrounding social associationism has been about its theoretical sufficiency. Can the simple process of association formation explain complex social behaviours such as cooperation at work, speech and writing, or games like football and chess? So critics have repeatedly argued that the evidence for "central processes" is too strong to ignore. Whereas learning theorists have insisted that complex social behaviours can only be understood by breaking them down into simple units (and ignoring any unobservable "cognitions"), others have argued that understanding cognition, its function in an overall "meaningful" context, and its creative role in organising behaviour, is the only true basis for understanding social behaviour. Bandura (1986) suggests that it involves some sort of abstract modelling, as well as other "information processing" routines such as symbolic coding, rehearsal, visualisation, and so on.

Another general criticism of social associationism is, of course, the tendency within it to demean human mentality. Compare, for example, the baby envisaged by Racklin in the quote given earlier, passively responding to rewards, with the active, creative being envisaged by Piaget and others. Stronger than this have been complaints about the social manipulation or even "brainwashing" implicit in social-associationist recommendations. For example, in favouring the application of operant conditioning principles in a human social context, Carpenter (1974, pp.192–193) admits that:

> In general, the socialisation of young people, that is, the shaping of their behavior so that they can function effectively and constructively in social settings, is a kind of brainwashing process. But it is a brainwashing that is necessary for a surviving society, which needs the cohesion supplied by mutual reinforcement. There is no possible way that a person can be socialised without also being controlled by the people in his environment. The person is always easier to change than the whole social system. Hence, it is most convenient and practical to shape the child's behavior so that it is reasonably compatible with that of his associates.

Of course, this contrasts starkly with social nativist models which would argue that such cohesion is already "shaped" by our genes. But neither of these indicates how it is that social *change* — often swift and radical – can occur in human societies. Other models suggest that it is due to the flexibility born within a quite different source of social cohesion, and it is to such models that I turn next.

Social constructivism

It will be remembered from Chapter 3 that constructivists have favoured the progressive build-up of representations and cognitive processes as a result of human actions on the world, and on the basis of very elementary biological "givens", themselves not determinate of the final cognitive structures. Social constructivists have stressed that the structured world for humans is very much a social world, and that this has fundamental consequences for the description and under-standing of knowledge and cognition. Although most constructivists, especially Jean Piaget, have indicated the importance of the social world for human development, one theorist has dominated the scene in the last 20 years or so, and that is the Russian psychologist L.S. Vygotsky. Although I will have occasion to refer to those other theorists, and will later make comparisons with the ideas of Piaget, it will perforce be the ideas of Vygotsky that will dominate the rest of this chapter.

Vygotsky's theory

Vygotsky spent only 10 years as a psychologist before he died of tuber-culosis at the age of 38 in 1934. But he has left a tremendous theoretical legacy. It is one based on the strongest assertion of the unavoidable reality of people's involvement in social life (Vygotsky & Luria, 1993, p.116):

> The entire history of the child's psychological development shows us that, from the very first days of development, its adaptation to the environment is achieved through social means, through the people surrounding it.

First I have to point out, however, that it is impossible to give a comprehensive account of Vygotsky's theory. The most important reason is that it consists more of general principles than a well worked-out model. Unlike the "rich description" of Piaget's accounts, we most often, in Vygotsky's accounts, get the merest allusions to "many experiments", vague descriptions of how they were conducted, and of their results. So we should perhaps start with its basic assumptions.

Basic constituents. Like Piaget, Vygotsky sought to describe and explain the development of that "higher" level of thought in humans, the hypothetico-deductive, "scientific", or what Bruner (1986; see Brockmeier, 1996) describes as the "paradigmatic" mode of thought (contrasting it with the "narrative" mode of thought common in everyday cultural activities).

One of the first of Vygotsky's arguments was that humans are "utterly different" from the rest of animal life. To understand the radical nature of this argument we have to remember how both nativists and associationists had, from the turn of the century, been keen to accept Darwinian principles, and stress the *continuity* between human and animal psychology, and thus a *competitive individualism*. In such a framework, even social life is seen merely as a means towards predominantly personal ends. But Vygotsky was operating in the Marxist Soviet Union, and throughout the long period of the rise of psychological individualism, Marx and Engels were among a very few who had sustained a view of humans as *social* beings, and contemporary individualism as a form of social ideology. Marx (1973, p.83) stated:

> In this society of free competition, the individual appears detached from natural bonds etc., which in earlier historical periods makes him the accessory of a definite human conglomerate ... The more deeply we go back into history, the more does the individual appear as dependent, as belonging to a greater whole.

It is in this "greater whole", argued Vygotsky and his followers, that we must look for an understanding of human cognition and human development (Luria, 1981, p.25; quoted by Wertsch & Sammarco, 1985):

> In order to understand the highly complex forms of human consciousness one must go beyond the human organism. One must seek the origins of conscious activity and "categorical" behaviour not in the recesses of the human brain or in the depths of the spirit, but of the external conditions of life. Above all, this means that one must seek those origins in external processes of social life, in the social and historical forms of human existence.

In this model, humans evolved to adapt to the world by means of social cooperation, and thus, from the first moments of birth, "meet" their world through and with other people in a definite cultural form. This cultural form consists of distinctive patterns of social relationships invariably involving social "tools" of various sorts. In addition to developing organic "tools" of survival, like the eye and the hand, human children acquire "cultural tools" that are far more adaptable. Among them Vygotsky (1978) included all cooperatively organised activities: organised industrial production; various inventions for "thought sharing" (e.g. number systems, language, and writing systems); schemes for cooperative action (such as shared plans); a myriad social rules and principles for managing resources and social relationships; as well as "hardware" tools and all human technological devices.

What the child is acquiring in the form of cultural tools are patterns (often highly abstract ones) of social interaction, sometimes moulded in the form of tangible instruments such as a bowl or a computer. The Soviet psychologist Leontiev (see Scaife, 1985) illustrated this with the example of a baby feeding with a spoon. At first the infant handles a spoon as he or she would any natural object. But this handling slowly, but radically, becomes reorganised by adult intervention to conform to a more specific social use (Fig. 4.3).

Cultural tools entail both social conventions and a logic of their social use. For example, all cultures have a number system — the

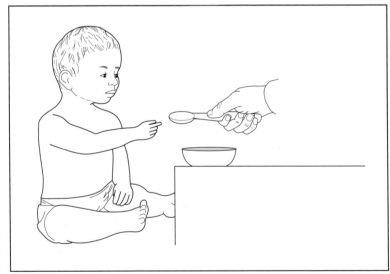

FIG. 4.3.
Development as
acquisition of cultural
tools.

system of reference by which information about the number of objects in a set can be exchanged. Our own culture uses the base 10, which dictates the logic of counting and embedded reference beyond 10, 10 10s, and so on. Other cultures may use other systems, such as the base 20, or even, as with the Oksapmin, of Papua New Guinea, simply the naming of body parts and the order in which they are named (Saxe, 1991; see Nunes & Bryant, 1996). But the specific cultural tool bears the same kind of logic. Measurement systems, too, vary with cultures. The Oksapmin, for example, use the length of body parts (e.g. arm length) as units of measurement but, again, within the constraints of an embedded logic, without which the system would be socially useless (Nunes & Bryant, 1996).

So acquisition of cultural tools consists of far more than mere convention. Even an infant's developing knowledge of an object consists of far more than isolated features, shape, weight, and so on. Rather, the objects mediate whole patterns of social relationships which individual cognitions "enable". As Scribner (1997, p.268) points out:

> In acting with objects the child is not merely learning the physical properties of things but mastering the social modes of acting with those things. These socially evolved modes of action are not inscribed in the objects themselves and cannot be discovered independently by the child from their physical properties — they must be learned through a socially-mediated process ... In embryonic form, the infant's relationships with others is mediated through objects — a bottle, a hand, a spoon ... The central point is that the child–object and the child–other interactions are part of a unitary process of activity for some purpose.

There are several crucial aspects of this internalisation of external social patterns to be noted. First, Vygotsky stressed how it "takes over" the human cognitive system, transforming and determining forms of knowledge and cognition as the child develops.

> By being included in the process of behaviour, the psychological tool alters the entire flow and structure of mental functions. It does this by determining the structure of a new instrumental act just as a technical tool alters the process of natural adaptation by determining the form of labour operation.

Development is thus quite clearly from the "outside in". Consequently, "... the very mechanism underlying higher mental functions is a copy from social interaction; all higher mental functions are internalised social relationships."

The second aspect is the way that, as a result of this process, knowledge and cognition become vastly extended beyond the limited forms present in other species, and inherent in our cognitive systems by themselves. We may illustrate this with the case of memory. As mentioned in Chapter 2, associationists instituted a prominent tradition of memory research which required subjects to learn, and immediately recall, lists of digits or nonsense syllables. The purpose of this immediacy and nonsensity has been to avoid the effects of background knowledge or use of learning strategies. Complex models of human memory have been based on these individualistic routines.

Yet Vygotskians would argue that they are the very opposite of the creative, social way that human memory is actually used. Very early in human social history, the demands of social cooperation and communication required counting and simple computation, as in the management and distribution of crops and animals. The interaction between social needs/regulations and cognitive ones led readily to the invention of simple tallies — auxiliary tools that, as Vygotsky and Luria (1993, p.177) explain, vastly expand the memory function, transforming the natural function in the process. Such auxiliary tools have of course been vastly augmented in more recent times by writing, libraries, calculators, and computers: "It is this transition from natural forms of memory to the cultural ones that constitutes development of memory from child to adult." Indeed, Nelson (1995) has argued that the function of autobiographical memory — the memory for personal episodes — is that of sharing experiences with others through the agency of language, and presents evidence suggesting that our childhood memories start from when we first started to talk about them.

The third aspect is the remarkable creativity that results from the dialectical process through which this takes place. Although the notion of "apprenticeship" is sometimes used as a "Vygotskian" metaphor of human learning, it can be misleading. As Vygotsky (1978) argued, cultural change, new practices, and new ideas arise because the relationship between individual and group is a dynamic, interactional one, not simply a handing-over of a tradition. The child's or novice's mind is not a computer passively waiting to be programmed, nor that of an apprentice simply "picking up" what the adult already knows and does. Rather it already contains representations of countless other experiences, themselves at various levels of abstraction. These will often conflict with, and react to, patterns currently being internalised (Vygotsky used the word "clash"), producing novel resolutions. "The very essence of cultural development is in the collision of mature cultural forms of behaviour with the primitive forms that characterise the child's behaviour" (Vygotsky, 1981, p.151). In this way, the cultural order is, in a sense, reconstructed in each developing child, emerging in "an individually differentiated fabric of meaning" (Brockmeier, 1996, p.133). This relationship between individual cognition and social forms allows the "original ideas and creative contributions of individual minds" while explaining "the achievement of social history" (Markova, 1990, p.191).

In each of these aspects Vygotsky argued that speech — the cultural tool *par excellence* — has a crucial role to play. So it is worth giving that aspect some special attention

Speech. For Piaget (1988, p.14), social experience, like experience in general, is significant for the child "only if he is capable of assimilating [them], and he can do this only if he already possesses the adequate instruments or structures." Moreover symbolic activity, including language, is an *outcome* of early cognitive development and, at first, merely runs in parallel with sensorimotor action, having no organisational role in it. The development of symbolic functions in the second year (play, mental images, drawing, and, above all, language itself) merely "enables the sensorimotor to extend itself" (Piaget, 1969/1991, p.9). In this respect human cognitive development in children is co-extensive with that in other animals, with language as a useful "add-on".

Vygotsky (Vygotsky & Luria, 1993, p.108) claimed that once children learn to speak their behaviour (especially that related to tool use) becomes entirely different from that of animals. Far from language being a mere extension of cognition, the very conjoining of thought and speech "results in symbolic activity's beginning to play a specific organizing part, penetrating into the process of tool use and giving birth to principally new forms of behaviour."

Some of the earliest research by Vygotsky and his colleagues involved giving to 3-year-old children simple problems such as how to recover an object that was out of reach, but with certain aids such as a box and a stick available. He compared their behaviours with that of apes given similar problems (as with food just outside the cage, or just out of reach within it). One of the first observations was that the child speaks spontaneously and continuously, throughout the task, its persistence increasing with the difficulties encountered. Attempts to block it experimentally are either futile or stop the activity altogether. Far from being loose "egocentric" babble, therefore, Vygotsky and Luria (1993, p.109) concluded that the speech is somehow integral to the cognitive functioning — so much so that without it the task cannot be completed: "the child solves a practical task with the help of not only eyes and hands, but also speech."

How, then, does this facilitation work? For a start, when associated with problems like those just mentioned, it seems to impart to the child greater freedom of operation — a detachment from the consuming predominance of the goal itself to allow careful planning, as in the preliminary gathering of a wider range of useful materials for tools, and the organisation of a chain of preliminary acts leading up to the goal. The impulsive, direct manipulations of the ape are replaced by the complex psychological processes of speech-planning and controlled motor organisation.

Speech, then, appears to help the child to master an object through mastery (organisation and planning) of his or her own behaviour. Indeed, over a course of experience with such tasks, the nature of the task itself, and thus the structure of responses, appear to "evolve" in the child, in contrast with the ape, where a stereotyped activity involving the tools emerges. According to Vygotsky and Luria (1993, p.111), "These entirely new psychological structures are absent in apes in even moderately complex forms."

This illustrates some crucial issues. Here speech seems to be acting like other symbol systems — auxiliary stimuli interposed between the child's actions and the outside world. "They serve the child first and foremost, as a means of social contacts with surrounding people, and are also applied as a means of self-influence ... creating thus a new and superior form of activity in the child" (Vygotsky & Luria, 1993, p.111). With the use of symbols the child is no longer a slave to the perceptual world, the immediate situation.

But the most important observation appears to be that the source of the developmental progression transcends the concrete task itself and has to be found in the social environment, even including, in the case of experiments, relations with the experimenter: "the child enters into relations with the situation, not directly, but through the medium of another person" (Vygotsky & Luria, 1993, p.115). This is how the child's development subsequently takes a radically different path compared with the ape: from a biological one to a *sociohistorical* one.

At first the child's response to a task is a strange mix of the practical and the social: direct attempts to solve the problem; emotional speech; appeals to the experimenter; and so on. There then usually transpires a suitable train of actions leading up to success. But just before the final, conclusive, step is taken, a remarkable event takes place: the child turns to the experimenter for help, usually consisting of some relatively trivial assistance like moving the object nearer. It is as if, as Vygotsky and Luria (1994, p.117) put it, the child is "showing that he knows what to do in order to attain his purpose, but cannot attain it by himself ... the plan of the solution is, in the main, ready, although beyond the limits of his own actions". In this way the child's intellect becomes socialised: the involvement of another person's behaviour "becomes ... a necessary part of the child's entire practical activity".

What happens at the next stage of development is that the child now turns this socialised speech in on him- or herself — so that a complex practical activity becomes an internalised social function, not the product of purely "internal" mechanisms. What was first only a reflective "verbal mould" of activity now comes to plan and direct action. By such means the child begins to be freed of slavishness to the immediate situation and becomes an active agent in foreseeing operations drawn out in time. As a result, the whole of the child's psychological development takes a new turn. Indeed the child appears to perceive not just with eyes and ears etc., but with its speech. For example, spontaneous action is restrained, and attention, perception, thought, and memory all begin to function in new ways.

The communicative intentions of the child even in the first year are taken over and shaped by social forces. For example (Vygotsky, 1966, pp.42–42):

> The pointing gesture is merely an unsuccessful grasping movement ... the child's unsuccessful grasping movement gives rise to a reaction not from the objects, but from another person. The original meaning of this grasping movement is thus imparted by others.

In this way the same action begins to obtain a completely different, communicative, function (1966, p.43): "from a movement directed towards the object, it becomes a movement directed towards another person, a means of communication: the grasping is transformed into pointing." Thus prelinguistic communication is not an offshoot of cognitive development, as Piaget may have argued, but arises from the acquisition of cultural tools through adults' contingent behaviour.

Thus we have the critical element of Vygotsky's more general "theory of signs". Sign systems such as language, tally systems in counting and memorising, and calculating devices, are the products of cultural evolution, not of individuals acting alone. They arise as a means of influencing others in cooperative activity, and then, by the process of internalisation, as a means of governing oneself.

Vygotsky's argument that language has its origins in prelinguistic, social, communication has led, since the 1970s to a series of studies of infant–parent social interaction and communication. Early studies (Bruner, 1975; Newson, 1974) showed how the infant is imputed with intentions, desires, and feelings from the start. In addition these early interactions in the first months of life — game-playing formats and routines — take on the structure of "proto-conversations".

It is in this way, these authors suggest, that the infant becomes incorporated into the structured world of "intersubjectivity", necessary for the development of language and "socialised" cognition. Indeed, Bruner (e.g. 1975) put forward the thesis that language development is based around the conceptual categories that emerge in early social interactions: the so-called "case" *categories* such as "agent", "object", and "experienced", and case *relations* such as "agent–object", "action–object", and so on. This became a very popular model for a while, but Bruner has weakened the model in recent years (Bruner, 1983; for discussion see Harris, 1993).

Finally, in analysing the relations between language and cognition, Vygotsky (1962, pp.148–149) noted several distinctive aspects of language or speech. External speech is that used in ordinary, explicit, social discourse. But individuals also use an *inner* speech: an abbreviated form, rather like the external speech used among acquaintances in familiar context, full of meaning, but with a special syntax and "draft form", used, as it were, "for oneself": "a distinct plan of verbal thought ... fluttering between word and thought". Furthermore, there is another level of verbal thought still more "inward". This is the level of thought itself, functioning according to its own principles (1962, p.149):

> The flow of thought is not accompanied by a simultaneous unfolding of speech. The two processes are not identical, and there is no rigid correspondence between the units of thought and speech ... Thought has its own structure, and the transition from it to speech is no easy matter.

From such an account it is difficult to overestimate the stunning skill that has to be mastered in the development of ordinary social intercourse in young children (Vygotsky, 1962, p.132):

from the motive which engenders a thought, to the shaping of the thought, first in inner speech, then in the meanings of words, and finally in words ... [all involving] an infinite variety of movements to and fro, of ways still unknown to us.

Vygotsky and education

Because Vygotsky's theory specifies a distinct role for the teacher or other expert in instruction and cognitive development, the last decade or so has witnessed enthusiastic attempts to institute Vygostkian principles in schools. These have, by and large, emphasised peer-group interactions and "collaborative learning" as basic principles. There have been so many excellent descriptions of these (e.g. contributions in Light, Sheldon, & Woodhead, 1991; Rogoff, Baker-Sennet, Lacasa, & Goldsmith, 1995) that I shall only offer a brief summary here.

The most popular Vygostkian idea has been that of the "zone of proximal development" (ZPD). Vygotsky defined this as that latent learning "gap" between what a child can do on his or her own and what can be done with the help of a more skilful other. Such "potential" cognition is a better index of a child's development, he argued, than the *apparent* level, as revealed, say, by a test score. The idea has been pursued through studies of adult–child, or expert–novice interactions "in" what is thus assumed to be the child's or novice's ZPD.

These studies have shown, first, how easily and rapidly children learn complex cultural tools, such as social skills, numeracy, and motor skills, when these are embedded in their cultural contexts. For example, in contrast with the turgidity of maths learning in schools, studies of everyday mathematics (e.g. Lave, 1988), even among 10-year-old street traders in Brazil (Nunes et al., 1993), shows that "quantitative relations are assembled inventively and effectively in everyday situations, independently of problem solvers' past school biographies" (Lave, 1994, p.318). In consequence many authors have contrasted the ease with which learning takes place in cultural context with the difficulties widespread in school learning (Bruner, 1985; Tharpe & Gallimore, 1991; Wood, 1991). Because "naturalistic" learning occurs in a social context, it is argued, it fuses motivational–need aspects of development and technical–operational ones.

Second, the studies have drawn attention to the structured *form* of such interactions. Typically, the adult/expert institutes an informal programme of instruction of progressively diminishing intervention. One example in a naturalistic setting is the teaching of weaving among the Zinacantecan of Southern Mexico (Childs & Greenfield, 1982). The novice (usually a child) has to learn six main steps, from setting up the loom to finishing off the garment. As each new step is tackled the "teacher's" intervention is, at first, frequent and detailed. But it reduces rapidly with practice: from 93% of the time with the child's first garment; through 50% of the time with the second garment, and so on.

In an experimental setting, Wood and Middleton (1975) devised a special set of wooden blocks which could only be put together by 4-year-olds with considerable help from an adult (usually the mother). In observing mother–child pairs it became clear that the "instruction" tended to take the form of "guided arrangement" in which the level of parental control gradually diminished as it became taken over by the child. The examples in Table 4.1 show reduced levels of control as we move up the Table.

TABLE 4.1

Levels of Control in Parent–Child Interactions
Modified from Wood, 1991

Level	Example
1. General verbal prompts	"Now you make something"
2. Specific instructions	"Get four big blocks"
3. Indicates materials	Points to blocks needed
4. Prepares materials	Orients blocks correctly
5. Demonstrates	Assembles two pairs

(Modified from Wood, 1991)

In such observations it is clear that instruction takes place by a method of "arranging experience", rather than didactic teaching. Wood, Bruner, & Ross (1976) used the term "scaffolding" to describe the support through which the child can extend or construct current skills to higher levels of competence and control — during which progression the scaffolding is slowly removed. This has, in turn, inspired attempts in educational settings to find explicit forms of scaffolding and support "designed to provoke zones of proximal development" (Brown et al., 1996, p.160).

A distinctive Vygotskian rhetoric of education has thus emerged in the last decade or so. It is too early to tell whether it will have durable practical consequences in schools. One of the great difficulties, of course, is that of transposing "culturally embedded" learning, which is usually on a one-to-one basis, to the setting of the typical classroom with one teacher to 30 or more pupils. Another is that of simply attempting to apply Vygotskian pedagogical "methods" for the attainment of traditional curriculum goals, without appreciation of how the latter, too, will need to be radically re-cast (Richardson, 1998).

Criticisms of Vygotsky and social constructivism

One criticism of Vygotsky (as well as social-constructivism in general) is similar to that levelled against other models of cognitive development. Yet again the contents and processes remain unspecified, except at an idealistic, generalised level. If Piaget was concerned to detail the inside with one form of idealism, based on formal logic, Vygotsky put the child in social context, but his attempts to show how this shaped the inside remained sketchy. This criticism applies especially to the crucial process of "internalisation" and resultant cognitive reconstruction. Without clear characterisation, we remain uncertain about whether development has taken place at all. Thus Wozniak (1996, p.17) complains of "its failure to address the issue of a normative criterion for development". And as Brockmeier (1996, p.132) reminds us, many current neo-rationalists are questioning assumptions that children can just "pick up" cultural forms and conventions "simply because they are there and children grow up in them". Thus, according to Chesnokova (1994, p.91), "The main research problem of this approach is how the knowledge structure, originating in the course of interaction, develops from the intermental level to the intramental level."

Without such description we can have little more than the rudiments of a theory of development. Indeed, Smith (1996b, p.112) has suggested that "There is actually no theory at all in the writings of Vygotsky, assuming standard criteria as to what counts as a scientific theory." Van der Veer and Valsiner (1991) have also argued that many of Vygotsky's key ideas were derivative, only half-formed and thin on empirical support. This, of course, might have been expected from a theorist whose work was so tragically cut short. Indeed, it can be argued that, as Vygotsky's main objective was to reconstruct *general principles* of psychology, on the basis of fresh presuppositions, he has been remarkably successful. It remains for others to flesh out those general principles in the form of explicit, testable theory. Judging from the amount of work that has been done in the relatively few years since Vygotsky's work became known in the West — especially regarding areas like pedagogy, and cognition in context — there is reason to be optimistic about that.

Piaget and Vygotsky compared

Vygotsky was born in the same year (1896) as Piaget, and their work has often been compared. Indeed, Vygotsky often wrote in praise of Piaget's work, although he became opposed to some of its basic principles. As a result there has been much debate about the relative virtues of their respective theories — debate that became much aired during a number of celebratory conferences and workshops in their centenary year (see e.g. Smith, Dockrell, & Tomlinson, 1996; Tryphon & Voneche, 1996). I think such comparisons have been instructive, and this seems a good place to try to summarise them.

There are undoubtedly commonalities in the theories of Piaget and Vygotsky. They have common epistemological and methodological principles: these include a developmental perspective, an anti-reductionism, a belief in the importance of action, and qualitative changes in cognition in the course of development. Both wished to explain the development of mature rational knowledge and scientific thinking. Both adopted dialectical conceptions of development in which opposites, created by an active organism, become transcended in new structures which become hierarchically organised (Wozniak, 1996). New structures of thought emerge at succeeding levels. Finally, they used similar research methods.

However, the differences are just as obvious. Piaget's model is described by Marti (1996, p.66) as an "individual, endogenous, operatory, universal constructivism": it stresses the progressive autonomy of the inside from the outside, through the process of equilibration. Social forms of knowledge and action are simply another form of disturbance, or, in the form of symbols (gestures, movements, images) or semiotic forms (language, mathematical notations), are "simply props for operatory thinking" — i.e. detached from their communicational context.

Vygotsky's theory stresses a "social, exogenous, semiotic, and contextual development" (Marti, 1996, p.57). Vygotsky sees the external social plane as original and constitutional to thought, not merely disturbing to it. But, like Piaget, he sees internalisation of these patterns as critical. Also, like Piaget, he sees it not merely as a transfer of pattern, but as reconstruction on the individual, internal plane, leading to successively new levels of regulation.

It is just as true, then, as Marti (1996) notes, that a simple "inside–out and outside–in" opposition fails to appreciate the complexity in *both* theories of the relation between the "inside" and the "outside'. It has been said that Piaget *ignored* the child's social context — his view was that in which a "lone child struggles single-handed to strike some equilibrium between assimilating the world to himself or himself to the world" (Bruner, 1985, p.25). Alternatively, it has been said that he simply neglected it. It is now clear, however, that Piaget saw peer interaction as an important source of disequilibrium (and subsequent re-equilibration/decentration) in development (Doise, 1988). And he saw inside–outside relations as part of a unified process: "asking whether intra-individual operations generate interindividual operations or the reverse amounts to asking which is first from the hen or the egg" (Piaget, 1960, p.234, translated and cited by Tryphon & Voneche, 1996, p.8).

Smith (1996b) claims, with numerous quotes, that there is considerable overlap between Piaget and Vygotsky as regards the importance of social context. However, for Piaget, social experience was necessary but not sufficient for development. As Piaget (1977/1995) quoted by Brockmeier, 1996, p.132) said: "Each individual is called upon to think and to rethink ... on his own account and by means of his own system of logic ... the system of collective notions." It seems likely, therefore, that, for Piaget, "thinking socially" is different from what it is for Vygotsky (Piaget, 1923/1974, quoted by Brown et al., 1996, p.147):

> The adult, even in his most personal and private occupation ... thinks socially, has continually in his mind's eye his collaborators or opponents ... to whom sooner or later he will announce the results of his labours. This mental picture pursues him throughout his task. The task itself is henceforth socialised at almost every stage of its development ... the need for checking and demonstrating calls into being an inner speech addressed throughout to a hypothetical opponent ... When, therefore, the adult is brought face to face with his fellow beings, what he announces to them is something already socially elaborated and therefore roughly adapted to his audience.

This view of "social" influence, as that of audience, contrasts with that of Vygotsky, who stresses the structure of human relations around cultural tools, wherein lie the roots of the structure of cognition — a developmental transformation of mind according to the historically constructed tools of the culture.

Although they shared many objectives (as already noted), they also had certain *different* aims. Piaget was interested, as an epistemologist, in the history and validation of knowledge: Vygotsky was interested in the historical genesis of revolution and change. Accordingly they adopted different *criteria* of development. Piaget's description was that of a domain-general or domain-independent system of increasingly higher forms of equilibration or logical operations. A sociohistorical description of individual cognitive development (of how one psychological state is more developed than another) is more problematic, and Vygotsky never explicitly addressed it thoroughly (Wozniak, 1996).

This debate seems crucial because of the issues it draws into focus, which can only be overcome in clearer theory. There are a number of current attempts to overcome the strictures of either or both theories by incorporating other principles. Most interesting have been attempts to show the role of social cooperation in performance on conservation tasks. For example Doise and his colleagues (see Doise, 1988), using a number of studies, have attempted to extend Piaget's theory into a more general theory of socioconstructivism. In one experiment, they had young children who had failed conservation tasks repeat the process in pairs. After that experience, their conservation status was much improved. The "conflict" or disequilibrium presented by another point of view appeared to have the effect of inducing or explicating the necessary coordinations that were seemingly absent before. Although it is unclear whether or not one of the children needs to be already at a conserving level, such an explanation seems promising at least of the applicability of Piaget's theory to social problem situations.

Other authors have sought a rapport between Piaget and Vygotsky by introducing additional assumptions. For example, Marti (1996) suggests a role for "innate constraints" along the lines of Karmiloff-Smith (1992) (and thus the very kind of nativist predeterminism that Piaget was striving to overcome). Elman et al. (1997) go even further in suggesting an amalgamation of nativist constraints with Piagetian constructivism and Vygotskian social constructivism, using connectionism as a means of description of products and processes. I shall have more to say about these increasingly "mixed" models in Chapter 5.

Models mixed and models new 5

Introduction

So far I have attempted to describe currently popular, basic ideas in the field of cognitive development in a way that might help students simplify the "Tower of Babel" that many complain about. As explained in the Preface, I hope that describing the assumptions underlying these ideas will help students obtain a critical purchase on the numerous models that abound. The basic ideas of rationalism, associationism, and constructivism are still very much alive, but as I also warned at the outset, my intention has been to describe these as distinctive *ingredients* of models, and not necessarily "pure" models in themselves. Although the accounts in Chapters 1–4 have rather tightly segregated these ingredients for purposes of understanding, they do not always exist in such pristine isolation. For example in Chapters 1 and 2, I mentioned the dual system implicit or explicit in modern associationism, and indeed pervading most of cognitive psychology.

Thus, it has become increasingly the case, over the last decade or so, that theorists have attempted to compensate for the obvious deficiencies underlying assumptions in one pedigree of model by "blending" in some of the assumptions of another. In this chapter, I want to do two things: first to emphasise, with further illustrations, the way in which such ingredients have been mixed in recent models. Then I want to consider some new models, stemming from these, some of which have attracted a great deal of attention in recent years. I hope this will bring us up to date across the contemporary spectrum of models.

Nativism with constructivism

Although there are still those theorists who postulate "strong" nativism in the form of genetically determined knowledge and cognitive processes, there are now many who favour less specific genetic information which only "constrains" the constructive development of knowledge and cognition in interaction with actual experience (albeit retaining some structural determination throughout). Thus there are now nativists who readily subscribe to the principles of genetic constraint, and some of the principles of Piaget's theory, in a single model — or, conversely, who have added a touch of nativism to a constructivist formulation. This was mentioned in Chapter 1, so I will be brief.

Perhaps the best example is that of Karmiloff-Smith (1992), who argues in favour of early genetic constraints, and subsequent "epigenetic" cognitive development within those constraints. Others (Plunkett & Sinha, 1992, p.212) describe the biological and social as part of a harmonious stream, and thus view "biological processes of growth and development as being continuous with psychological development, and the human mind as a product of a developmental unfolding of biological potential in a given sociocultural context". As Keil (1988, p.85) put it: "Under this view, acquiring complex knowledge would be impossible, if all of us did not share certain a priori constraints that restrict the range of hypotheses to be made about the structure of what is learned."

As for what these constraints consist of, Keil (1988, p.92) envisages a "conceptual core or core competency that is defined by sets of rigorous constraints and which is supplemented by a periphery that is governed much more loosely." Many, if not most, of the "modularity" models described in Chapter 2 fall into this category (see contributions in Carey & Gelman, 1991; and Hirschfeld & Gelman, 1994). Conversely, Case (e.g. 1992) and others have introduced the notion of an innate conceptual control structure to a Piagetian model of development.

The problem is, how well do these disparate assumptions actually mix in complex, evolved characters? Keil (1988, p.92) argues, with reference to the hypothetical "genetic skeleton", that "... dramatic shifts can occur in the periphery provided they honour the general boundaries of the skeleton. Because the core is only a skeletal framework, it does not completely constrain the structures within it...". But real-life structures, anatomies, and architectures that are associated with an underlying skeleton remain closely determined by it. Dramatic changes in specific aspects of animal anatomies, or in their general form, do not occur without changes in the skeleton; and we can hardly argue that dramatic changes in the shape of a building, say, can occur without a change in its foundations.

Yet it is precisely such dramatic changeability in cognition that has most characterised human cognition. Consider, for example, the evolution from an abacus to a modern processor as a mode of computation; from the foot to the motor car, as a form of transport; drastic changes in the ways in which we make a living; or the radically changing forms of scientific knowledge. All this has happened without any changes in genes and their hypothetical constraints. In any case, as described in Chapter 1, cognitive and sociocognitive abilities not only evolved as devices for dealing with highly changeable (especially social) circumstances, but in the way in which *they* regulate epigenetic regulations, which in turn regulate genomic regulations, which in turn regulate genetic regulations. So the simple mix of genes plus epigenesis may be too simplistic — and indeed, dysfunctional — in the kinds of environment in which humans evolved. This — plus the fact, of course, that there is little direct evidence for it — needs to be borne in mind whenever this "mix" is encountered.

Nativism with associationism

As pointed out in Chapters 1 and 2, much of cognitive psychology since the 1970s actually reflects an amalgamation between nativism and neo-associationism. In such models a number of innate cognitive processes act on "information" (itself conceived in various ways), either in current input or existing knowledge stores, to establish or update a knowledge store envisaged, in turn, as a network of associations. In the guise of Artifical Intelligence, this has probably been mainstream "cognitive science" over the last 20 years, although it has not been so prominent in the area of cognitive development, where some forms of nativism and constructivism have long held sway. However, a number of models were mentioned in Chapter 2 that come into this category.

As was also mentioned in Chapter 2, the problem with such models is that the positing of the innate processes, although very convenient from the point of view of model-making, is largely an act of faith. Their nature is invariably left mysterious, as is the way in which they actually work in extracting features, symbols, and their associations, from raw, fragmentary inputs. Moreover there are reasons to believe that such "simple" associations, whether in the form of S–R bonds, symbolic networks, or prototypes, cannot account for the richness of human reasoning. Finally, they have not offered convincing accounts of the nature of cognitive development, or at least not one that a majority of developmental psychologists might share. This is one reason why more recent associationist models have taken their leave of many of these assumptions, as I shall describe shortly.

Nativism with constructivism and associationism

There have been attempts to amalgamate associationism and constructivism, usually in the guise of two levels of reasoning. And it has been considered that, in order to get this arrangement to work, some sort of innate constraints are necessary. For example, Halford (1993), while stressing the role of mental models, acknowledges that associationist processes will sometimes operate in reasoning. Indeed, Halford (1993, p.9) states: "where these mechanisms suffice they will tend to be preferred, because they impose smaller processing loads and understanding will tend to be used only where associative processes are inadequate." He also argues that development of these can only take place on the basis of innate constraints like those proposed by Keil and by Gelman and associates (see Chapter 1).

In the last few years, a new kind of synthesis has emerged. This involves nativist (genetic) constraints and a new kind of associationism that allegedly manifests itself through constructivist principles. This new kind of associationism is known as "connectionism" and it has created a great deal of enthusiasm as the latest cutting edge of developmental theory. Thus, in a major collaborative work, Elman et al. (1997, p.147) claim to offer us rich examples "of the use of connectionist simulations for understanding the intricate interactions between mind and environment during development"; that these "permit ever more sophisticated interpretations of the domain being learned" (p.168); and that even "the functional processes of assimilation, accommodation and equilibration invoked by Piaget seem to be very well captured in the dynamics of the network architecture and learning algorithm" (p.166).

In the face of such strong claims we obviously need to examine the underlying models in some detail. What follows, then, is a brief account of what is the first of the new perspectives that the rest of this chapter is about.

Connectionism

As the brain is the seat of knowledge and cognition, a reasonable-sounding research strategy may be to attempt to model it, and its richly interconnected network of neurons, in some way, to discover what it can tell us about cognition that we haven't been able to discover by other means. Over the last decade or so, then, the computer metaphor of the mind, prominent since the 1960s, has been replaced by a "brain metaphor" in which learning and cognition take place via simplified models called "neural networks". As Hanson and Burr (1990, p.472) note, "Connectionism consists of old ideas about representation, spreading activation, semantic decomposition, and associative memory all packaged in something that looks like a cartoon brain with cartoon neurons, connected by cartoon synapses."

Modern connectionist models consist of:

1. large numbers of input–output units receiving inputs from, and making outputs to, potentially large numbers of other units;
2. each unit having a level of activation, or activation value, at any point in time;
3. "output" from, or "firing" of, the unit depending on an activation threshold being exceeded;
4. depending in turn on the summed "strengths" of potentially numerous inputs;
5. rich interconnections, such that most if not all of one set of units may connect to all or most of those of another set;
6. efficacy of inputs to units modifiable through changes in connection "strengths" or "weights" resulting from previous activations (and according to various "learning rules").

Figure 5.1. shows some of these features. The connection strengths or weights are the crux of the matter. These moderate the input from one node to the other and thus help to determine whether or not the receiving node's activation value is exceeded (and it fires in turn). It is the overall pattern of connection strengths (and ultimately of patterns of firing) that is said to constitute the network's representations. In so-called "distributed" models, and unlike the nodes in a "symbolic"

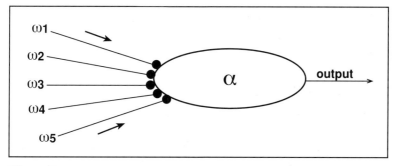

FIG. 5.1.   The basic "unit" in connectionist models; $\omega 1$–$\omega 5$ are the weights on synapses (black blobs) between input axons and the unit; α is the activation threshold that the sum of the inputs, as moderated by those weights, must exceed for the unit to "fire".

associator (see Chapter 2), they "stand for" and mean nothing in themselves. For example, the "units" or nodes in the kind of semantic network described in Chapter 2 are "localist" in that each one stands for a specific feature, concept, or proposition. In connectionist models it is in the interplay between nodes and their weights, and the overall patterns of activity, where "meaning" emerges and where most of the current mystique surrounding connectionist networks resides.

A simple "pattern-associator" network is shown in Fig. 5.2. Here the patterns are labelled features of dogs or birds. When features of dogs are activated in input units (filled circles), output units to which they are connected may be activated. A learning-rule is usually implemented such that, if one feature is associated with another frequently in experience then the connection between the nodes coding them will become more heavily weighted (the weight is adjusted): activity in one node will then be more likely to trigger activity in the other in future (a notion stemming from Hebb, 1949). By adjusting weights (connection strengths) between units through a feedback algorithm, then, appropriate combinations of features can be associated in output units, and discriminated from other associations. As shown in the histogram in Fig. 5.2., after such training only certain output units (filled circles) are activated upon presentation of "dog" features.

FIG. 5.2. A simple pattern-associator network: the histogram to the right shows relative levels of activation of respective output units after the network has been trained.

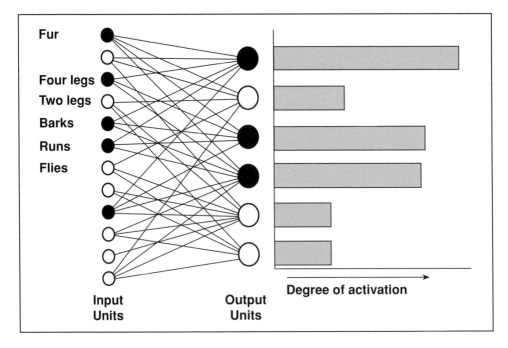

By taking account of the presence and absence of other features at the same time (in parallel), complex patterns of weights can form which approximate complex, abstract rules, such as those involved in categorisation and in language production. That is, they may exhibit "emergent properties", at least superficially resembling those actually implemented in real brains/minds, purely on the basis of strengths of association. Note that, in this particular network, nearly all cells in the input layer connect to all cells in the output layer, but the degree of connectivity can be varied Finally, (but not shown here) some of the connections can be inhibitory instead of excitatory (input suppresses activation in the recipient unit).

Note that the "representation" does not consist of a singular composite, but is "distributed" among many units which are activated in parallel. This arrangement furnishes several advantages. One is that an input image bearing only a few of the features of a dog (perhaps a partially occluded one) will still result in an activation of the entire representation. Also, damage to some of the output units will result in marginal, or "graceful", degeneration of activation (representation), rather than a cataclysmic breakdown as in a traditional "symbolic" processor (for fuller descriptions, simulations and results see Rumelhart & McClelland, 1986).

Most interest has been attracted to the properties of "multilayered" networks. A simple multilayered network is shown in Fig. 5.3. To simplify description, instead of, perhaps, dozens of units on each layer, and corresponding density of interconnections, I have reduced these to two, and my description will follow that of Plunkett and Sinha (1992).

The circles (a–e) are the units or cells in the network. These are organised in layers, as shown. Arrows represent the connections and

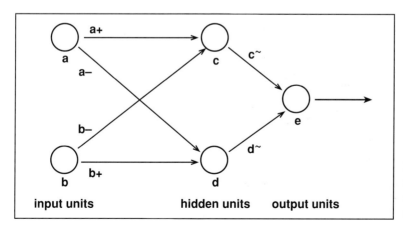

Fig. 5.3.
A fragment of a multilayered connectionist network.

direction of activation, and indicate that the input units, which get specific "environmental" values keyed in (e.g. light in a certain place; a letter-feature, such as the cross on a "t"; or a letter itself), feed into the hidden units, which, in turn, activate the output unit. The connections may be excitatory or inhibitory as indicated by the plus and minus signs. Again, a learning rule is usually implemented such that, if one feature is associated with another frequently in experience, then the connection between the nodes coding them will become more heavily weighted.

Most connectionist modelling has in fact consisted of attempts to simulate well-known, but relatively simple and isolated cognitive phenomena in equally simple networks. The prime motivation seems to have been to show that such networks *can in principle* do what the cognitive system does (with the implication that the latter must do it in the same way, whatever exactly that is — which is another question I will be returning to later). In practice, a network is "set up" on a computer according to a set of assumptions (of which more later), themselves dependent on the kind of "learning" or "task" we want the network to do. Processing commences with activation of input units by the investigator from the keyboard, each particular key standing for a value on a variable, or "vector". This activation is then propagated to other units via the connections. An output results from the output unit, and some feedback is keyed in by the investigator (e.g. "correct", "incorrect"). Both input and feedback produce changes in connection weights between some of the units according to a learning equation or algorithm. Series of subsequent inputs and feedback thus enable the network to "settle into" a configuration of connection weights which tends to produce the correct output whatever the input.

The results of such simulations have certainly been impressive. For example, even the simple multilayered network shown earlier can "learn" logical functions such as the EXCLUSIVE OR (or XOR) problem. In this problem the network (or a real person) is presented with pairs of numbers which fall into one or other of two categories, as shown below, and the task is to learn the categorisation correctly.

Number pairs		Category (Output)
0	0	0
1	1	0
0	1	1
1	0	1

As you may be able to see, the solution cannot be learned by an additive rule, or simple combination of the values of the pairs. But it is quite easy to train a simple network to learn the solution by presenting it with the inputs (in sufficiently large numbers) and keying in the feedback, which adjusts the connection weights until performance is satisfactory. Note that, for reasons that are not entirely clear (see later) only a network with hidden units can solve such a problem. Because of this, a kind of mystique has grown around them (Elman et al., 1997, p.64):

> They are equivalent to the internal representations we invoke in psychological theorising ... Hidden units are extra-ordinarily powerful; they make it possible for networks to have internal representations of inputs which capture the more abstract, functional relationships between them.

By such training, networks (usually much more complex than this in the sense of having more input units and more hidden units) have been shown to be capable of learning a wide variety of tasks. They can learn to form apparent prototypic representations (see Chapter 2) from variable input patterns, responding to "old" and "new" exemplars in a way similar to human subjects (Plunkett & Sinha, 1992). They can learn words, such as to recognise distorted or "smudged" versions, and the difficult (irregular) past tense forms of English verbs (Rumelhart & McClelland, 1987).

In a particularly impressive demonstration, Elman (1990) trained a network to predict successive words in sentences. The sentences were input one word at a time, and the network was required to predict what the next word would be. Feedback was given to allow weight adjustment, and so on over thousands of sentences. The network seemed to learn more than the next word in each case, however. It also appeared to acquire a "classification" of the various words in the form of at least some rudimentary grammar. This was shown when the activation patterns in the hidden units corresponding with different words were compared for their "similarity" (using a parameter known as Euclidean distance). The clustering shown in Fig. 5.4. resulted, and suggested that the network was rating verbs as more similar than nouns, and animate nouns as more similar than inanimate nouns.

Not surprisingly, the developmental implications of such findings have been emphasised. Although essentially associationist in origins, it has been said of networks that they illustrate the "construction" of knowledge; "epigenesis" of cognitive development; "emergent" cognitive abilities; a decisive refutation of pure nativism (at least in the form of strongly preformed or pre-coded structure), and so on (e.g.

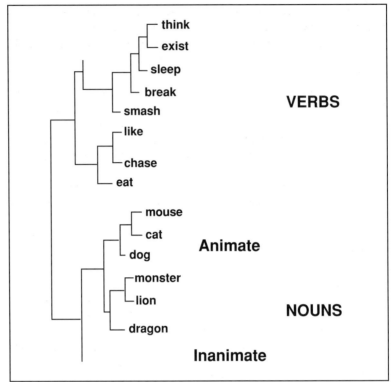

Elman et al., 1997; Plunkett & Sinha, 1992; Quartz, 1993). Ironically, they have also been taken to support notions of weaker nativist constraints in development. Thus, Elman et al. (1997) take the fact that networks require a number of computational "constraints" to be set up, before they will work, as evidence for *genetic* constraints in the development of human cognition.

In addition, much has been made of the "brain-like" structure of connectionist networks. This structure has been said to offer neural plausibility, and thus biological credibility, and with it a number of other brain-like properties. Damage or remove part of the network, and it continues to function more or less normally, rather than suffering dramatic collapse, and this is what is usually found in brain damage in children (Bechtel & Abrahamsen, 1991). Input only part of a regular input and spreading activation through the network, according to the learned weights, will "fill-in" the missing information, again allowing more or less normal function. Finally, each unit will participate in any number of different learned responses so that, in effect, a large number of "memories" are overlain in the same set of units, albeit with different patterns of activation. All of these have made the connectionist network a potent and tangible metaphor for development in real brains/minds.

Criticisms of connectionism

This is, of course, a very skimpy look at the principles of connectionism, and those who want to do it more justice are urged to consult some of the standard texts mentioned. But we do need to ask: is this really the breakthrough that cognitive developmental theory has been waiting for (as, for example, Elman et al., 1997, suggest)? Is it really the correct balance of nativism, associationism, and constructivism that cognitive developmentalists have been looking for? Here I want to mention some of the many problems about the enterprise that draw such claims into doubt.

The first problem is that although networks can be shown to simulate some aspects of human cognition, this doesn't just "happen" from within the network, on the basis of the naturalistic experience typical of real brains/minds. The outcomes are "made" to happen in all kinds of subtle and not-so-subtle ways on the basis of the various assumptions and expectations of the modeller. As Bechtel and Abrahamsen (1991, p.265) remind us, there has been a major debate about whether the "achievements" of networks are simply side-effects of manipulations on input and output, and thus the extent to which the results follow from analyses previously worked out.

A typical connectionist network, that is, has to be "set up" by the modeller, and many people have criticised the seemingly *ad hoc* ways in which this is done. Major prior decisions and manipulations cover such crucial aspects as: the extent of connectivity between layers; whether it is uni- or bi-directional; how many units; the numbers of layers of units; initial connection weights on units; initial activation values on units; the rate at which the net is "permitted" to learn; the nature of the learning (i.e. feedback) algorithm; the ordering of inputs in the training regime; and so on. These are all ways adopted for nudging the network into behaving in the way we want and producing the outcomes we then claim to be the miraculous properties of the network *itself*. It is, perhaps, hardly surprising that some authors, such as Shepard (1988, see Haberlandt, 1990, p.495) have criticised the "haphazard and idiosyncratic" method of "guess and test" that characterises connectionist modelling.

Quartz (1993) has suggested that the high performances of connectionist models stem from the very restrictions built into their formation — i.e. that they are virtually *guaranteed* to work by the way that they are set up beforehand in a self-fulfilling ordinance. There is a certain irony, then, in the way that Elman et al. (1997) take the need for such preparation as good evidence of the need for genetic constraints in real brains/minds.

This pragmatism leads to the second problem, which is that, when all is said and done, we remain remarkably naive about what is being "learned" or "developed" in connectionist nets, and how, exactly, it happens. The "knowledge" formed is certainly based on associations; but not simple, transparent, associations like those discussed in Chapter 2. Then what? "Knowledge ultimately refers to a specific pattern of synaptic connections in the brain ... knowledge is the representations that support behaviour", say Elman et al. (1997, p.359). But, as we are not told what a "specific pattern" consists of, how are we to describe this knowledge? What is the nature of these representations? The only answer we get is: a distributed pattern of connection weights. Remarkably, in the drive to get learning algorithms to "work" in a practical sense, there has been little analysis of the nature of the "knowledge" that results: as Hanson and Burr (1990, p.472) pointed out, "the relationships between the learning algorithms and the representations that support them still remain largely unanalysed."

To put it another way, connection weights may be the bearers of knowledge, but this doesn't tell us anything about the structure of knowledge itself, any more than describing the orientation of molecules on a magnetic tape tells us about the message recorded upon it. Even if we were to undertake the tedious task of specifying connection weights or weight changes across thousands of connections, this still wouldn't describe the knowledge that had been acquired.

This descriptive hollowness leaves many problems. For example, we must assume that knowledge improves and develops with experience: how are we to describe such changes in the language of weight changes alone? And what do connection weights tell us about how to intervene in a knowledge deficiency, or to generally promote knowledge development, in real brains/minds? Without more principled description, we are surely in danger of treating the cognitive system as another "black box", and learning as more akin to "forcing", or even the "shaping" of behaviourists. Indeed, as Varela, Thompson, & Rosch (1991, p.92) point out, "... in experimental psychology connectionist models facilitate a return to a behaviourist orientation, which circumvents theorizing in terms of high-level common-sense, mentalistic constructs."

The grand claims of the advocates of connectionism must also be tempered by the realisation that connectionist modelling, so far, has been confined to "toy" problems, using highly tailored processing constraints. Thus all current nets are very simple, and rapidly break down when attempts are made to "scale up". They don't tell us how reasoning develops and is used productively, as is conspicuously the case in real life (Billman, 1996). Furthermore, their neural and biological plausibility has probably been exaggerated. As Elman et al. (1997, p.316) conclude, while some aspects of brain structure are compatible with connectionism, others raise serious problems for it: "Similarities between real and artificial development are seductive, but it has been argued that they are too superficial to hold up under further scrutiny." And as Reilly (1989, p.165) points out:

> With regard to the neural plausibility of connectionist models, few connectionists see their models as anything more than schemata for what goes on in the brain ... For example Smolensky (1987) has argued that "the principles of cognition being explored in the connectionist approach are better *not* construed as the principles of the neural level" (author's emphasis).

Finally, we have to stress another limitation of networks compared with real brains and minds. This is that they cannot *act* on the world — they can "read" it (or rather have it "read" to them) but they cannot change it. This "sensation of action" is a crucial aspect of constructivism, and, of course, of what we know of how the brain works. In conclusion, as Bechtel and Abrahamsen (1991, p.263) point out, "Current models are exploratory, and a very large promissory note remains due." In other words it remains to be seen whether connectionism can provide convincing models of real cognitive development, and this may require greater attention to the contents of representation over and above the highly general notion of patterns of connection weights.

Ecological realism theory

The school of perception fostered by J.J. and E.J. Gibson does not fall easily into any of the major classes of theory described so far. It argues that the brain/mind does not have to be burdened with native structures, accumulated associations, or constructed schemas at all, because there is enough information in the flow of natural experience itself to provide the "affordances" needed for fruitful action. "The *affordances* of the environment are what it *offers* the animal, what it *provides* or *furnishes*, either for good or ill" (J.J. Gibson, 1986, p.127, emphases in original).

That information, in other words, is structured by natural events, as well as the explorations, movements, and manipulations of the individual, in systematic ways. All this reveals the "higher-order" invariants in objects and events — the characteristic flight of a bird, the ripples and sounds of water, and so on — to which the individual attunes through perceptual learning. When this happens, as in the course of development, there is improved attention to significant detail, improved discrimination, and thus sensitivity to affordances (J.J. Gibson, 1986). So the information in the environment is itself a sufficient basis for perception and action, requiring no appeal to innate ideas, associations, concepts, or schemas. What is needed is not so much a cognitive system, but appropriate *perceptual* systems which can "pick up" that information (Reed, 1996). There are no representations, only perceptual processes. The mind has "interpretive powers" (Reed, 1996) but it simply acts to coordinate this process across the sensory receptors, and integrate the information picked up, without the need to represent it in any way. As J.J. Gibson (1986, p.267) puts it:

> The evidence ... shows that the available information surrounding an organism has structure, both simultaneous and successive, and that this structure depends on sources in the outer environment. If the invariants of this structure can be registered by a perceptual system, the constants of neural input will correspond to the constants of stimulus energy, although the one will not copy the other. But then meaningful information can be said to exist inside the nervous system as well as outside. The brain is relieved of the necessity of constructing such information by any process — innate rational powers (theoretical nativism), the storehouse of memory (empiricism), or form-fields (gestalt theory). The brain can be treated as the highest of several centres of the nervous system governing the perceptual systems. Instead of postulating that the brain constructs information from the input of a sensory nerve, we can suppose that the centres of the nervous system, including the brain resonate to information.

According to E.J. Gibson, the utilisation of affordances begins from birth. Indeed, a number of studies in infants have supported this idea. For example, infants as young as 1 month old can "pick up" information about the properties of objects provided by motion. Using the habituation technique described in Chapter 1, Gibson and her colleagues obtained evidence suggesting that infants could detect the higher-order invariances indicative of different kinds of substance (forms showing rigid motion versus forms showing deforming motion; or the relative elasticity, "chewability" or "squeezability" detected by 4-week-old infants: Walker-Andrews & Gibson, 1986). And such invariances may generalise across modalities — for example, across vision and touch. It has also been shown how infants will blink and show head withdrawal to a looming shadow, as if it is that of a fast-approaching object (e.g. Yonas, Petterson, & Lockman, 1979).

Most famous is Gibson's work on the visual cliff (Gibson & Walk, 1960). The visual cliff consists of a sheet of plate glass supported above a deep "drop" in the surface, the whole surface being covered with a chequerboard pattern (Fig. 5.5). Gibson had reckoned that by the time they can crawl infants will be able to discriminate the affordances signifying depth (or, rather, lack of support). This is achieved by movement specifying transformations of variables like texture, density, motion parallax, occlusion, binocularity, and so on, which distinguish the "drop" in the cliff. It was indeed shown that babies from 6 months to 1 year old had developed an aversion response in the face of those affordances.

Development according to this view, then, consists of the progressive attunement of perceptual systems to the distinctive features and invariants of objects, and thus better utilisation of their affordances. This results in greater economy of attention and processing of information. Thus, as new actions become available to the young infant in the course of development — crawling, walking, climbing, etc. — so *new* affordances will be revealed. In a number of studies with infants, E.J. Gibson and her colleagues showed how the kinds of actions performed in confrontation with certain barriers or obstacles seemed to be dependent on the affordances perceived (e.g. Adolph, Eppler, & Gibson, 1993).

Accordingly, E.J. Gibson (1991) recommends a programme of research aimed at specifying the perceptual information that signals an affordance, and analyses and measures the action–affordance "fit". In opposition to the associationists she argues that learning is a change in what is perceived, not a change in response. This process is self-motivating. Thus, in a number of studies in the 1950s and 1960s she showed how mere experience with objects or shapes facilitated discrimination learning, even though no reward or other reinforcers had been used (for review see E.J. Gibson, 1991).

FIG. 5.5.
The "visual cliff" as
used by Gibson and
Walk (1960).

Critics of the ecological realism view accept many of these presuppositions. They agree that traditional views, that information for perception and cognition from outside is impoverished and intrinsically inadequate, are wrong; that the structure is "all there" in experience; and that higher-level "invariants" need to be abstracted. But we still need to give more principled descriptions of that structure, and a more principled account of how the system utilises it. We can use terms like the brain "resonating", or becoming "attuned" to external invariants, but these are only metaphors, and we need to know the real content behind them. There is some *sense* of what is meant by invariance: but what *kind* of invariances over what kind of transformations, and — more importantly — how does the system capture and use them? All these need to be specified. In the absence of such specification it is hardly surprising that critics find, within ecological psychology, a "nativist stance" (Rutkowska, 1993, p.9).

A similar criticism applies to the most central, yet most difficult, of Gibsonian ideas, that of "affordance". The argument (E.J. Gibson, 1991, p.559) that "an affordance implies perception that is meaningful, unitary, utilitarian and continuous over time ..." has a vaguely meaningful ring. But it it is hardly crystal clear. In sum, the theory of direct or ecological perception is beguiling. There is little doubt that dynamic perception in time and space is important, that it is relational, and multiply-determined, and so on. But the theory, so far, is couched in abstract generalisations that are difficult to pin down.

Dynamic systems theory

Attempts to oppose reductionism and "mechanicism" in science have commonly consisted of appeals to organised *structures* and *systems*, involving ideas like transformations and self-regulation, rather than independent controlling factors. Piaget (1971), indeed, followed the biologist L. von Bertalanffy in attempting to develop a "general theory of systems" based on a structured "organicism" (Von Bertalanffy, 1968). Such efforts have become more widespread in recent times, and are attracting more general attention. Indeed, as a general approach to scientific theorising, they now form such a coherent movement as to have acquired a distinctive title: "dynamic systems theory". It is a view that eschews reductionist, monocausal schemes for modelling complex systems and, instead, attempts to capture "the mutual dependence of causes ... an entire ensemble of influences" (Oyama, 1985, p.15).

In many ways it is a reaction to the whole "metaparadigm" governing science in the last two centuries, whereby causes and effects have been sought, and systems described, in terms of a few, "push–pull" linear relationships. Although the traditional approach has obviously been enormously beneficial, its limitations are being increasingly realised: natural systems tend to be "complex" in the sense of consisting of many variables, mutually dependent on each other, often in non-linear relationships, conditioned by others at a "higher" level, reacting adaptively to those in their surround, the whole system often changing or evolving over time. If this is true of physical and physiological systems, it is likely to apply even more to something as complex as the human cognitive system and *its* development.

Dynamic systems theory demands a radical change in the way we think, scientifically, about both cognition and its development. What Fraser (1988, p.1) says about the development of physical systems —

that "the Aristotelian search for a prime mover" is unnecessary — is even more applicable to cognitive development, in such a view. Far from being dependent on isolated factors operating independently, functional organisation and development arise out of the interactions among the multiple factors within the system as a whole in interaction with its surround. In this view, according to Van Gelder & Port, 1995, p.3), "The cognitive system is not a computer ... not a discrete sequential manipulator of static representational structures ... Its processes ... unfold in the real time of on-going change in the environment, the body and the nervous system."

Thelen and Smith (e.g. 1994) have been most vigorous in their advocacy of such a view in helping to understand cognitive development. Acknowledging that Piaget's theory fitted "the orderliness of development on the large scale" they argue (1994, pp.21–22), that "it dramatically failed to capture the complexity and messiness of cognitive development in detail ... if we vary the tasks and nudge and push at the child's mind, we see instabilities, context-dependencies, and fluidity in cognition." But just as they reject much of Piaget's view, Thelen and Smith also strongly reject nativist views (especially the stronger versions such as that of Spelke).

Thelen and Smith (1994), offer a number of illustrations in support of their arguments. For example, careful recording shows how the intricate pattern of bipedal walking appears to "emerge" out of the interactions of bones, joints, and muscles, and internal and external constraints and freedoms, rather than being dictated by a precise neural program (although simple changes in neural inputs may alter the rate and/or pattern of interaction, as in the transition from walking to running).

Moreover, Thelen and Smith argue that the initial structures of development (no matter how far "back" we go), which are themselves the emergent products of complex interactions, also create the conditions for further development, sometimes in surprising ways. For example, the heartbeat in the chick embryo causes the head to jerk up and down slightly in the egg. It is from just such movement that the pecking in the newly hatched chick develops (Kuo, 1967; see Thelen & Smith, 1994): what is usually thought of as an "innate" behaviour pattern, somehow encoded in genes, emerges instead from the interactions within the system as a whole.

The most basic idea of self-organising systems is that of multiple, interacting forces, which can "settle into" a "preferred state", known as an attractor. Among the myriad such systems described to date are included dripping taps, cloud formation, heart rhythms, electroencephalograms (EEGs or "brain waves"), animal (and human) walking, and so on. Although organised, and often "developing", such systems have no controlling codes, programs, blueprints, or schemas, only internal interactions, and their reactivity to external conditions. The most common descriptive tool is that of a "state–space" graph — for example a plot of the states through which a system can pass as defined by two or more coordinates. For example, the picture on the left of Fig. 5.6 plots position against velocity for a frictionless pendulum; the picture on the right shows the state space for a more realistic, normal one. The attractor of the first is its continuous circular orbit; that of the second is its final position of rest. By analogy, development in biological and cognitive systems can be viewed as the transition from one attractor to another as new conditions are revealed by the individual's increasing action on the world and/or changes in its own components.

Thelen and Smith (1994) have made great efforts to describe development in these terms, and offer samples of developmental data in dynamic terms. One example is the case of infant kicking. When placed on their backs, infants perform rhythmic kicking movements which increase in frequency in the first six months of life until the infants begin to sit, crawl, and stand. The movements consist of synchronous flexions and extensions of the joints, with frequent switches between alternate legs. This basic, stable set of coordinations can be seen as an attractor state.

But it is one from which the infant needs to move if development is to proceed. Thelen (1985; see Thelen & Smith, 1994) followed changes in coordination of supine kicking from 2 weeks to 10 months. Early coupling of extensions and flexions between hip, knee, and ankle decreased drastically after 8 months, permitting individual joint actions and thus new coordinations. Such instability was also seen in inter-limb

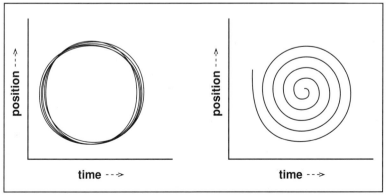

FIG. 5.6.
State–space diagrams
of the movements of a
frictionless pendulum
(left) and a normal
pendulum (right).

coordination. And again, new forms of coordination became possible. This transition indicates how an initial attractor state must become unstable in order for new patterns of coordination to emerge. Thelen and Smith argue that development of limb coordinations from newborn kicking, through stepping, standing, walking (and then skipping, hopping, jumping etc.) consists of a succession of such attractor states, each one emerging as a result of changes (e.g. weight, size) in the limbs and joints and in their interface with the physical world. They use "ontogenetic landscapes" like those of Waddington (1957) to illustrate this idea of development as progress from one attractor state to others (Fig. 5.7).

As a more cognitive example, Thelen and Smith (1994) consider the case of conceptual representation. Recall from Chapter 2 Lakoff's point about the multiple disjunctive nature of representation (e.g. the concept of "mother") and how it poses a problem for traditional models. As Thelen & Smith (1994, p.166) argue, however:

> These insights are not troubling if we view categories as embodied — living — processes that are creative because they emerge from the interactions of multiple disjunctive glosses on the same reality ... [and] if we view our multiple understandings of mother with all their subtle and perfectly apt nuances as the products of a dynamic system that leaps from the basin of one attractor to that of another.

FIG. 5.7. A developmental landscape depicted as movement of the system (the ball) from one attractor state to new ones over time (redrawn from Thelen & Smith, 1994).

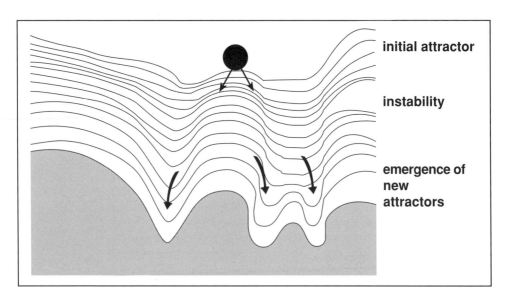

initial attractor

instability

emergence of new attractors

They offer similar accounts to explain some of the "smart infant" data, such as those of Kellman & Spelke (1983) and Baillargeon (1994) (see Chapter 2), again without recourse to innate knowledge or constraints.

Thelen and Smith eschew the idea of stable representations and processes as *the* basis of cognitive development. Likewise, they dismiss specific end-states as the best descriptions of "what develops". Rather it is developmental change itself that should be modelled (1994, p.44, emphasis in original):

> [I]n our view, development does not "know" where it is going from the start. There are no constraints on development that act like levees on a flooding river, keeping it from going where it ought not to go. There is no set end-state other than the end of life itself. We propose instead that development is the outcome of the self-organising processes of continually active *living* systems.

Of course, dynamic systems theory can account for stability as well as change. Some of the patterns that emerge from the interactions may, given certain recurring conditions, be very predictable and ultimately stable because the system has reached an intrinsically "preferred" state. Goodwin (e.g. 1988) and others have long argued that the development of body form in animals — morphogenesis — reflects such self-organising interactions arriving at preferred states rather than the direct "intentions" of genes. That preference does not reflect the "intentions" of a single creative agent, nor a determinate case. As Thelen (1995, p.100) states: "Although some behavioural preferences are so stable that they they take on the qualities of a developmental stage, the stability is a function of the organism-in-context, not a set of prior instructions." Thus the *appearance* of an ability as "innate" merely reflects such an equilibrium state (one that is theoretically moveable to another state). Development is then seen as the transition from one such preferred state to another, as one or other factor(s) in the system (internal or external) changes and creates a disequilibrium.

Although appealing, because of its recognition of complexity, of dynamic states, and state changes, there are obvious problems with the approach as presented so far. First, it is purely *descriptive* of states and state-change rather than offering "laws" of organisation and of change, as in traditional science. For example, we get interesting general accounts of state changes, but without a "causal" picture, in the sense of one that would allow us to intervene in development. This, many people would argue, is what we most need in order to promote development, or to compensate for possible defects.

Also, accounts such as those of Thelen and Smith sometimes almost appear "magical", in the sense of offering something seemingly emergent out of nothing. But this may simply reflect the need to adjust our own minds to new ideas: after all, this has been a criticism often made against nativist and other models. Finally, dynamic systems accounts are inevitably complex, and require a language with which few students of psychology are conversant. We need to ask whether this is just substituting one set of terms for another without any increase in understanding. For example, it is only fair to point out that descriptive tools like ontological landscapes have also been used by nativists and neo-nativists (e.g. Elman et al., 1997; see Chapter 1), as well as epigeneticists, with whose principles they are equally consistent.

Dynamic systems theory certainly offers a way of thinking that is consistent with many aspects of development: for example, becoming "stuck" in a deep attractor, and thus remaining refractory to efforts to change it (Thelen & Smith, 1994), is a picture many parents and teachers will be familiar with. However, it is still thinking with metaphors rather than real structures. The danger is that, when taken too literally, such metaphors can also be traps. Thus, Thelen and Smith (1994, p.245) see an intelligent system "as one that lives on the edge of many close attractors — dipping in along the side of an attractor and out again, perhaps never falling all the way to the bottom." This *doesn't* present a picture of an intentional, mindful cognitive system. In any case, as Hopkins and Butterworth (1997, p.81) put it, "the introduction of the problem of intentionality presents serious challenges yet to be overcome by the approach."

In sum, it is probably too early to tell whether this approach will yield better models of cognitive development, or whether it will fizzle out through lack of appropriate detail. An obvious danger is that dynamic systems theory could simply present us with yet another set of shadowy metaphors for development.

Cognitive hyperstructures

One regular criticism that applies almost universally to models discussed so far is the widespread uncertainty about real contents and mechanisms — as opposed to metaphors — of cognition and its development. Where there are "genetic codes" for basic processes or constraints, as in nativist models, such codes are invariably vague, and almost always based on mechanical or logical metaphors.

Where they are more clear, as in associationist models, they are usually condemned for being unrealistically shallow. And constructivist models are sometimes described as near-miraculous in failing to specify the origins of constructions, as well as their products, clearly and without resort, again, to convenient (but perhaps misleading) metaphors. So a model that is explicit about "starting points", can go beyond shallow associations, and be clearer about "what is constructed" and how, is the great contemporary challenge in the area of cognitive development.

Believe it or not, this is what I try to do in the remainder of this chapter! As it is the author's bias it will, perforce, be rather short of criticism, compared with what has been levelled against the assumptions of others throughout this book. I thus leave the reader with an important responsibility, which is that of "ripping it apart" (by, I hope, identifying assumptions, implicit or explicit, and showing how they may be invalid, as well as exposing illogicalities and other inconsistencies)! My own immediate responsibility is to first put the model to you as briefly, yet as clearly, as possible.

The model I have proposed with a number of colleagues over the last few years starts by attempting to grasp the "real" information that is most useful to adaptable organisms, and thus likely to constitute the informational fodder of cognition. Then I have tried to show how that information enters into the dynamic system of cognition, forming knowledge and cognitive processing, and how it changes over time. However, the identification of that information — and, subsequently, how it is used in cognition — is based on several assumptions, and I suggest it is worth considering these in some detail first.

The challenge of change

It is now well known that humans evolved in very highly changeable environments. Human ancestors evolved from tree-dwelling primates at least 15 million years ago when climatic changes led to thinning of the forests. Little is really known about the habits of these forebears, but they were obviously forced into dealing with less predictable conditions, with much less of the food they had been used to, more patchy availability, and much greater exposure to predators. By about about four million years ago, they had become bipedal (walking more or less upright on hind limbs). By two million years ago, they had clearly compensated for their lack of *natural* foraging, hunting, and defensive equipment, by producing tools. More significantly, at about the same time, they were cooperating socially on a vastly increased scale and with greater complexity.

Most theorists have stressed the importance of these new social relations for brain and psychological evolution, and, in particular, the benefits of cooperative foraging, hunting, and defence. Lovejoy (1981, quoted in Richards, 1987, p.162), explains how social cooperation

> ... puts a premium on the ability to exchange information and to make arrangements regarding future movements of group members. It also increases the importance of regulating social relations among individuals. All these influences might be expected to favour the evolutionary development of an effective communication system, such as protolanguage, and of sharpened socio-intellectual capabilities.

Up to that time, brain size had increased only slightly from the primate equivalent. But it suddenly underwent a rapid and massive expansion (Bilsborough, 1976). It seems that human brain functions evolved not simply to create individual "cleverness", so much as to meet the needs of an increasingly successful social way of life. The complexity of social-technical life itself became the context of increased brain complexity, which made even more complex social-technical life possible, and so on, in a spectacular, and unique, virtuous spiral. "Modern" humans appeared only about 100,000 years ago and rapidly displaced all competitors such as the Neanderthals. Nearly all human change since then has consisted of social and technological change on the basis of developmental systems that had, by then, evolved.

It is important to stress how the regulatory demands on the brain of operating jointly with other individuals are far more complex than those presented by the physical world alone (Doise, 1988; Humphrey, 1976). If you have any doubts about this, consider moving a wardrobe downstairs with two other people. You need to integrate a multitude of stimuli, changing over fractions of seconds, continually adjust personal actions correspondingly, regulate personal feelings, and communicate rapidly and efficiently. There are few humans who cannot perform tasks like this or, indeed, others far more complex; there are no other animals who can do it.

The same point has been put in different ways by many authors. Richards (1987, p.171; see also Byrne, 1995) states:

> The intense social interaction and regulation of social relationships required is ... a more likely single cause for the origin of human intelligence than any other ... demands on

intelligence are greater in dealing with the social world than in tackling the external environment.

Or, as Dunn (1988, p.5) put it, from a developmental perspective:

> To become ... a member of that complex world — children must develop powers of recognising and sharing emotional states, of interpreting and anticipating other's reactions, of understanding the relationships between others, of comprehending the sanctions, prohibitions and accepted practices of their world.

Increasingly complex, and cooperative, social life also demanded new forms of communication. The crucial role of a uniquely structured language for mediating joint-attention and joint-action rapidly and smoothly has been described by a number of psychologists (Bruner, 1983; Vygotsky, 1962). But such communication became important in another sense, too. If a member of a group can pass on the acquired structural representations of a class of problems to other group members, or to the young, then the behaviours of others are modified, and become "pre-adapted" for those situations, with a minimum of actual experiences of them. What was a mountainous problem for an individual becomes a "zone of proximal development" (to use Vygotsky's, 1981, famous terminology) for a member of a communicating group. The means by which such transmission of representations and behaviours (in short, cultures) is passed on, has recently become a very fertile field of research (Cole, 1988; Rogoff & Chavajay, 1995).

In sum, humans appear to have evolved a still further method of "information acquisition and storage" — an *interpersonal*, as well as an *intrapersonal* one — and to support such a system is, at least partly, the purpose of our huge brains. It is not difficult to see how the other evolved regulations I described in Chapter 1 (from the genetic level to the cognitive level) are nested in and conditioned by it (Fig. 5.8). Human knowledge, cognitions, needs, and motivations become contained and expressed within a social frame. Just as cognitive regulations "opened up" epigenetic regulations (and these opened up genomic regulations etc.) so social regulations have opened up cognitive regulations, permitting dazzling new potentials to be created perpetually in the interactions between these levels. Indeed, humans now largely adapt the world to themselves, rather than vice versa. We don't have the genetic or epigenetic regulations that provide wings — but this has not prevented us from flying, thanks to another,

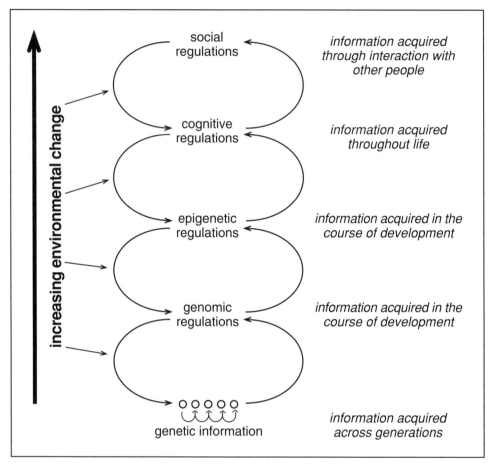

FIG. 5.8. sociocognitive, level of regulation. Much the same can be said across the
Cognitive (and other) spectrum of human activities.
regulations have

become nested in ## The structure of change

social regulations. But what do we mean by "complexity" of change and variability?
Precisely *what* sociocognitive abilities are needed to deal with it?
Entertaining these questions means considering predictability. All of
life is based on predictability, as many authors have pointed out (see
Plotkin & Odling-Smee, 1979). In traditional neo-Darwinism, the
important genes we possess have been selected precisely because they
are associated with certain characters which themselves are
functionally associated, in some way, with specific, but predictable
(i.e. recurrent) aspects of environments. This predictability makes life

itself possible. This *direct* predictability is the basis of all simpler forms of life: certain cell structures or absorbent surfaces for predictable kinds of food, light, oxygen, and so on; defensive structures against the predictable presence of predators; enzyme structures that operate in predictable ranges of temperature, and so on.

In changeable environments, however, such simple kinds of predictability, by definition, are more difficult to establish. In addition, the "environment" for more complex organisms, which move around, consists of arrays of *objects*, rather than mere concentration gradients of substances, forces, or factors. The kinds of things it is necessary to predict from objects include things like edibility, danger, size and/or weight (for moving them or moving around them), or just their identity (perhaps for communicating to someone else). Nearly all models of cognition and development posit some kind of internal representation of objects for inferring "unseen" properties from those "seen". The problem is that our experience of objects is fragmentary, as they move, or as we move around or manipulate them. Our experience even of a single object is one of constant novelty. A typical visual scene will contain up to, say, 50 objects in passive or active motion, partially occluding one another, and so on. How could we ever form a stable representation of the world in such circumstances? How could we ever make events, and our action on them, predictable?

My view is that we do this by finding structure, and thus predictability, at "deeper" levels, namely in the simple and complex covariation structures that characterise so much of the natural world. There are "simple" covariations when the value of a target variable (e.g. food present/absent) is predicted by the values of some other variable (e.g. time of day). For example, a blue-tit may have registered a covariation between time of day and the fullness of a bird-feeder. But things are usually far more complicated than that in complex environments. For example, natural food availability changes seasonally, dependent on location. Organisms such as migratory birds have adapted to this fluctuation, although it only becomes predictable because it embodies a "deeper" covariation structure (Fig. 5.9). That structure is itself signalled by some environmental factor, such as temperature or duration of day-light, *here and now*. By adapting to one factor (temperature, say), organisms that start migrating now are adapting to that deeper covariation structure. Such covariation structure is so stable that it can be adapted to by epigenetic regulations (see Chapter 1), requiring no cognitive regulation at all (we often, in fact, refer to it as a kind of "instinct").

FIG. 5.9.
A hypothetical
seasonal effect. An
association between
food availability (low
or high) and location
(A or B) depends on
season (Time 1 or
Time 2). In order to
feed continuously
organisms need to
adapt to this deeper
covariation structure.

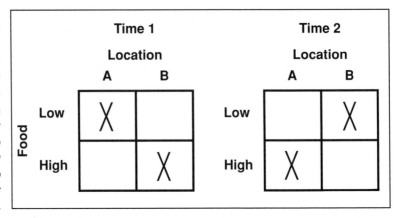

This is not the case, however, for covariation structures that can themselves change rather quickly and frequently. Consider, for example, a squirrel that experiences nuts sometimes in location A and sometimes in location B, but doesn't have the energy to reach both locations in a single day. Even by randomly setting its targets, the animal will, at best, be eating irregularly. Now assume that the location varies with some other variable, such as the weather (A when it's fine, B when it's wet). If the squirrel has a behavioural regulatory system sensitive to such environmental covariation it will feed much better. In doing so it is creating an internal representation of a deeper covariation structure than simple association:

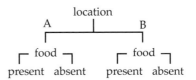

But that covariation may be also be weak — giving better, but still insufficient, predictability about food location. Now consider how that covariation may itself be conditioned by another variable such as temperature, so that the food is most likely to be in location A when it is wet and warm, but location B when it is dry and warm; A when it's dry and cool, but B when it's wet and cool. A squirrel that is able to capture this "deeper" covariation structure will render food availability far more predictable than may seem possible from casual inspection. In the process it has come to represent a still deeper covariation structure:

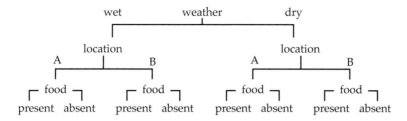

It is important to note that these relations are interactive ones, in the sense that the association between two variables is "conditioned by" the level of another, rather than an array of additive, independent factors. This is what imparts predictability. For example, predicting food availability from location in Fig. 5.9. is only possible *in the context of time*. It has long been recognised that a description of a system in terms of the *interactions* of its components or variables — rather than simply enumerating independent factors — is a natural measure of its "complexity" (Bozdogan, 1990; Van Embden, 1971). But it is the predictability that arises from such structure that is important in the present context. Although "surface" variations of single factors, or even bivariate associations, may appear too capricious for adaptation to them to be possible, deeper interactions among them, where they exist, can help to make complex environments predictable. Obviously, an organism that can "tune in" to such structure may thus flourish where others would not.

Such structures, which are not simple inclusion hierarchies, but ones in which the information at one level *interacts with*, or is *conditioned by*, the information at other levels, have been called *hyperstructures* (Baas, 1994). They may, of course, be much more complex than those mentioned so far, including many more values/variables and hierarchical levels of conditioning or interaction. And any such hyperstructure may be conditioned by, or interact with, others to form a *hyperstructural network*, or *hypernetwork*, as between, for example, two objects from the same category, or in event schemas, or the actions of two or more people cooperating around a common task or cultural tool.

This latter example hints at the significance of such structures for cognitive systems. Although stable environmental associations — even deeper ones as in seasonal effects — can be, as it were, "built-in" to the organism's epigenetic system, this cannot be the case with environments that change more erratically, and *throughout life*. Consider, for example, a monkey that feeds on fruit in the upper canopy of a rain forest (having discovered a covariation between elevation and food abundance). The monkey also learns that nearer the forest margins the fruit lies lower down (a height/abundance covariation conditioned by location). But those marginal locations, at certain times of the year, are also more frequently scanned by monkey eagles (the conditioning itself conditioned by a correlation between predator presence and season). This whole covariation structure — which, again, makes the environment predictable through its "deep" contingencies — may change completely when the monkey troop moves to another forest because of fruit depletion (i.e. its own activity).

As I will go on to argue later, cognitive systems evolved for the rapid abstraction and frequent updating of such "deep" covariation structures. As such complex contingencies became deeper and deeper, in more complex environments, especially human social ones, so more capacity for abstracting them became necessary. This necessity explains the rapid evolution of brains in mammals, especially humans, and all the other attributes of "advanced" cognition. I will pick up on all of these points later, but there is another one worth making at this stage.

If even remotely correct, such analyses suggest how ordinary experience must be, as Baldwin (1901, quoted by Butterworth, 1992, p184) put it, "a voracious datum of consciousness". This must put into perspective to some extent models of cognitive development based on notions of "the poverty of the stimulus" (e.g. Chomsky, 1980) or of "the indeterminacy or inadequacy of experience" (Hirschfeld & Gelman, 1994). Far from our cognitive structures being "underdetermined" by the data of experience (Chomsky, 1980), I suggest that the data of experience may themselves have been seriously underestimated by psychologists.

Cerebral hyperstructures

There is little doubt that the cerebral cortex, with its richly intersecting, and reciprocally connecting, layers of units, is eminently suited for just such abstraction of complex covariation structures, or hyperstructures. Instead of hypothetical, pre-adapted structures or constraints, all we need to suggest that the cerebral system underlying the cognitive system "comes with" is units, or groups of units, sensitive to the complex covariations in experience. It is these, after all — and not directly encodable "features", "object images", symbols", or whatever — that are the only invariants of experience. Indeed, there is abundant evidence that neurons in cerebral cortex, and elsewhere in the brain, are sensitive to covariations; that the covariation patterns to which they are attuned at any one time constitute these neurons' functional properties; and that such attunements may change with further experience on a life-long basis.

Mackay (1986) postulated such "covariation units" on the basis of neurophysiological evidence. He argued that what the system is registering in the maintenance of multiple information parameters is not features or other "coded" symbols, but covariations, and, indeed, that much of sensory behaviour (hearing while looking; moving eyes and head to sample a range of views; tactile exploration while seeing) has the purpose of collecting "sample" covariations, rather then preformed features or images. Mackay (1986, p.368) explains: "Exploratory probing of the environment, as by a moving fingertip or a moving retina ... gives rise to covariation between sensory signals and the exploratory motor action." In the presence of analysers of covariation, even minimal input can give rise to complex form. "A blind man, for example, can recognise the location and shape of a manhole cover by probing it with the tip of his cane. A coat button can be perceived in considerable detail by exploring it with the finger nail."

Zeki (1993) reviews evidence of cells in the visual cortex that are sensitive, not only to direct inputs, but also to what other cells are "doing" at the same time. Even the early work on the retina (Barlow, 1985, p.125) suggested that "the eye was not so much a detector of light as a detector of patterns created by those objects and events in the environment that were important for the animal". This suggested (Barlow, 1985, p.133) that "exploitation of the redundancy in the input that results from the complex structure of associations it contains must play an important part in the process" (note that the term redundancy refers to the "extra" information provided by covariations and interactions). Correlated activity between groups of neurons widely dispersed in the cortex is now well known (Singer & Gray, 1995); the recording of correlated activity in groups of neurons that have been active in a learning experience strongly indicates increased "cooperativity" associated with changes in what they actually respond to (Dinse, Recanzone, & Merzenich, 1993). Changes in the "the functional specificity of cells" have been traced to "interaction between disparate points in the visual field", suggesting the involvement, not of independent processing units with predetermined functions, but a whole "neuronal ensemble" (Gilbert & Weisel, 1990, p.1699–1700; see also Gilbert, 1996). As Weinberger (1995, p.153) notes in his review of such effects, this plasticity appears to be a life-long capacity, and the "dynamic regulation" implied "constitutes a severe blow to the hypothesis that cortical perceptual functions are based on static properties of individual cells". In other words, the activity of at least some neurons is not simply dependent on independent "inputs", but is conditioned by what other neurons are "doing" or have recently done.

Interestingly, Phillips, Kay, and Smyth (1994, p.117) have examined the possibility that cortical processors "perform a kind of statistical latent structure analysis that discovers predictive relations between large and diverse data sets". They point to a "redundancy-reducing" strategy in cortical processing, which they describe (p.118) as that of "maximizing the mutual information between output and input under a constraint that ensures data reduction". As Bozdogan (1990) notes, mutual information (a concept arising out of information theory) is an index of the covariation complexity in a data set.

There is abundant evidence, in other words, that what the most evolved cerebral/cognitive systems are most "interested" in are the complex covariations in moment-to-moment experience, internalised as cognitive hyperstructures. That they are *not* interested in stable features or images is suggested in another, rather startling, way. When a perfectly stable visual image is projected onto the retina (a technically difficult feat), the result is not a perfectly formed replica in the perceptual and/or cognitive system. Instead, the very opposite happens — the image *disappears*. As Mackay (1986, p.371) explains:

> Stabilisation, even if it does not abolish all retinal signals, eliminates all covariation. If no correlated changes take place, there is nothing for analysers of covariation to analyse. If, then, seeing depends on the results of covariation analysis, there will be no seeing.

This, of course, should not be surprising when we come to fully recognise that, in complex environments, stable features or images rarely exist. The only consistent information that an object presents to the nervous system is the complex pattern of covariations inherent in the spatio-temporal arrangements of its parts as it is experienced in an infinite diversity of orientations, distances, and so on. These are the "invariants" that provide the predictabilities which are most useful to the system. This is what a cognitive system most needs to represent.

The formation of representational hyperstructures

How, then, does a cognitive system actually use this deeper information? Again this means thinking in terms of interactions, and emergent functions, among a constellation of forces, rather than of nodes or modules responding according to predetermined functions or constraints. Properties of inputs, such as lines, sub-features, features, and images of whole objects, are not "out there" waiting to be picked up by a corresponding "detector", but a product of synthesis between the fragmentary input and a representational hyperstructure, which itself reflects a history of experience with that and other similar inputs.

First let me attempt to explain how represented hyperstructures are "creative" in the sense of furnishing predictabilities (about object recognition, values of specific variables) from novel or fragmentary inputs. The workings of a simple (indeed almost the very *simplest*) environmental hyperstructure can be demonstrated at the level of cognition about objects as follows. Imagine we experience apples, which vary in size, colour, and sweetness, in the frequencies shown in the cross-classification in Fig. 5.10 (top). Statistical analysis of these frequencies reveals that the dimensions are not independent: all pairs of variables covary, and the three-way covariation is also statistically significant. The latter signifies an interaction in which at least one of the two-way covariations is conditioned by values of the third variable. This nested relation, if registered in a suitable system, can generate structures and predictions that would not otherwise be possible.

	pale			pink			red		
	sour	medium	sweet	sour	medium	sweet	sour	medium	sweet
small	0	30	0	30	0	0	0	0	30
medium	30	0	0	0	0	30	0	30	0
large	0	0	30	0	0	0	30	0	0

'Expected Frequencies'

	pale			pink			red		
	sour	medium	sweet	sour	medium	sweet	sour	medium	sweet
small	6	8	10	8	10	13	10	13	17
medium	7	9	11	9	9	9	11	9	7
large	9	11	12	10	8	6	12	6	3

FIG. 5.10.   Top: Apples cross-classified from frequencies of experience according to variable values shown in the table. Bottom: When the association interactions have been registered, they "generate" the predicted frequencies as shown, including predictions for combinations of variable values not previously experienced.

For example, imagine we come across an apple that is large and pink. Because that combination has not actually been experienced before, it cannot be used as a simple cue to sweetness. However, predictions about its sweetness can be made if the environmental hyper-structure has been registered and represented in some way (e.g. in a cognitive system). One way of modelling what might happen is to generate the "expected" frequencies from a statistical model that includes those interactions (see Richardson & Carthy, 1990). Those expected frequencies are shown in Fig. 5.10 (bottom) and indicate that the novel apple is much more likely to be sour than sweet. The important point is that the full "image" of this novel feature, and with it a novel apple, is an emergent structure from the represented hyper-structure. Of course, much greater precision of prediction could arise if the hyperstructure included still further variables.

I believe the natural world is full of such hyperstructurally nested information, and that it is just such hyperstructures that make the world predictable and permitted the entry of animal life into complex, dynamic environments at all. Of course, if these change in structure in the course of a life-time, this could only be done, as just mentioned, if the hyperstructures can be "abstracted" and "represented" by the organism in some way as a continually updated process. Although it is tempting to identify singular cognitive agents (such as preadapted nodes or modules) carrying out pre-specified functions, it is just as clear that those adaptive functions in complex environments are only really possible when the depth of information in the world as experienced has been abstracted and represented.

In the visual conception of an object I see this process happening as follows. The model starts from basic sensory parameters "up". For example, visual experience of objects starts with light spots on the retina. Figure 5.11 shows a series of snapshots of an "object" moving in space, or as viewed by a person moving around it (it's actually a paperclip with its ends bent out, and viewed from different angles). Although actually experienced as thousands of light spots on the retinae, I concentrate on only five of them for illustrative purposes. The point is that, under typical spatio-temporal transformation, the only stable information consists of the covariation between these points, although that information may lie very deep.

For example, the translation of point A may covary with that of point B, but only very weakly. However, we may find that the covariation is strongly conditioned by point C — there is a three-way statistical interaction. So that, in the context of the position of point C, in which the relation is embedded, prediction of the location of point B

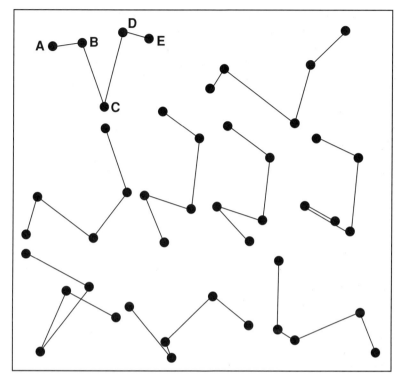

FIG. 5.11.
A series of images of
a pseudo-object in
spatio-temporal
translation, illustrating
the covariations
between combinations
of selected light spots.

from point A becomes far more possible. Furthermore, the structural relation between these three points may be further embedded in another point, or perhaps a covariation between two or more other points. Such structure is, of course, analogous to that of our imaginary apple described earlier.

Again, a system that can register such nested *covariations* is in a much stronger position than one that seeks to "encode" even simple features such as lines and edges, if only because the latter rarely appear in experience as stereotyped patterns. Having registered them, the same object may be "recognised" in future inputs even though the experienced image is entirely novel (for example the "object" experienced on a trajectory different from that shown in Fig. 5.11, or perhaps partially occluded). Instead of simply firing to the rare features that fit some rigid response specifications, an image of a line or an edge (or other features) can now be "created" from novel or fragmentary input. That is, the instantiation of lines or features in recognition or identification is an emergent property of the hyperstructure first registered at the level of primary sensory parameters.

This, of course, is only the first level of representation, and utilisation, of a visual hyperstructure for an object. It should also be clear that these emergent properties *will themselves tend to covary in more or less complex, but characteristic, ways for that object,* thus giving rise to a second-order hyperstructure, perhaps reflecting more complex features or feature-combinations (Fig. 5.12). These second-order hyperstructures will in turn give rise to nested covariations that create *tertiary-order* structures ... and so on. In a system which is "looking" for covariations, therefore, the original hyperstructure becomes nested in others emergent from it. This evolutionary process continues so long as interaction emerges from the evolved structures — for example, up to the level of object and event-schema hyperstructures (in humans, complex social regulations).

The system of representational hyperstructures functions overall at *any one* of these emergent levels in a way analogous to its function at the level of primary sensory parameters. When "new" input presents to the system specific sets of variable-values or "sample" covariations (as is the case with any moving object), these will almost always be novel and/or highly fragmentary. It may be, for example, a novel view of the same object in Fig. 5.12, consisting of only the handle and one side

FIG. 5.12.
Diagram indicating how simple features, as emergent properties of hyperstructural information at the sensory level, become further nested to form hyperstructures nested in each other at "higher" levels (which can be further nested "horizontally" to form hypernetworks).

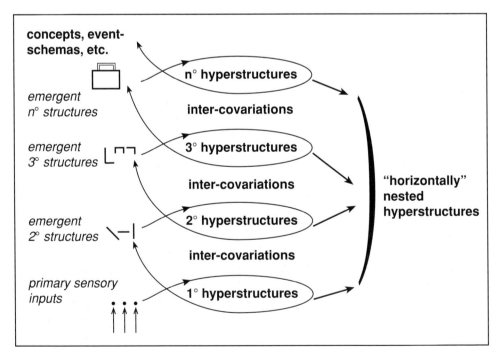

(the others being obscured by another object). But the characteristic covariations in the input access the representational hyperstructure at whatever level they find correspondence, and a process of spreading activation among a network of registered covariations "fills-in" the most probable missing details. Recognition/classification or other predictions can be made from this super-image generated "on-line" (Fig. 5.13).

Of course, this simple picture describes a "vertical" nest of hyperstructures based on passively experienced visual parameters. These hyperstructures can also be nested *horizontally* in various ways. Objects from the same category will share much covariation structure, and this shared hyperstructure will form the concept of those objects. In addition, nearly all visual experience of objects is associated with motor action, even if it is just characteristic eye-movements. More typically, it will include direct actions on objects, themselves entailing kinaesthetic and other motor covariation hyperstructures with which the visual ones will also covary. There will be complex covariations with other sensory modes, and, most importantly, with affective variables. At the level of event schemas, object hyperstructures will be nested horizontally in "event" and "social" hyperstructures. The result is really a system of "hypernetworks".

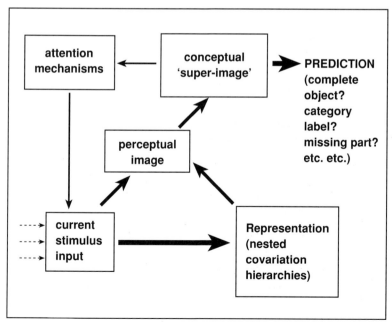

FIG. 5.13.
General process of conceptualisation on the basis of conceptual hyperstructures (nested covariation hierarchies).

Again it is necessary to emphasise that there are no discrete features, images, symbols, or whatever, as grist of this model. Rather these are created in distributed form among the interactions within and between hyperstructures. For example, a "bottom-up" view of the briefcase in Fig. 5.12 will also generate an image of the out-of-sight handle by spreading activation within that hyperstructure. This process, in turn, provides an "affordance" for action (e.g. turning the briefcase around for lifting), to use a Gibsonian term.

There are a number of other aspects of the model that I cannot go into here, except for two important things. First, note how it dissolves the distinction between knowledge and cognition. A hyperstructural representation *is* knowledge, which *is* simultaneously the structure of cognition. The structure of that knowledge, that is, also guides inference and deduction, without the need to erect other independent processes to "work" on it. The same structure is, of course, far more complex than that envisaged in typical associationist models. The model *is* constructivist, but it indicates tractable principles and *substance* of construction, not mere metaphors. And there is nothing innate in terms of preformed knowledge, processes, or even constraints, only those that arise from a dynamic system interactively "attuning" to its environment.

The second thing is how human social relations, themselves intricate covariation structures especially in the form of cultural tools, come to dominate hyperstructural contents in humans. The social covariation patterns focus attention on those covariations in the physical world that, in turn, become incorporated into them — a process that, as Vygotsky (1981, p.165) put it, "alters the entire flow and structure of mental functions". The best example of this is the role that language — itself an intricate hyperstructural system — comes to play in human cognition, and in the definition and perception of the physical world.

Development of cognitive hyperstructures

So what has all this got to do with cognitive development? The most straightforward implication is that development consists of the build-up of hyperstructures in corresponding domains of experience. These consist of ever deeper covariation hierarchies, as shown in the progressive formation of "higher" levels in Fig. 5.13. At first sight, of course, these may not seem to be much different from a simple associationist hierarchy, as discussed in Chapter 3. The difference is that here the "nodes" are not features or symbols, but covariations; the hierarchy is an interactive one, not one of additive inclusion; and the associations may be non-linear, and consist of continuous, as well as nominal or ordinal variables, with, potentially, many more values. In addition, each of these hyperstructures may become nested in others to which they give rise. All of this imparts far more creativity and predictability, in constructing objects, and event schemas "on-line" on the basis of sparse inputs.

Even more interesting, developmentally, is the potential for cognitive hyperstructures (through the same common principle of covariation sensitivity) for overlapping, or nesting "horizontally", with other hyperstructures. For example, overlapping hyperstructures of objects from the same category (whose covariation patterns also covary) is how object concepts are formed. Such a view is consistent with most research findings on object concepts (see Chapter 2 for review; also Hampton, 1997), but, I believe, adds coherence to them. Such a complex hyperstructure will lead to graded membership, or "prototypicality", among members of a category, but on the basis of covariation patterns, not feature associations. And it indicates how, in a sense, all exemplar information is included, as a number of "exemplar-based" models have suggested — although it is information about their covariations, not their featural composition as such, that is included. The idea would also explain the role of "background knowledge" or "theories" in studies of concept learning (e.g. Murphy, 1993), the hyperstructure itself being indistinguishable from such "knowledge".

A "vertical" nesting of hyperstructures may form the basis of the well-known distinctiveness, arising in the course of development, between "basic", "subordinate" and "superordinate" levels of representation — often described as taxonomic structures (see Chapter 2). Such taxonomic structure has usually been described, at least at the basic and subordinate levels, in terms of overlapping features (e.g. Rosch, 1978). Structure at the superordinate level has then been described, more or less vaguely, in terms of the overlap of *functions* (as in, for example, vehicles, or tools, or kitchen utensils). Considerable debate has arisen about the age at which children have (or theoretically *can* have) such conceptual structures. A number of studies have shown, for example, that taxonomic reasoning, even at the superordinate level, is possible among children as young as 2 or 3 years (see Walsh, Richardson, & Faulkner, 1993, for review).

Again, I would argue that this distinction is best seen as the consequence of the nesting of hyperstructures — one level (basic) being distinguished largely by "perceptual" covariations (vision, hearing, taste, smell, touch, and combinations of these), the other (superordinate level) including covariations of kinaesthesia and motor and social action. One piece of evidence for this is that even 4-year-olds can easily switch from matching objects by perceptual attributes, to matching by taxonomic group, to matching by thematic association (i.e. involvement in common event schemas) according to current task demands. This suggests that these are far from being mutually exclusive levels of development (Walsh et al., 1993).

Finally, the same principle can also account for the spatio-temporal nesting of object hyperstructures in event schemas. I suspect *most* conceptual hyperstructures will be of this kind, especially as most of what people do involves other people in cooperative action around shared cultural tools and sequences of action on objects. This view is entirely consistent with that of Nelson (1986), and other advocates of "script" and other event-schema representation — except that, here, I am trying to give them "real", rather than metaphoric, substance. More generally, as cognitive hyperstructures are closely tied in with structures of experience, especially as revealed by specific actions on the world, the model explains why cognition and its development is so closely tied in with social and physical contexts, as described in Chapters 3 and 4.

Not even hinted at, so far, is the way that other emergent concepts can arise from nested hyperstructures by virtue of shared covariation structures. These include all the action concepts of "on", "under", "through", and so on, and "abstract" concepts like obligation, permission, duty, and so on. The model of cognitive hyperstructures also indicates why metaphoric, or analogical, thinking is so pervasive in human cognition, developing rapidly even in very young children (Goswami, 1996).

Empirical evidence for representational hyperstructures

In a general sense, evidence for this model comes from the basic everyday fact that people can make sense of the world of experience in spite of the fact that the latter continually bombards us with fragmentary and novel information, and with structure that is continually changing. Dealing with this simple fact has always presented a stumbling block to theorists, as mentioned several times in Chapters 1 to 3. Particularly strong forms of such evidence come from studies describing "full" conceptual functions, such as recognition of, and predictability about, objects on the basis of extremely sparse sensory information. For example, the recognition of objects and events from even a few point lights, displaying appropriate covariations, on a computer screen, is now well known. In a number of studies, film of sets of luminous dots, either pasted to critical points such as moving joints of the body, or moving parts of faces, or generated from computer programs, has been presented to subjects. Subjects from infants to adults appear to be acutely sensitive to, and even report detailed recognition of, objects from such displays (Fox & McDaniel, 1982; Johansson, 1985). Fig. 5.14 shows a short series of snapshots from the most famous of these, the "point light walker" (Richardson & Webster, 1996a).

In spite of widespread demonstration of such functioning, however, there is still considerable uncertainty about how it is achieved. Lappin (1994, p.360) states: "... global organization of the whole pattern is implicitly assumed to require integration and reconstruction by higher order neural mechanisms. Precisely how such global organization may be accomplished, however, is seldom discussed." I believe that recognition from point light stimuli is simply a spectacular example of the general capacity for predictability furnished by the hyperstructures I have been trying to describe.

Evidence that such recognition is based on covariation "samples" in the stimuli was shown in an experiment in which the point light walker was reduced to ten different permutations of four points each. These seemingly *very* sparse inputs displayed different degrees and "depths" of covariation complexity, as measured statistically (Richardson & Webster, 1996a). Across the range of stimuli, there was a significant association between this complexity and the numbers of subjects who recognised a person walking in the display (Richardson & Webster, 1996a). We found similar results with point light stimuli derived from a variety of inanimate objects (e.g. kettle, vacuum-cleaner, iron) filmed in normal use (Richardson, Webster, & Cope, submitted). Because such recognition *is* related to the covariation complexity in stimuli (bearing in mind that there are no recognisable features in

FIG. 5.14.
A sequence of images from a point light walker — a person walking is quickly recognised from such a display (NB the images are "spaced out" for this presentation).

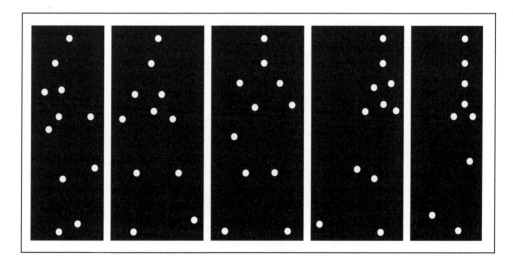

them), it suggests that what is represented "internally" are covariation patterns, and not discrete features or images.

The growth of conceptual hyperstructures with age is also suggested in a study I did with David Webster (Richardson & Webster, 1996a) in which 7- to 11-year-olds were shown point light stimuli derived from a number of animate objects such as an animal walking, a dog barking, a sheep baa-ing, and so on. Each of the stimuli only contained four points, yet most children were able to recognise objects approximating the originals within a few seconds. However, although the responses of the younger children were rapid, they were relatively diffuse, in the sense of offering a wider range of possible categories of objects *more or less* like the originals. The older children were slower, but significantly more accurate. This suggests that the latter group had more "structure" to search, but with ultimately more precision.

In another study, children between 7 and 14 years of age were shown a set of pictures of children riding bikes, displaying different combinations of values on three variables: size of rider; size of bike; and roughness of road surface (Fig. 5.15; Richardson, 1992). In each case they were asked to predict the speed at which the rider would be able to go. Such a situation, of course, consists of a natural hyperstructure of interacting variables. For example, although the bigger riders might be generally expected to go faster, this would be conditioned by size of bike and roughness of road surface: in some combinations, smaller riders might be expected to ride faster than bigger ones, and so on. In making these predictions, the older children displayed much greater appreciation of the interactions involved between the variables, although even the younger ones recognised that the variables were not independent (Fig. 5.16). Again, this supports the idea that more extensive representational hyperstructures had developed with age.

Such coordination of variables is, of course, at the heart of Piaget's theory of knowledge and reasoning, except that here I am trying to show how the "logical structures" can be modelled by "real" information structures, without resort to other logical metaphors. The example just given is one of conservation, but suggests the *informational* basis of the development of the requisite operatory structure. I believe the same kind of operatory (hyper)structure can be seen at work in any of Piaget's conservation experiments.

A confluence of models?

Although this is not the place for an extensive or technical discussion, I would like to indicate, finally, how the model of cognitive

Fig. 5.15.

Two pictures from the "bikes" study: a small child on a big bike on a rough road (top); and a larger child on a small bike on a smooth road (bottom).

hyperstructures is perfectly compatible with the theories of Piaget and Vygotsky, and may even help elucidate and reconcile them. At the heart of Piaget's theory are the coordinations of variables, and part–whole relations, and the powers of reversibility they furnish. However, the terms in which they have been expressed (including the "new theory" terms of morphisms and correspondences) have always been something of a stumbling block for Piaget's theory.

Nested covariation hierarchies, which we know exist in nature, and which neuronal groups are sensitive to, may offer a more substantive medium for much the same ideas. Covariations are, almost by definition, reversible, and their incorporation into perceptual-action hyperstructures indeed offers the basis of a kind of cognitive logic, in the sense of coherent and necessary predictabilities. In addition, it is not difficult to see how such hyperstructures become re-equilibrated, and

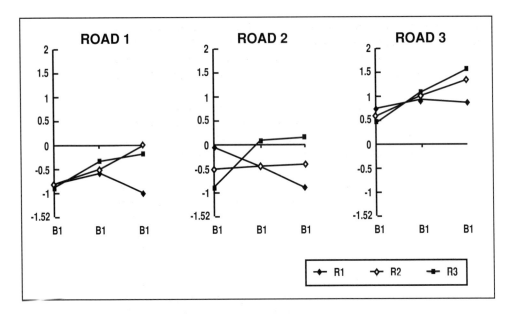

FIG. 5.16.
Seven-year-olds'
predictions of bike
speed (vertical axes
— expressed in
standardised units)
from rider size (R1,
R2, and R3), bike size
(B1, B2, and B3 on
horizontal axes) and
road surface
(Road 1: smooth;
Road 2: medium;
Road 3: rough),
showing appreciation
of interactions
between variables.
This appreciation
increased with age
(from Richardson,
1992).

grow in extensiveness, with new experiences in a domain, and, eventually, may transcend domains.

I believe, however, that the apparent stages that Piaget described are based more on an "explicitation" of these conceptual hyperstructures for purposes of social interaction and discourse, rather than an increase in their logical structure *per se* (although, as just mentioned, this does happen). Karmiloff-Smith (1992) and Mandler (1993) suggest a cognitive "redescription" process at the roots of this progression (in Karmiloff-Smith's account the process is based on genetic constraints). But this suggests a separate (innate) cognitive mechanism which I think is unnecessary. Instead I see it as part of a difficult "unpacking" process from the multidimensional weave of a hyperstructure into the linear and "flatter" forms required for human communication.

Let us first consider the classic conservation study. The child who is used to drinking from vessels has a perfectly adequate knowledge of the complex covariations involved, but may stumble when asked to represent these covariations in a drawing, or to predict the volumes of liquids in vessels of different shape. In the conservation task, then, the child is being asked to socially explicate the "deep" covariations already acquired — i.e. not only those that create the "images" of vessel and liquid, but also the fact of the relation between height of liquid and volume being dependent on its width, or vice versa. The (social) need to make predictions based on this covariation structure, to recognise their logical necessity, and to communicate them explicitly in the linear form of speech, requires a renewed and *different* attention to the variables and their interrelations. To quote Vygotsky again (1962, p.149): "... there is no rigid correspondence between the units of thought and speech ... Thought has its own structure, and the transition from it to speech is no easy matter." I suggest that it is just such "guided" attending for social purpose that is the basis of reflective abstraction and the explicitation of the covariation structure (read "operatory structure" or "morphism") .

In the disc and weights problem described in Chapter 3 (see Fig. 3.17) children have to discover a nested covariation relation — a hyper-structure — in which a covariation between weight and size of effect is conditioned by (nested in) disc size. This is done with considerable attentional guidance from the experimenter's questioning. Children tend to already have, from general experience, a representation of the covariation between weight and effect. They next discover, from guided experience with the apparatus, the covariation between disc size and effect; and then the nested covariation structure of the whole. Finally they have to "unpack" and communicate this nested structure in the special linear form of speech. Again, I suggest that it is such guided attending for social purpose that forms the reflective abstraction, and the explicated hyperstructure that forms the "morphism" or "operatory structure".

Recent years have seen intense interest in the distinction between implicit and explicit forms of knowledge since the early work of Reber (e.g. 1989) and others, although this has not yet had a major impact in the developmental literature. So the ideas of socially guided devel-opment of, and social unpacking of, cognitive hyperstructures may have wider heuristic value, especially in relating cognition to cultural and historical variation. For example, it has often been claimed that the emergence of scientific thinking — i.e. "formal operations" — accel-erated when scientists began to communicate their findings, publish papers, and so on, in which they were obliged to make explicit the structure of their theories, teasing out variables, clearly describing relations between them in a way that could be replicably tested, and so on. By analogy, it may well be the growth of social, *communicational* demands that best explains the advent of explicit scientific and logical thinking in adolescence.

As with nearly all models, however, this idea requires far more clari-fication. But it may have the potential for reconciling a sociohistorical view of development with Piaget's aim of establishing a valid genetic epistemology. Such a model, which reconciles what happens "outside" with what happens "inside", is what, I suggest, is most needed in future research. Let me, then, finally indicate what the model suggests with regard to the other classes of models described in this book:

1. There is no cognitive nativism in the sense of prescriptions for cognitive functions, structures, or constraints "written" in genes, the information in which is determinate of information and structures in cognition. In itself this would be a naive view of the nature of genes, as I tried to explain in Chapter 1. Instead it is best to think of the role of genes as *resources for development* in nested levels of regulation. Genes associated with complex characters — especially those having to cope with rapidly changeable aspects of environments — have been organised into self-organising genomic regulations with powerful emergent properties. The nesting of genomic regulations in "higher" epigenetic regulations, which in turn have been nested in cognitive, and then sociocognitive, regulations, has opened up vast new possibilities for survival in changeable environments.

2. It is true that humans can form associations at all levels of the cognitive system: between sensory qualities, simple features, concepts, and so on. But it is demeaning to suggest that such simple association is all the system is capable of. Instead, I have argued that such associations are merely a very simple rendering of the more critical capacity for abstracting associations in their "deeper", hyperstructural form — the form in which we generally find them, *by* our actions upon them, in complex (especially social) environments.

3. It is these socially embedded, self-organising systems of representational hyperstructures that form the "constructions" of the cognitive system in my view. As these develop with experience in specific domains, especially under socially guided attention, they become related across domains, and "unpacked" in social discourse. In the end they furnish all the intricate knowledge and patterns of reasoning that have been so conspicuous in human history.

References

Acredolo, C. (1997). Understanding Piaget's new theory. *Human Development, 40,* 235–237.

Adolph, K.E., Eppler, M.A., & Gibson, E.J. (1993). Development of perception of affordances. In C. Rovee-Collier & L. Lipsitt (Eds.), *Advances in infancy research.* Norwood, NJ: Ablex.

Allan, L.G. (Ed.) (1993). Human contingency judgements: Rule based or associative. *Psychological Bulletin, 114,* 435–448.

Allen, R.E. (1993). *The Concise Oxford Dictionary* (8th ed.). Oxford: Oxford University Press.

Alloy, L.B., & Tabachnik, N. (1984). Assessment of covariation by humans and animals: The joint influence of prior expectations and current situational information. *Psychological Review, 92,* 112–149.

Anderson, J.R. (1983). *The architecture of cognition.* Cambridge, MA: Harvard University Press.

Anderson, J.R. (1991). *The adaptive character of thought.* Hillsdale, NJ: Erlbaum.

Anderson, J.R., & Bower, G.H. (1973). *Human associative memory.* Washington: Hemisphere Publishing.

Anisfeld, M. (1996). Only tongue protrusion modeling is matched by neonates. *Developmental Review, 16,* 149–161.

Antell, S.E., & Keating, D.P. (1983). Perception of numerical invariance in neonates. *Child Development, 54,* 695–701.

Ashcraft, M.H. (1995). Cognitive psychology and simple arithmetic: A review and summary of new directions. In B. Butterworth (Ed.), *Mathematical cognition, vol 1.* Hove, UK: Psychology Press.

Baas, N.A. (1994). Emergence, hierarchies and hyperstructures. In C.G. Langton (Ed.), *Artificial life III, (Santa Fe Institute Studies in the Science of Complexity).* New York: Addison-Wesley.

Baddeley, A.D. (1990). *Human memory: Theory and practice.* Boston: Allyn & Bacon.

Baddeley, A.D. (1992). Is working memory working? The fifteenth Bartlett lecture. *The Quarterly Journal of Experimental Psychology, 44A,* 1–31.

Baeyens, F., Heremans, R., Eelen, P., & Crombez, G. (1993). Hidden covariation detection and imagery ability. *European Journal of Cognitive Psychology, 5,* 435–456.

Baillargeon, R. (1987). Object permanence in $3^{1}/_{2}$- and $4^{1}/_{2}$-month-old infants. *Developmental Psychology, 23,* 655–664.

Baillargeon, R. (1994). Physical reasoning in young infants: Seeking explanations for impossible events. *British Journal of Developmental Psychology, 12,* 9–33.

Baillargeon, R., & Graber, M. (1987). Where is the rabbit? 5.5 month old infants' representation of the height of a hidden object. *Cognitive Development, 2,* 375–392.

Baillargeon, R., Spelke, E.S., & Wasserman, S. (1985). Object permanence in 5-month-old infants. *Cognition, 20,* 191–208.

Baker, A.G., Mercier, P., Vallee-Tourangeau, F., Frank R., & Pan, M. (1993). Selective associations and causality judgements: Presence of a strong causal factor may reduce judgements of a weaker one. *Journal of Experimental Psychology: Learning, Memory & Cognition, 19,* 414–432.

Baldwin, J.M. (1901). *Dictionary of philosophy and psychology.* New York: Macmillan.

Bandura, A. (1989). Social cognitive theory. *Annals of Child Development, 6,* 1–60.

Bandura, A., Barbaranelli, C., Caprara, G.V., & Pastorelli, C. (1996). Multifaceted impact of self-efficacy beliefs on academic functioning. *Child Development, 67,* 1206–1222.

Barlow, H. (1985). The twelfth Bartlett memorial lecture: The role of single neurons in the psychology of perception. *The Quarterly Journal of Experimental Psychology, 37A,* 121–145.

Barrouillet, P., & Poirier, L. (1997). Comparing and transforming: An application of Piaget's morphisms theory to the development of class inclusion and arithmetic problem solving. *Human Development, 40,* 216–234.

Bartlett, F.C. (1932). *Remembering: A study in experimental and social psychology.* Cambridge: University of Cambridge Press.

Bartlett, F.C. (1958). *Thinking: An experimental and social study.* London: Allen & Unwin.

Bates, E.A., & Elman, J.L. (1993). Connectionism and the study of change. In M.H. Johnson (Ed.), *Brain development & cognition: A reader.* Oxford: Blackwell.

Bauer, P.J., Dow, G.A., & Hertsgaard, L.A. (1995). Effects of prototypicality on categorization in 1- to 2-year-olds: Getting down to basics. *Cognitive Development, 10,* 43–68.

Beale, J.M., & Keil, F.C. (1995). Categorical effects in the perception of faces. *Cognition, 51,* 1–23.

Bechtel, W., & Abrahamsen, A. (1991). *Connectionism and the mind.* London: Blackwell.

Beilin, H. (1985). A view of current American psychology through Piagetian glasses. In J. Montangero (Ed.), *Genetic epistemology: Yesterday and today; with a contribution by Harry Beilin.* New York: City University of New York.

Beilin, H. (1987). Current trends in cognitive development research: Towards a new synthesis. In B. Inhelder, D. de Caprona, & A. Cornu-Wells (Eds.), *Piaget today.* Hove, UK: Lawrence Erlbaum Associates Ltd.

Beilin, H. (1992). Piaget's enduring contribution to developmental psychology. *Developmental Psychology, 2,* 191–204.

Benbow, C.P., & Lubinski, D. (1993). Psychological profiles of the mathematically talented: Some sex differences and evidence supporting their biological basis. In *CIBA Foundations Symposium 1978.* Chichester, UK: Wiley.

Bentham, J. (1789/1966). An introduction to the principles of morals and legislation. Reprinted in C.W. Everett (Ed.), *Jeremy Bentham* (p.111). London: Weidenfeld & Nicolson.

Bertenthal, B.L., Proffitt, D.R., & Cutting, J. (1984). Infant sensitivity to figural coherence in biomechanical motion. *Journal of Experimental Child Psychology, 37,* 213–230.

Bickhard, M.H. (1997). Piaget and active cognition. *Human Development, 40,* 238–244.

Bijou, S.W. (1984). Cross-sectional and longitudinal analysis of development: The interbehavioral perspective. *The Psychological Record, 34,* 525–535.

Bijou, S.W. (1992). Behaviour analysis. In R. Vasta (Ed.), *Six theories of child development: Revised formulations and current issues.* London: Jessica Kingsley.

Billman, D. (1996). Structural biases in concept learning: Influences from multiple functions. *The Psychology of Leaning and Motivation, 35,* 283–320.

Bilsborough, A. (1976). Patterns of evolution in Middle Pleistocene hominids. *Journal of Human Evolution, 5,* 423–439.

Bogartz, R.S., Shinskey, J.L., & Speaker, C.J. (1997). Interpreting infant looking: The event set x event set design. *Developmental Psychology, 33,* 408–422.

Bozdogan, H. (1990). On the information-based measure of covariance complexity and its application to the evaluation of multivariate linear models. *Communications in Statistics: Theory & Methodology, 19,* 221–278.

Brazelton, T.B., & Cramer, B.G. (1991). *The earliest relationship: Parents, infants and the drama of early attachment.* London: Karnac Books.

Bremner, J.G. (1997). From perception to action. In J.G. Bremner, A. Slater, & G. Butterworth (Eds.), *Infant development: Recent advances.* Hove, UK: Psychology Press.

Brockmeier, J. (1996). Construction and interpretation: Exploring a joint perspective on Piaget and Vygotsky. In A. Tryphon & J. Voneche (Eds.), *Piaget–Vygotsky: The social genesis of thought.* Hove, UK: Psychology Press.

Brothers, L., & Ring, B. (1992). A neuroethological framework for the representation of minds. *Journal of Cognitive Neuroscience, 4,* 107–118.

Brown, A.L., Metz, K.E., & Campione, J.C. (1996). Social interaction and individual understanding in a community of learners: The influence of Piaget and Vygotsky. In A. Tryphon, & J. Voneche (Eds.), *Piaget–Vygotsky: The social genesis of thought.* Hove, UK: Psychology Press.

Bruce, V., & Young, A. (1986). Understanding face recognition. *British Journal of Psychology, 77,* 305–327.

Bruner, J.S. (1975). From communication to language – a psychological perspective. *Cognition, 3,* 255–287.

Bruner, J.S. (1983). *Child's talk.* Cambridge: Cambridge University Press.

Bruner, J.S. (1985). Vygotsky: A historical and conceptual perspective. In J.V. Wertsch (Ed.), *Culture, communication and cognition: Vygotskian perspectives.* Cambridge: Cambridge University Press.

Bruner, J.S. (1986). *Actual minds: Possible worlds.* Cambridge, MA: Harvard University Press.

Bruner, J.S. (1990). *Acts of meaning.* Cambridge, MA: Harvard University Press.

Bruner, J.S. (1992). On searching for Bruner. *Language & Communication, 1,* 75–78.

Bryant, P.E., & Trabasso, T. (1971). Transitive inferences and memory in young children. *Nature, 232,* 456–458.

Bullock, M., Gelman, R., & Baillargeon, R. (1982). *The development of causal reasoning.* New York: Academic Press.

Butterworth, G. (1992). Context and cognition in models of cognitive development. In P. Light & G. Butterworth (Eds.), *Context and cognition: Ways of learning and knowing.* Hemel Hempstead, UK: Harvester Wheatsheaf.

Byrne, R. (1995). *The thinking ape: Evolutionary origins of intelligence.* Oxford: Oxford University Press.

Byrne, R.M.J., & Johnson-Laird, P.N. (1990). Models and deductive reasoning. In K.J. Gilhooly, M.T.G. Keane, R.H. Logie, & G. Erdos (Eds.), *Lines of thinking: Reflections on the psychology of thought. Vol 1: Representation, reasoning, analogy and decision making.* London: Wiley.

Cain, W. (1992). *Theories of development: Concepts and applications.* Englewood Cliffs, NJ: Prentice-Hall.

Cairns, R.B. (1990). Towards a development science. *Psychological Science, 1,* 42–44.

Carey, S. (1982). Semantic development: The state of the art. In E. Wanner & L.A. Gleitman (Eds.), *Language acquisition: The state of the art*. Cambridge: Cambridge University Press.

Carey, S. (1985). *Conceptual change in childhood*. Cambridge, MA: MIT Press.

Carey, S. (1988). Are children fundamentally different kinds of thinkers and learners than adults? In K. Richardson & S. Sheldon (Eds.), *Cognitive development to adolescence*. Hove, UK: Lawrence Erlbaum Associates Ltd.

Carey, S. (1994). On becoming a face expert. *Philosophical Transactions of the Royal Society of London, B, 335*, 95–103.

Carey, S., & Gelman, R. (Eds.)(1991). *The epigenesis of mind: Essays on biology and knowledge*. Hillsdale, NJ: Erlbaum.

Carpenter, F. (1974). *The Skinner primer*. New York: Free Press.

Carpenter, P.A., Just, M.A., & Shell, P. (1990). What one intelligence test measures: A theoretical account of the processing in the Raven Progressive Matrices Test. *Psychological Review, 97*, 404–431.

Case, R. (1985). *Intellectual development: A systematic reinterpretation*. New York: Academic Press.

Case, R. (1992). The role of central conceptual structures. In A. Demetriou, M. Shayer, & A. Efklides (Eds.), *Neo-Piagetian theories of cognitive development*. London: Routledge.

Ceci, S.J. (1980). A developmental study of multiple encoding. *Child Development, 51*, 892–895.

Ceci, S.J., & Roazzi, A. (1994). Cognition in context. In R.J. Sternberg & R.K. Wagner (Eds.), *Mind in context: Interactionist perspectives on human intelligence*. Cambridge: Cambridge University Press.

Chalmers, M. (1997). Review of T.S. Kendler, 'Levels of cognitive development'. *British Journal of Developmental Psychology, 15*, 144–145.

Chapman, M. (1988). *Constructive evolution: Origins and development of Piaget's thought*. Cambridge: Cambridge University Press.

Cheng, P.W., & Holyoak, K.J. (1985). Pragmatic reasoning schemes. *Cognitive Psychology, 17*, 391–416.

Cheng, P.W., & Novick, L.R. (1992). Covariation in natural cause induction. *Psychological Review, 99*, 365–382.

Chesnokova, O.B. (1994). The role of interaction in mental action formation. In J. ter Laak, P.G. Heymans, & A.I. Podolskij (Eds), *Developmental tasks*. Kluwer Academic.

Chi, M., & Ceci, S.J. (1987). Content knowledge: Its role, representation, and restructuring in memory development. *Advances in Child Development & Behavior, 18*, 91–142.

Chi, M., Hutchinson, J.E., & Robin, A.F. (1989). How inferences about novel domain-related concepts can be constrained by structured knowledge. *Merrill-Palmer Quarterly, 35*, 27–62.

Chi, M., & Koeske, R. (1983). Network representation of a child's dinosaur knowledge. *Developmental Psychology, 19*, 29–39.

Chi, M.T.H. (1978). Knowledge structures and memory development. In R.S. Siegler (Ed.), *Children's thinking: What develops?* Hillsdale, NJ: Erlbaum.

Childs, C.P., & Greenfield, P.M. (1982). Informal modes of learning and teaching: The case of Zinacenteco basket weaving. In N. Warren (Ed.), *Advances in cross-cultural psychology* (Vol. 2). London: Academic Press.

Chomsky, N. (1959). Review of 'Verbal Behavior' by B.F. Skinner. *Language, 35*, 26–58.

Chomsky, N. (1980). *Rules and representations*. Oxford: Blackwell.

Cohen, L.B. (1991). Infant attention: An information processing approach. In M.J.S. Weiss & P.R. Zelazo (Eds.), *Newborn attention: Biological constraints and the influence of experience*. Norwood, NJ: Ablex.

Cole, M. (1988). Cross-cultural research in the sociohistorical tradition. *Human Development, 31,* 137–152.

Colledge, R.G., Smith, T.R., Pellegrino, J.W., Doherty, S., & Marshall, S.P. (1995). A conceptual model and empirical analysis of children's acquisition of spatial knowledge. In C. Spencer (Ed.), *Readings in environmental psychology.* London: Academic Press.

Collins, A.M., & Loftus, E.F. (1975). A spreading activation model of semantic processing. *Psychological Review, 82,* 407–428.

Corrigan, R., & Denton, P. (1996). Causal understanding as a developmental primitive. *Developmental Review, 16,* 162–202.

Cosmides, L. (1997). *Evolutionary psychology.* Paper presented at the Annual Conference of the British Psychological Society, Edinburgh, 3–6 April, 1997.

Cosmides, L., & Tooby, J. (1994). Origins of domain-specificity: Evolution of functional organization. In L.A. Hirschfeld & S.A. Gelman (Eds.), *Mapping the mind: domain specificity in cognition and culture.* Cambridge: Cambridge University Press.

Cowan, R. (1987). When do children trust counting as a basis for relative number judgement? *Journal of Experimental Child Psychology, 43,* 328–345.

Cowan, R., Foster, C.M., & Al-Zubaidi, A.S. (1993). Encouraging children to count. *British Journal of Developmental Psychology, 11,* 411–420.

Damon, W. (1997). The Handbook's back pages – and ours. *Human Development, 40,* 74–86.

Davidson, D. (1996). The role of schemata in children's memory. *Advances in Child Development & Behaviour, 26,* 35–58.

Davis, A. (1991). Piaget, teachers and education: Into the 1990s. In P. Light, S. Sheldon, & M. Woodhead (Eds.), *Learning to think.* London: Routledge, in association with the Open University.

Deary, I.J., & Caryl, P.G. (1997). Neuroscience and human intelligence differences. *Trends in Neuroscience, 20,* 365–371.

Dennett, D. (1978). *Brainstorms.* Montgomery: Bradford Books.

De Paolis, P., Doise, W., & Mugny, G. (1987). Social marking in cognitive operations. In W. Doise & S. Muscovi (Eds.), *Current issues in European social psychology. Vol III.* Cambridge: Cambridge University Press.

Depew, D.J., & Weber, B.H. (1995). *Darwinism evolving.* Cambridge, MA: MIT Press.

Dinse, H.R., Recanzone, G.H., & Merzenich, M.M. (1993). Alterations in correlated activity parallel ICMS-induced representational plasticity. *NeuroReport, 5,* 173–176.

Dobzhansky, T. (1962). *Mankind evolving: The evolution of the human species.* New Haven: Yale University Press.

Doise, W. (1988). On the social development of the intellect. In K. Richardson & S. Sheldon (Eds.), *Cognitive development to adolescence.* Hove, UK: Lawrence Erlbaum Associates Ltd.

Donahoe, J.W., & Palmer, D.C. (1995). *Learning complex behaviour.* Boston: Allyn & Bacon.

Donaldson, M. (1978). *Children's minds.* London: Fontana.

Dreyfus, H.L., & Dreyfus, S.E. (1987). The mistaken psychological assumptions underlying belief in expert systems. In A.Costall & A.Still (Eds.), *Cognitive psychology in question.* New York: St Martin's Press.

Driver, R., & Bell, B. (1985). Students thinking and the learning of science: A constructivist view. *School Science Review, 67,* 443–456.

Dumont, L. (1965). The modern conception of the individual: Notes on its genesis and that of concomitant institutions. *Contributions to Indian Sociology, 8,* 13–61.

Dunn, J. (1988). *The beginnings of social understanding.* Oxford: Blackwell.

Eames, D., Shorrocks, D., & Tomlinson, P. (1992). Naughty animals or naughty experimenters? Conservation accidents revisited with video-simulated commentary. In L. Smith (Ed.), *Jean Piaget: Critical assessments, Vol. 2*. London: Routledge.

Eimas, P. D., Miller, J.L., & Jusczyk, P.W. (1987). On infant speech perception and the acquisition of language. In S. Harnad (Ed.), *Categorical perception: The groundwork of cognition*. Cambridge: Cambridge University Press.

Elliot, A., & Donaldson, M. (1982). Piaget on language. In S. Modgill & C. Modgill (Eds.), *Jean Piaget: Consensus and controversy*. London: Holt, Rinehart, & Winston.

Elman, J.L. (1990). Finding structure in time. *Cognitive Science, 14,* 179–211.

Elman, J., Bates, E., Karmiloff-Smith, A., Johnson, M., Parisi, D., & Plunkett, K. (1997). *Rethinking innateness: A connectionist perspective on development*. Cambridge, Mass: MIT Press.

Evans, S.H., & Dansereau, D.F. (1991). Knowledge maps as tools for thinking and communication. In R.F. Mulcahy, R.H. Short, & J. Andrews (Eds.), *Enhancing learning and thinking*. New York: Praeger.

Flavell, J.H., & Wellman, H.H. (1977). Metamemory. In R.V. Kail Jr. & J.W. Hagen (Eds.), *Perspectives on the development of memory & cognition*. Hillsdale, NJ: Erlbaum.

Fodor, J. (1983). *The modularity of mind*. Cambridge, MA: MIT Press.

Fodor, J. (1985). Precis of 'The Modularity of mind'. *Behavioral & Brain Sciences, 8,* 1–42.

Fodor, J. (1994). Concepts: A potboiler. *Cognition, 50,* 95–113.

Fodor, J., & Lepore, E. (1996). The red herring and the pet fish: Why concepts still can't be prototypes. *Cognition, 58,* 253–270.

Fox, R., & McDaniel, C. (1982). The perception of biological motion by human infants. *Science, 218,* 486–487.

Fraser, A.M. (1988). *Information and entropy in strange attractors*. Doctoral Dissertation, University of Texas at Austin.

Freeman, N.H., Lloyd, S., & Sinha, C.G. (1980). Infant search tasks reveal early concepts of containment and canonical use of objects. *Cognition, 8,* 243–262.

Frye, D. (1993). Causes and precursors of children's theories of mind. In D. Hay & A. Angold (Eds.), *Precursors and causes in development and psychopathology*. London: Wiley.

Gardner, H. (1984). *Frames of mind: The theory of multiple intelligences*. London: Heinemann.

Gathercole, S.E., & Hitch, G.J. (1995). Developmental changes in short-term memory: A revised working-memory perspective. In A.F. Collins, S.E. Gathercole, M.E.Conway, & P.E. Morris (Eds.), *Theories of memory*. Hove, UK: Lawrence Erlbaum Associates Ltd.

Geary, D.C. (1995). Reflections of evolution and culture in children's cognition. *American Psychologist, 50,* 24–37.

Geary, D.L. (1996). Sexual selection and sex differences in mathematical abilities. *Behavioral & Brain Sciences, 19,* 167–228.

Gelman, S.A., & Markman, E.M. (1986). Categories and induction in young children. *Cognition, 23,* 183–209.

Gelman, S.A., & Markman, E.M. (1987). Young children's inductions from natural kinds: The role of categories and appearances. *Child Development, 58,* 1532–1541.

Gentner, D. (1988). Metaphor as structure mapping: The relational shift. *Child Development, 59,* 47–59.

Gibson, E.J. (1991). *An Odyssey in learning and perception*. Cambridge, MA: MIT Press.

Gibson, E.J., & Walk, R.D. (1960). The visual cliff. *Scientific American, 202,* 64–71.

Gibson, J.J. (1986). *The ecological approach to visual perception.* Hillsdale, NJ: Erlbaum.

Gigerenzer, G. (1995). The taming of content: Some thoughts about domains and modules. In J. St. B.T. Evans (Ed.), *Thinking & reasoning, Vol 1.* Hove, UK: Psychology Press.

Gilbert, C.D., & Weisel, T.N. (1990). The influence of contextual stimuli on the orientation selectivity in the cells of primary visual cortex of the cat. *Vision Research, 30,* 1689–1701.

Gilbert, I.D. (1996). Plasticity in visual perception and physiology. *Current Opinions in Neurobiology, 6,* 269–274.

Gilhooly, K.J. (1995). *Thinking: Directed, undirected and creative (3rd ed.).* London: Academic Press.

Gil-Perez, D., & Carrasco, J. (1990). What to do about science 'misconceptions'. *Science Education, 74,* 531–540.

Ginsburg, H.P. (1988). Piaget and education: The contribution and limits of genetic epistemology. In K. Richardson & S. Sheldon (Eds.), *Cognitive development to adolescence.* Hove, UK: Lawrence Erlbaum Associates Ltd.

Girotto, V., Light, P., & Colbourn, C. (1988). Pragmatic schemas and conditional reasoning in children. *The Quarterly Journal of Experimental Psychology, 40(A),* 469–482.

Glaser, R. (1984). Education and thinking: The role of knowledge. *American Psychologist, 39,* 93–104.

Gobbo, C., & Chi, M. (1986). How knowledge is structured and used by expert and novice children. *Cognitive Development, 1,* 221–237.

Goodnow, J. (1997). Change within limits. *Human Development, 40,* 91–95.

Goodwin, B. (1988). Morphogenesis & heredity. In M.W. Ho & S.W. Fox, (Eds.),*Evolutionary processes and metaphors.* Chichester, UK: Wiley.

Gopnik, A., & Meltzoff, A.N. (1992). Categorisation and naming: Basic level sorting in 18-month-olds and its relation to language. *Child Development, 63,* 1091–1103.

Goswami, U. (1996). Analogical reasoning and cognitive development. *Advances in Child Development and Behaviour, 26,* 92–139.

Grize, J.B. (1987). Operatory logic. In B. Inhelder, D. de Caprona, & A. Cornu-Wells (Eds.), *Piaget today.* Hove, UK: Lawrence Erlbaum Associates Ltd.

Gruber, H. (1974). *Darwin on Man: A psychological study of scientific creativity.* London: Wildwood House.

Haberlandt, K. (1990). Expose hidden assumptions in network theory. *Behavioral and Brain Sciences, 13,* 495–496.

Halford, G.S. (1993). *Children's understanding: The development of mental models.* Hillsdale, NJ: Erlbaum.

Hall, R.H., & Sidio-Hall, M.A. (1994). The effects of colour-enhancement on knowledge map processing. *Journal of Experimental Education, 62,* 209–217.

Hampton, J.A. (1997). Psychological representation of concepts. In M.A. Conway (Ed.), *Cognitive models of memory.* Hove, UK: Psychology Press.

Hanson, S.J., & Burr, D.J. (1990). What connectionist models learn: Learning and representation in connectionist networks. *Behavioral & Brain Sciences, 13,* 471–518.

Harnad, S. (1987). *Categorical perception: The groundwork of cognition.* Cambridge: Cambridge University Press.

Harnad, S. (1990). The symbol grounding problem. *Physica D, 52,* 335–346.

Harré, R., & Gillett, G. (1994). *The discursive mind.* London: Sage.

Harris, M. (1993). *Language experience and early language development: From input to uptake.* Hove, UK: Lawrence Erlbaum Associates Ltd.

Hebb, D.O. (1949). *The organisation of behavior.* New York: Wiley.

Henriques, G. (1992). Morphisms. In T. Brown (Ed.), *Morphisms and categories: Comparing and transforming.* Hillsdale, NJ: Erlbaum.

Henry, L.A., & Millar, S. (1993). Why does memory span improve with age? A review of the evidence for two current hypotheses. *European Journal of Cognitive Psychology, 5,* 241–287.

Herrnstein, R.J., & Murray, C. (1994). *The bell curve: Intelligence and class structure in American life.* New York: Free Press.

Hirschfeld, L.A., & Gelman, S.A. (Eds.) (1994). *Mapping the mind: Domain specificity in cognition and culture.* Cambridge: Cambridge University Press.

Hirst, W., & Manier, D. (1995). Opening vistas for cognitive psychology. In L.M. Martin, K. Nelson, & F. Tobach (Eds.), *Sociocultural psychology: Theory and practice of doing and knowing.* Cambridge: Cambridge University Press.

HMSO (1967). *Children and their primary schools.* (The Plowden Report). London: HMSO.

Hobson, P. (1993). *Autism and the development of mind.* Hove, UK: Lawrence Erlbaum Associates Ltd.

Holland, J.H., Holyoak, K.J., & Nisbett, R.E. (1986). *Induction: Processes of inference, learning and induction.* Cambridge, MA: MIT Press.

Holyoak, K.J., & Cheng, P.W. (1995). Pragmatic reasoning with a point of view. In J. St.B.T. Evans (Ed.), *Thinking and reasoning* (Vol. 1). Hove, UK: Psychology Press.

Hopkins, B., & Butterworth, G. (1997). Dynamical systems approaches to the development of action. In G. Bremner, A. Slater, & G. Butterworth (Eds.), *Infant development: Recent advances.* Hove, UK: Psychology Press.

Howe, M.J.A. (1997). *IQ in question: The truth about intelligence.* London: Sage.

Humphrey, N.K. (1976). The social function of intellect. In P.P.G. Bateson & R.A. Hinde (Eds.), *Growth points in ethology.* Cambridge: Cambridge University Press.

Inhelder, B., & Piaget, J. (1958). *The growth of logical thinking from childhood to adolescence.* New York: Basic Books.

Isaacs, N. (1966). Critical Notice. *Journal of Child Psychology and Psychiatry, 7,* 155–158.

James, W. (1890/1950). *Principles of psychology.* New York: Dover Publications.

Janowsky, J.R. (1993). The development and neural basis of memory systems. In M.H. Johnson (Ed.), *Brain development & cognition: A reader.* Oxford: Blackwell.

Jensen, A.R. (1969). How much can we boost IQ and educational achievement? *Harvard Educational Review, 39,* 1–123.

Johansson, G. (1985). About visual event perception. In R.E. Shaw & W.H. Warren (Eds), *Persistence and change.* Hillsdale, NJ: Erlbaum.

Johnson, M.H., & Morton, J. (1991). *Biology and cognitive development: The case of face recognition.* Oxford: Blackwell.

Johnson-Laird, P.N. (1983). *Mental models.* Cambridge: Cambridge University Press.

Johnston, T.D. (1994). Genes, development, and the 'innate' structure of the mind. *Behavioral and Brain Sciences, 17,* 721–722.

Jones, S.S., & Smith, L.B. (1993). The place of perception in children's concepts. *Cognitive Development, 8,* 113–139.

Just, M.A., & Carpenter, P.A. (1992). A capacity theory of comprehension: Individual differences in working memory. *Psychological Review, 99,* 122–149.

Kail, R. (1990). *The development of memory in children.* New York: Freeman.

Kant, I. (1781/1968). *Critique of pure reason* (trans. N.K. Smith). London: Macmillan.

Kareev, Y. (1995). Positive bias in the perception of covariation. *Psychological Review, 102,* 490–502.

Karmiloff-Smith, A. (1992). *Beyond modularity: A developmental perspective on cognitive science.* Cambridge, MA: MIT Press.

Karmiloff-Smith, A. (1993). Self-organisation and cognitive change. In M.H. Johnson (Ed.), *Brain development and cognition.* Oxford: Blackwell.

Karmiloff-Smith, A. (1994). Precis of *Beyond modularity*: A developmental perspective on cognitive science. *Behavioural and Brain Sciences, 17,* 693–745.

Karmiloff-Smith, A., Klima, E., Bellugi, U., Grant, J., & Baron-Cohen, S. (1995). Is there a social module? Language, face processing, and theory-of-mind in individuals with Williams syndrome. *Journal of Cognitive Neuroscience, 7,* 196–208.

Kaye, K. (1977). Towards the origins of dialogue. In H.R. Schaffer (Ed.), *Studies in mother--infant interaction.* London: Academic Press.

Kee, D.W. (1994). Developmental differences in associative memory: Strategy use, mental effort, and knowledge access interactions. *Advances in Child Development & Behavior, 25,* 7–38.

Keil, F.C. (1986). The acquisition of natural kinds and artifact terms. In W. Demopolous & A. Marras (Eds.), *Language learning and concept acquisition.* Norwood, NJ: Ablex.

Keil, F.C. (1988). On the structure-dependent nature of stages of cognitive development. In K. Richardson & S. Shelson (Eds.), *Cognitive development to adolescence.* Hove, UK: Lawrence Erlbaum Associates Ltd.

Keil, F.C. (1990). Constraints on constraints: Surveying the epigenetic landscape. In M.D. Ringle (Ed.), *Cognitive Science, 14,* 135–168.

Kellman, P.J., & Spelke, E.S. (1983). Perception of partly occluded objects in infancy. *Cognitive Psychology, 15,* 483–524.

Kendler, T.S. (1995). *Levels of cognitive development.* Hillsdale, NJ: Erlbaum.

Kessel, F.S. (1969). The philosophy of science as proclaimed and science as practiced. *American Psychologist, 24,* 999–1004.

Kessen, W., & Resnick, J.S. (1992). Constraining constraints. *Cognitive Development, 8,* 105–112.

Kitcher, P. (1985). *Vaulting ambitions: Sociobiology and the quest for human nature.* Cambridge, MA: MIT Press.

Klahr, D. (1992). Information processing approaches. In R. Vasta (Ed.), *Six theories of child development: Revised formulations and current issues.* London: Jessica Kingsley.

Kulhavy, R.W., Stock, W.A., Verdi, M.P., Rittschof, K.A., & Savenye, W. (1993). Why maps improve memory for text: The influence of structural information on working memory operations. *European Journal of Cognitive Psychology, 5,* 375–392.

Kuo, Z. (1967). *The dynamics of behavior development: An epigenetic view.* New York: Random House.

Laird, J. (1932/1967). *Hume's philosophy of human nature.* London: Archon Books.

Lakoff, G. (1987). Cognitive models and prototype theory. In U. Neisser (Ed.), *Concepts and conceptual development: Ecological and intellectual factors in categorisation.* Cambridge: Cambridge University Press.

Lambiotte, J.G., Dansereau, D.F., Cross, D.R., & Reynolds, S.B. (1989). Multirelational semantic maps. *Educational Psychology Review, 1,* 311–367.

Lappin, J.S. (1994). Sensing structure in space–time. In G. Jansson, S.S. Bergstrom, & W. Epstein (Eds.), *Perceiving events and objects.* Hillsdale, NJ: Erlbaum.

Lave, J. (1988). *Cognition in practice: Mind, mathematics and culture in everyday life.* Cambridge: Cambridge University Press.

Lave, J. (1994). The culture of acquisition and the practice of understanding. In J.W. Stigler, R.H. Shweder, & G. Herdt (Eds.), *Cultural Psychology*. Cambridge: Cambridge University Press.

Lawrence, P.A. (1992). *The making of a fly: The genetics of animal design*. Oxford: Blackwell.

Leach, E. (1964). Anthropological aspects of language. In E.H. Lenneberg (Ed.), *New directions in the study of language*. Cambridge, MA: MIT Press.

Leahy, T.H. (1987). *A history of psychology*. Englewood Cliffs, NJ: Prentice Hall.

Leslie, A.M. (1987). Pretence and representation: The origins of "theory-of-mind". *Psychological Review, 94*, 412–426.

Leslie, A.M. (1992). Pretence, autism and the 'theory-of-mind' module. *Current Directions in Psychological Science, 1*, 18–21.

Leslie, A.M. (1994). ToMM, ToBy, and Agency: Core architecture and domain specificity. In L.A. Hirschfeld & S.A. Gelman (Eds.), *Mapping the mind: Domain specificity in cognition and culture*. Cambridge: Cambridge University Press.

Levicki, P., Hill, T., & Czyzewska, M. (1997). Hidden covariation detection: A fundamental and ubiquitous phenomenon. *Journal of Experimental Psychology: Learning, Memory & Cognition, 23*, 221–228.

Levin, J.R. (1988). Elaboration based learning strategies: Powerful theory = powerful application. *Contemporary Educational Psychology, 13*, 191–295.

Lewis, C. (1995). Episodes, events and narratives in the child's early understanding of mind. In C. Lewis & P. Mitchell (Eds.), *Children's early understanding of mind*. Hove, UK: Lawrence Erlbaum Associates Ltd.

Lewis, C., Freeman, N.H., Kyriakidou, C., Marridaki-Kassotaki, K., & Berridge, D. (1996). Social influences on false belief access: Specific sibling influences or general apprenticeship. *Child Development, 67*, 2930–2947.

Lewontin, R.C. (1974). *The genetic basis of evolutionary change*. New York: Columbia University Press.

Light, P., Buckingham, N., & Robbins, A.H. (1979). The conservational task as an interactional setting. *British Journal of Educational Psychology, 49*, 304–310.

Light, P., Sheldon, S., & Woodhead, M. (Eds.) (1991). *Learning to think*. London: Routledge; in association with the Open University.

Little, A.H., Lipsitt, L.P., & Rovee-Collier, C.K. (1984). Classical conditioning and retention of the infant's eyelid response: Effects of age and interstimulus interval. *Journal of Experimental Child Psychology, 37*, 512–524.

Logie, R.H., & Pearson, D.G. (1997). The inner eye and the inner scribe of visuo-spatial working memory: Evidence from developmental fractionation. *European Journal of Cognitive Psychology, 9*, 241–257.

Lumsden, C. J., & Wilson, E.O. (1981). *Genes, mind & culture*. Cambridge, MA: Harvard University Press.

Mackay, D.M. (1986). Vision – the capture of optical covariation. In J.D. Pettigrew, K.J. Sanderson, & W.R. Levick (Eds.), *Visual neuroscience*. Cambridge: Cambridge University Press.

Mandler, J.M. (1992). The foundations of conceptual thought in infancy. *Cognitive Development, 7*, 273–285.

Mandler, J.M. (1993). On concepts. *Cognitive Development, 8*, 141–148.

Mandler, J.M., & McDonough, L. (1993). Concept formation in infants. *Cognitive Development, 8*, 299–318.

Markman, E.M. (1978). Empirical versus logical solutions to part–whole comparison problems concerning classes and collections. *Child Development, 49*, 168–177.

Markman, E.M. (1984). The acquisition and hierarchical organisation of categories by children. In M. Sophian (Ed.), *Origins of cognitive skills*. Hillsdale, NJ: Erlbaum.

Markova, I. (1990). Causes and reasons in social development. In G. Butterworth & P. Bryant (Eds.), *Causes of development.* Brighton, UK: Harvester.

Markovitz, H. (1993). The development of conditional reasoning: A Piagetian reformulation of mental models theory. *Merrill-Palmer Quarterly, 39,* 131–158.

Marti, E. (1996). Mechanisms of internalisation and externalisation of knowledge in Piaget's and Vygotsky's theories. In A. Tryphon & J. Voneche (Eds.), *Piaget–Vygotsky: The social genesis of thought.* Hove, UK: Psychology Press.

Marx, K. (1973). *Grundrisse.* Harmondsworth, UK: Penguin; in association with New Left Review.

McGarrigle, J., & Donaldson, M. (1975). Conservation accidents. *Cognition, 3,* 341–350.

McGaugh, J.L., Bermudez-Rattoni, F., & Prado-Alcala, R.A. (1995). *Plasticity in the central nervous system.* Hillsdale, NJ: Erlbaum.

Medin, D.L., Goldstone, R.L., & Gentner, D. (1993). Respects for similarity. *Psychological Review, 100,* 254–278.

Medin, D.L., & Ortony, A. (1989). Psychological essentialism. In S. Vosniadou & A. Ortony (Eds.), *Similarity and analogical reasoning.* Cambridge: Cambridge University Press.

Mehler, J., & Dupoux, P. (1994). *What infants know: The new cognitive science of early development.* Oxford: Blackwell.

Meltzoff, A.N., & Gopnik, A. (1993). The role of imitation in understanding persons and developing theories of mind. In S. Baron-Cohen, H. Tager-Flusberg, & D. Cohen (Eds.), *Understanding other minds: Perspectives from autism.* Oxford: Oxford University Press.

Meltzoff, A.N., & Moore, M.K. (1977). Imitation of facial and manual gestures by human neonates. *Science, 198,* 75–78.

Meltzoff, A.N., & Moore, M.K. (1992). Early imitation within a functional framework: The importance of personal identity, movement and development. *Infant Behavior & Development, 15,* 479–505.

Mervis, C.B., & Crisafi, M.A. (1982). Order of acquisition of subordinate-, basic-, and superordinate-level categories. *Child Development, 53,* 258–266.

Miller, P.H. (1993). *Theories of developmental psychology.* San Francisco: W.H. Freeman.

Mix, K.S., Levine, S.C., & Huttenlocher, J. (1997). Numerical abstraction in infants: Another look. *Developmental Psychology, 33,* 423–428.

Mowrer, O.H. (1960). *Learning theory and behavior.* New York: Wiley.

Munakata, Y., McClelland, J.L., Johnson, M.H., & Siegler, R.S. (1997). Rethinking infant knowledge: Towards an adaptive process account of successes and failures in object permanence tasks. *Psychological Review, 104,* 686–713.

Murphy, G.L. (1993). Theories and concept formation. In I.V. Mechelen, J. Hampton, R.S. Michalski, & P. Theuns (Eds.), *Categories and concepts: Theoretical views and inductive data analysis.* London: Academic Press.

Murray, D.J. (1997). *Gestalt psychology and the cognitive revolution.* Hemel Hempstead, UK: Harvester Wheatsheaf.

Murray, T.R. (1996). *Comparing theories of child development.* Pacific Grove, PA: Brookes/Cole.

Nelson, K. (1986). *Event knowledge.* Hillsdale, NJ: Erlbaum.

Nelson, K. (1995). Explaining the emergence of autobiographical memory in early childhood. In A.F. Collins, S.E. Gathercole, M.E. Conway, & P.E. Morris (Eds.), *Theories of memory.* Hove, UK: Lawrence Erlbaum Associates Ltd.

Newell, A. (1980). Physical symbol systems. *Cognitive Science, 4,* 135–183.

Newson, J. (1974). Towards a theory of infant understanding. *Bulletin of the British Psychological Society, 27,* 251–257.

Nunes, T., & Bryant, P. (1996). *Children doing mathematics.* Oxford: Blackwell.

Nunes, T., Schliemann, A.L., & Caraher, D. (1993). *Street mathematics and school mathematics.* Cambridge: Cambridge University Press.

Oakes, L.M., Coppage, D.J., & Dingel, A. (1997). By land or by sea: The role of perceptual similarity in infants' categorisation of animals. *Developmental Psychology, 33,* 396–407.

Oakhill, J. (1988). The development of children's reasoning ability: Information processing approaches. In K. Richardson & S. Sheldon (Eds.), *Cognitive development to adolescence.* Hove, UK: Lawrence Erlbaum Associates Ltd.

Oakley, D.A. (1985). Cerebral cortex and adaptive behaviour. In D.A. Oakley & H.C. Plotkin (Eds.), *Brain, behaviour and evolution.* London: Methuen.

Oates, J. (1994). Sensation to perception. In J. Oates (Ed.), *The foundations of development.* Oxford: Blackwell.

Overton, W.F. (1997). Marching toward the millennium. *Human Development, 40,* 102–108.

Owings, R.A., & Baumeister, A.A. (1979). Levels of processing, encoding strategies, and memory development. *Journal of Experimental Child Psychology, 28,* 100–118.

Oyama, S. (1985). *The ontogeny of information.* Cambridge: Cambridge University Press.

Paivio, A. (1986). *Mental representations: A dual coding approach.* Oxford: Oxford University Press.

Papert, S. (1992). Preface. In J. Piaget, G. Henriques, & E. Ascher, *Morphisms and categories: Comparing and transforming* (edited by T. Brown). Hillsdale, NJ: Lawrence Erlbaum Associates Inc.

Phillips, W.A., Kay, J., & Smyth, D.M. (1994). How local processors that maximize coherent variation could lay foundations for representation proper. In L.S. Smith & P.J.B. Hancock (Eds.), *Neural computation and psychology.* London: Springer.

Piaget, J. (1926/1972). *The child's conception of the world.* Totowa, NJ: Littlefield Adams.

Piaget, J. (1941). Le mécanisme du développement mental et les lois du groupement des opérations. *Archives de Psychologie, 28,* 215–285.

Piaget, J. (1954). *The construction of reality in the child* (trans. M. Cook). New York: Basic Books.

Piaget, J. (1969/1991). Science of education and the psychology of the child. In P. Light, S. Sheldon, & M. Woodhead (Eds.), *Learning to think.* London: Routledge.

Piaget, J. (1970/1988). Piaget's theory. In P.H. Mussen (Ed.), *Manual of child psychology.* London: Wiley. Reprinted in K. Richardson & S. Sheldon (Eds.), *Cognitive development to adolescence.* Hove, UK: Lawrence Erlbaum Associates Ltd.

Piaget, J. (1971). *Structuralism.* London: Routledge & Kegan Paul.

Piaget, J. (1972). *The psychology of intelligence* (trans. M. Piercy & D.E. Berlyne). Totowa, NJ: Littlefield, Adams & Co.

Piaget, J. (1973). *Main trends in psychology.* London: George Allen & Unwin.

Piaget, J. (1974/1976). *The grasp of consciousness* (trans. S. Wedgwood). Cambridge, MA: Harvard University Press.

Piaget, J. (1975). *The development of thought.* Oxford, Blackwell.

Piaget, J. (1977). *The origin of intelligence in children.* Harmondsworth, UK: Penguin.

Piaget, J. (1988). Piaget's Theory. In K. Richardson, & S. Sheldon (Eds.), *Cognitive development to adolescence.* Hove, UK: Lawrence Erlbaum Associates Ltd.

Piaget, J., & Garcia, R. (1991). *Towards a logic of meanings*. Hillsdale, NJ: Erlbaum.

Piaget, J., Henriques, G., & Ascher, E. (1992). *Morphisms and categories: Comparing and transforming* (edited by T. Brown). Hillsdale, NJ: Erlbaum.

Piaget, J., & Inhelder, B. (1969). *The psychology of the child*. New York: Basic Books.

Plotkin, H.C., & Odling-Smee, F.J. (1979). Learning, change and evolution: An inquiry into the teleonomy of learning. *Advances in the Study of Behavior, 10*, 1–42.

Plunkett, K., & Sinha, C. (1992). Connectionism and developmental theory. *British Journal of Developmental Psychology, 10*, 209–254.

Poulson, C.L., Nunes, L.R. de P., & Warren, S.F. (1989). Imitation in infancy: A critical review. *Advances in Child Development & Behavior, 22*, 271–298.

Quartz, S.R. (1993). Neural networks, nativism, and the plausibility of constructivism. *Cognition, 48*, 223–242.

Quillian, M.R. (1969). The teachable language comprehender. *Communications of the Association for Computing Machinery, 12*, 459–476.

Quinn, P.C., Eimas, P.D., & Rosenkranz, S.L. (1993). Evidence for representations of perceptually similar natural categories by 3-month-old and 4-month-old infants. *Perception, 22*, 463–475.

Rachlin, H. (1970). *Introduction to modern behaviorism*. San Francisco: Freeman.

Reber, A. (1989). Implicit learning and tacit knowledge. *Journal of Experimental Psychology: General, 118*, 219–235.

Reber, A.S. (1995). *Penguin dictionary of psychology (2nd ed.)*. London: Penguin.

Reed, E.S. (1996). *The necessity of experience*. New Haven, CT: Yale University Press.

Reese, H.W. (1979). *Basic learning processes in children*. New York: Holt, Rinehart, & Winston.

Reese, H.W. (Ed.). (1989). *Rule-governed behaviour: Cognition, contingencies and instructional control*. New York: Plenum Press.

Reilly, R. (1989). On the relationship between connectionism and cognitive science. *The Irish Journal of Psychology, 10*, 162–187.

Reykowski, J. (1982). Social motivation. *Annual Review of Psychology, 33*, 23–54.

Richards, G. (1987). *Human evolution*. London: Routledge & Kegan Paul.

Richardson, K. (1991). Reasoning with Raven – in and out of context. *British Journal of Educational Psychology, 61*, 129–138.

Richardson, K. (1992). Covariation analysis of knowledge representation: Some developmental studies. *Journal of Experimental Child Psychology, 53*, 129–150.

Richardson, K. (1998). *The origins of human potential: Evolution, development and psychology*. London: Routledge

Richardson, K., & Carthy, T. (1990). The abstraction of covariation in conceptual representation. *British Journal of Psychology, 81*, 415–438.

Richardson, K., & Webster, D.W. (1996a). Recognition of objects from point-light stimuli: Evidence of covariation structures in conceptual representation. *British Journal of Psychology, 87*, 567–591.

Richardson, K., & Webster, D. (1996b). Analogical reasoning in context: A research note. *British Journal of Educational Psychology, 66*, 23–32.

Richardson, K., Webster, D., & Cope, N. (submitted). *Conception of form from point-light stimuli.*

Rips, L.J, Shoben, E.J., & Smith E.E. (1973). Semantic distance and the verification of semantic relations. *Journal of Verbal Learning & Verbal Behavior, 12*, 1–20.

Robinson, D.N. (1981). *An intellectual history of psychology*. New York: Macmillan.

Rogoff, B., Baker-Sennet, J., Lacasa, P., & Goldsmith, D. (1995). Development through participation in sociocultural activity. In J.J. Goodnow, P.J. Miller, & F. Kessel (Eds.), *Cultural practices as contexts for development*. San Francisco: Jossey-Bass.

Rogoff, B., & Chavajay, P. (1995). What's become of research on the cultural basis of cognitive development? *American Psychologist, 50*, 859–877.

Rollo, D.C. (1994). *Phenotypes: Their epigenetics, ecology and evolution*. London: Chapman & Hall.

Rosch, E. (1978). *Principles of categorization*. Hillsdale, NJ: Erlbaum.

Rosch, E., & Mervis, C.B. (1975). Family resemblances: Studies in the internal structure of categories. *Cognitive Psychology, 7*, 573–605.

Rosch, E., Mervis, C.B., Gray, W.D., Johnson, D.M., & Boyes-Braem, P. (1976). Basic objects in natural categories. *Cognitive Psychology, 8*, 382–429.

Rose, S., Kamin, L.J., & Lewontin, R.C. (1984). *Not in our genes*. Harmondsworth, UK: Penguin.

Ross, G.S. (1980). Categorization in 1- to 2-year olds. *Developmental Psychology, 16*, 391–396.

Rumelhart, D.E., & McClelland, J.L (1987). Learning the past tenses of English verbs: Implicit rules of parallel distributed processing? In B. MacWhinney (Ed.), *Mechanisms of language acquisition*. Hillsdale, NJ: Erlbaum.

Rumelhart, D.E., & McClelland, J.L. (Eds.) (1996). *Parallel distributed processing: Explorations in the microstructure of cognition, Vol. 1. Foundations*. Cambridge, MA: MIT Press.

Rushton, P. (1995). *Race, evolution & behavior*. New Brunswick, NJ: Transaction Publishers.

Rutkowska, J.C. (1993). *The computational infant*. Hemel Hempstead, UK: Harvester Wheatsheaf.

Saxe, G. (1991). *Culture and cognitive development: Studies in mathematical understanding*. Hillsdale, NJ: Erlbaum

Scaife, M. (1985). The implications of a structural biology for developmental psychology (commentary on Goodwin). In G. Butterworth, J. Rutkowska, & M. Scaife (Eds.), *Evolution and development theory*. Brighton, UK: Harvester.

Scarr, S. (1992). Developmental theories for the 1990s: Development and individual differences. *Child Development, 63*, 1–19.

Schaffer, H.R. (1991). Early social development. In P. Light, S. Sheldon, & M. Woodhead (Eds.), *Learning to think*. London: Routledge; in association with the Open University.

Schanks, R.C., & Abelson, R.P. (1977). *Scripts, plans, goals and understanding*. Hillsdale, NJ: Erlbaum.

Schneider, W., & Pressley, M. (1989). *Memory development between 2 and 20*. New York: Springer-Verlag.

Scholnick, E.K. (1994). Redescribing development. *Behavioral & Brain Sciences, 17*, 727–728.

Scribner, S. (1997). Mind in action: A functional approach to thinking. In E. Tobach, L.M.W. Martin, R.J. Falmagne, A.S. Scribner, & M.B. Parlee (Eds.), *Mind and social practice: Selected writings of Sylvia Scribner*. Cambridge: Cambridge University Press.

Seigal, M. (1997). *Knowing children: Experiments in conversation and cognition*. Hove, UK: Psychology Press.

Shaklee, H., Holt, P., Elek, S., & Hall, L. (1988). Covariation judgement: Improving rule use among children, adolescents and adults. *Child Development, 59*, 755–768.

Shanks, D.R. (1995). *The psychology of associative learning*. Cambridge: Cambridge University Press.

Shepard, R.W. (1988). How fully should connectionism be activated? *Behavioral and Brain Sciences, 11*, 52.

Shockley, W. (1972). Dysgenics, geneticity and raceology. *Phi Delta Kappan, 53,* 297–307.

Siegler, R.S. (1978).The origins of scientific reasoning. In R.S. Siegler (Ed.), *Children's thinking: What develops?* Hillsdale, NJ: Erlbaum.

Siegler, R.S. (1991). *Children's thinking.* Englewood Cliffs, NJ: Prentice Hall.

Siegler, R.S., & Crowley, K. (1994). Constraints on learning in nonprivileged domains. *Cognitive Psychology, 27,* 194–226.

Siegler, R.S., & Shipley, C. (1987). The role of learning in children's strategy choices. In L.S.L. Gened (Ed.), *Development and learning: Conflict or congruence.* Hillsdale, NJ: Erlbaum.

Silverman, I., & Eals, M. (1992). Sex differences in spatial abilities: Evolutionary theory and data. In J.H. Barkov, L. Cosmides, & J. Tooby (Eds.), *The adapted mind.* Oxford: Oxford University Press.

Sinclair, H. (1982). Piaget on language: A perspective. In S. Modgill & C. Modgill (Eds.), *Jean Piaget: Consensus and controversy.* London: Holt, Rinehart, & Winston.

Singer, W., & Gray, C.M. (1995). Visual feature integration and the temporal correlation hypothesis. *Annual Review of Neuroscience, 18,* 555–586.

Skinner, B.F. (1948). *Walden Two.* New York: Macmillan.

Skinner, B.F. (1972). *Beyond freedom and dignity.* London: Cape.

Skinner, B.F. (1985). Cognitive science and behaviourism. *British Journal of Psychology, 76,* 291–301.

Slater, A. (1989). Visual memory and perception in early infancy. In A. Slater & G. Bremner (Eds.), *Infant development.* Hove, UK: Lawrence Erlbaum Associates Ltd.

Slater, A., & Butterworth, G. (1997). Perception of social stimuli: Face perception and imitation. In J.G. Bremner, A. Slater, & G. Butterworth (Eds.), *Infant development: Recent advances.* Hove, UK: Psychology Press.

Slater, A., & Morison, V. (1985). Shape constancy and slant perception at birth. *Perception, 14,* 337–344.

Slater, A., Morison, V., Town, C., & Rose, D. (1985). Movement perception and identity constancy in the new-born baby. *British Journal of Developmental Psychology, 3,* 211–220.

Smith, E.E., & Medin, D.L. (1981). *Categories and concepts.* Cambridge, MA: Harvard University Press.

Smith, L. (1993). *Necessary knowledge: Piagetian perspectives on constructivism.* Hove, UK: Lawrence Erlbaum Associates Ltd.

Smith, L. (Ed.) (1996a). *Critical readings on Piaget.* London: Routledge.

Smith, L. (1996b). The social construction of understanding. In A. Tryphon & A. Voneche (Eds.), *Piaget–Vygotsky.* Hove, UK: Psychology Press.

Smith, L. (1997). Necessary knowledge and its assessment in intellectual development. In L.Smith, J. Dockrell, & P. Tomlinson (Eds.), *Piaget, Vygotsky and beyond.* London: Routledge.

Smith, L., Dockrell, J., & Tomlinson, P. (Eds.) (1996). *Piaget, Vygotsky and beyond.* London: Routledge.

Smith, L.B., & Jones, S.S. (1993). Cognition without concepts. *Cognitive Development, 8,* 181–188.

Smith, S. (1979). *Ideas of the great educators.* New York: Barnes and Noble.

Smyth, M., Collins, A.F., Morris, P.E., & Levy, P. (1994). *Cognition in action.* Hove, UK: Lawrence Erlbaum Associates Ltd.

Spelke, E. (1994). Initial knowledge: Six suggestions. *Cognition, 50,* 431–445.

Spelke, E.S., Brienlinger, K., Macombre, J., & Jacobson, K. (1992). Origins of knowledge. *Psychological Review, 99*, 605–632.

Sperber, D. (1986). The mind as a whole. *Times Literary Supplement,* 21 Nov.

Sperber, D. (1994). The modularity of thought and the epidemiology of representations. In L.A. Hirschfeld & S.A. Gelman (Eds.), *Mapping the mind: Domain specificity in cognition and culture.* Cambridge: Cambridge University Press.

Stearns, S.C. (1989). The evolutionary significance of phenotypic plasticity. *BioScience, 39,* 436–447.

Sternberg, R.J. (1982). A componential approach to intellectual development. In R.J. Sternberg (Ed.), *Advances in the psychology of human intelligence, vol 1.* Hillsdale, NJ: Erlbaum.

Sternberg, R.J. (1984). Towards a triarchic theory of human intelligence. *Behavioral & Brain Sciences, 7,* 269–315.

Still, A., & Costall, A. (1987). Introduction. In A.Costall & A.Still (Eds.), *Cognitive psychology in question.* New York: St Martin's Press.

Strauss, M. (1979). Abstraction of prototypical information by adults and 10-month-old infants. *Journal of Experimental Psychology: Human Learning & Memory, 5,* 618–632.

Sullivan, K., & Winner, E. (1993). Three year olds' understanding of mental states: The influence of trickery. *Journal of Experimental Child Psychology, 56,* 135–148.

Tharpe, R., & Gallimore, R. (1991). A theory of teaching as assisted performance. In P. Light, S. Sheldon, & M. Woodhead (Eds.), *Learning to think.* London: Routledge; in association with The Open University.

Thelen, E. (1985). Developmental origins of motor coordination: Leg movements in human infants. *Developmental Psychobiology, 18,* 323–333.

Thelen, E. (1995). Time-scale dynamics and the development of an embodied cognition. In R.F. Port & T. van Gelder (Eds.), *Mind as motion: Explorations in the dynamics of cognition.* Cambridge, MA: MIT Press.

Thelen, E., & Smith, L.B. (1994). *A dynamic systems approach to the development of cognition and action.* Cambridge, MA: MIT Press.

Thorndike, E.L. (1911). *Animal intelligence.* New York: Macmillan.

Thorndyke, P.W. (1984). Applications of schema theory in cognitive research. In J.R. Anderson & S.M. Kosslyn (Eds.), *Tutorials in learning and memory.* San Francisco: W.H. Freeman.

Tolman, E.C. (1948). Cognitive maps in rats and men. *Psychological Review, 55,* 189–205.

Tomlinson-Keasey, C. (1982). Structures, functions and stages: A trio of unresolved issues in formal operations. In S. Modgill & C. Modgill (Eds.), *Jean Piaget: Consensus and controversy.* London: Holt, Rinehart & Winston.

Trevarthen, C. (1977). Descriptive analysis of infant communicative behaviour. In H.R. Schaffer (Ed.), *Studies in mother–infant interaction.* London: Academic Press.

Trevarthen, C. (1979a). Communication and cooperation in early infancy: A description of primary intersubjectivity. In M. Bullowa (Ed.), *Before speech.* Cambridge: Cambridge University Press.

Trevarthen, C. (1979b). Instincts for human understanding and for cultural cooperation: Their development in infancy. In M. von Cranach, K. Foppa, W. Lepenies, & D. Ploog (Eds.), *Human ethology: Claims and limits of a new discipline.* Cambridge: Cambridge University Press.

Trevarthen, C. (1983). Interpersonal abilities of children as generators for transmission of language and culture. In A. Oliverio & M. Zappella (Eds.), *The behavior of human infants, vol 2*. New York: Plenum Press.

Tryphon, A., & Voneche, J. (Eds.) (1996). *Piaget–Vygotsky: The social genesis of thought*. Hove, UK: Psychology Press.

Van der Veer, R. (1996). Structure and development. Reflections by Vygotsky. In A. Tryphon & J. Voneche (Eds.), *Piaget–Vygotsky: The social genesis of thought*. Hove, UK: Psychology Press.

Van der Veer, R., & Valsiner, J. (1991). *Understanding Vygotsky: A quest for synthesis*. Oxford: Blackwell.

Van Embden, M.H. (1971). *An analysis of complexity*. Amsterdam: Mathematical Centre Tracts 35.

Van Gelder, T., & Port, R.F. (1995). It's about time: An overview of the dynamical approach to cognition. In R.F. Port & T. Van Gelder (Eds.), *Mind as motion: Explorations in the dynamics of cognition*. Cambridge, MA: MIT Press.

Varela, F.J., Thompson, E., & Rosch, E. (1991). *The embodied mind: Cognitive science and human experience*. Cambridge, MA: MIT Press.

Vera, A.H., & Simon, H.A. (1994). Reply to Touretzky and Pomerleau: Reconstructing physical symbol systems. *Cognitive Science, 18*, 355–360.

Vernon, P.A. (Ed.) (1987). *Speed of information processing and intelligence*. New York: Ablex.

Vernon, P.E. (1979). *Intelligence, heredity and environment*. San Francisco: Freeman.

Von Bertalanffy, L. (1968). *General systems theory*. New York: George Braziller.

Vygotsky, L.S. (1962). *Thought and language* (trans. E. Hanfmann & G. Vakar). Cambridge, MA: MIT Press.

Vygotsky, L.S. (1966). Development of the higher mental functions. In A. Leontiev, A. Luria, & A. Smirnov (Eds.), *Psychological research in the USSR, Vol I*. Moscow: Progress Publishers.

Vygotsky, L.S. (1978). *Mind in society: The development of higher psychological processes*. Cambridge, MA: Harvard University Press.

Vygotsky, L.S. (1981). The genesis of higher mental functions. In J.V. Wertsch (Ed.), *The concept of activity in Soviet psychology*. Armonk, NY: Sharpe.

Vygotsky, L.S., & Luria, A.R. (1993). *Studies on the history of behaviour* (edited and translated by V.I. Golod & J.E. Knox). Hillsdale, NJ: Erlbaum.

Waddington, C.H. (1957). *The strategy of the genes*. London: Allen & Unwin.

Waddington, C.H. (1966). *Principles of development and differentiation*. London: Macmillan.

Wagner, R.K., Torgesen, J.K., & Rachotte, C.A. (1994). Development of reading-related phonological-processing abilities: New evidence of bi-directional causality from a latent variable longitudinal study. *Developmental Psychology, 30*, 73–87.

Walker-Andrews, A.S., & Gibson, E.J. (1986). What develops in bimodal perception. In C. Rovee-Collier & L. Lipsitt (Eds.), *Advances in infancy research*. Norwood, NJ: Ablex.

Walsh, M., Richardson, K., & Faulkner, D. (1993). Perceptual, thematic and taxonomic relations in children's mental representations. *European Journal of Psychology of Education, 8*, 85–102.

Walsh, W.H. (1968). Schematism. In R.P. Wolff (Ed.), *Kant: A collection of critical essays*. London: Macmillan.

Walton, G., Bower, N.G.A., & Bower, T.G.R. (1992). Recognition of familiar faces by newborns. *Infant Behaviour and Development, 15*, 265–269.

Wason, P.C., & Johnson-Laird, P.N. (1972). *Psychology of reasoning: Structure and content*. London: Batsford.

Wasserman, E.A., Elek, S.M., Chatlosh, D.L., & Baker, A.G. (1993). Rating causal relations: The role of probability in judgements of response–outcome contingencies. *Journal of Experimental Psychology: Learning, Memory & Cognition, 19*, 174–188.

Wattenmaker, W.D. (1996). Knowledge structures and linear separability: Integrating information in object and social categorisation. *Cognitive Psychology, 28*, 274–328.

Waxman, M.S.R., & Markow, D.B. (1995). Words as invitations to form categories: Evidence from 12- to 13-month-old infants. *Cognitive Psychology, 29*, 257–302.

Weinberger, N.M. (1995). Dynamic regulation of receptive fields and maps in the adult sensory cortex. *Annual Review of Neuroscience, 18*, 129–158.

Weitz, L.J., Bynum, T.W., & Steger, J.A. (1973). Piaget's system of 16 binary operations: An empirical investigation. *Journal of Genetic Psychology, 123*, 279–284.

Wellman, H.M. (1990). *The child's theory-of-mind.* Cambridge, MA: MIT Press.

Wertsch, J.V., & Sammarco, J.G. (1985). Social precursors to individual cognitive functioning: The problem of units of analysis. In J.V. Wertsch (Ed.), *Vygotsky and the social formation of mind.* Cambridge, MA: Harvard University Press.

Whaley, D.L., & Malott, R.V. (1968). *Elementary principles of behavior.* New York: Appleton-Century-Crofts.

Wilson, E.O. (1975). *Sociobiology: The modern synthesis.* Cambridge, MA: Harvard University Press.

Wilson, K.V. (1980). *From associations to structure.* Amsterdam: North Holland.

Winn, W.D. (1990). A theoretical framework for research on learning from graphs. *International Journal of Educational Research, 6*, 553–564.

Wittgenstein, L. (1958). *Philosophical investigations.* Oxford: Blackwell.

Wood, D. (1991). Aspects of teaching and learning. In P. Light, S. Sheldon, & M. Woodhead (Eds.), *Learning to think.* London: Routledge; in association with The Open University.

Wood, D.J., Bruner, J.S., & Ross, G. (1976). The role of tutoring in problem-solving. *Journal of Child Psychology & Psychiatry, 17*, 89–100.

Wood, D. J., & Middleton, D.J. (1975). A study of assisted problem-solving. *British Journal of Psychology, 66*, 181–191.

Wozniak, R.H. (1996). Qu'est-ce que l'intelligence? Piaget, Vygotsky and the 1920s crisis in psychology. In A. Tryphon & J. Voneche (Eds.), *Piaget–Vygotsky: The social genesis of thought.* Hove, UK: Psychology Press.

Wynn, K. (1992). Addition and subtraction by human infants. *Nature, 358*, 749–750.

Yolton, J.W. (1977). *The Locke reader: Selections from the works of John Locke.* Cambridge: Cambridge University Press.

Yonas, A., Petterson, L., & Lockman, J.J. (1979). Young infants' sensitivity to optical information for collision. *Canadian Journal of Psychology, 33*, 269–276.

Younger, B.A., & Cohen, L.B. (1983). Infant perception of correlations among attributes. *Child Development, 54*, 858–867.

Zeki, S. (1993). *A vision of the brain.* Oxford: Blackwell.

Author index

Subject index

importance of context, 119–120
social cooperation, 168
CONSPEC, 146
Constructivism, 87–142, 154–168, 214
applications, 139–141
criticisms, 141–142, 165
schema, 87, 89–91
social, 154–158
with associationism, 172
with nativism, 169–171, 172
Content knowledge, 65
Context
cognition, 119–126
learning, 163
Cooperation, 168, 191–193
Coordinations, 96–97
Cortical covariation units, 198–200
Cortical hyperstructures, 198–200
Covariation
causal reasoning, 73–76, 84
cortical units, 198–200
environmental, 195–198
rules, 73–74
social, 206
unconscious, 76, 84
Cultural tools, 156–157, 163

Developmental defect theories, 29
Dialects of personal growth, 88
Digit span memory, 8–9
Dinosaur knowledge, 64
Disturbances, 103–104
Drawing studies, 27–28
Dynamic systems theory, 185–190
attractors, 186, 187, 188
interpreting infancy data, 36–37, 189
state-space diagrams, 187
Dyscalculia, 29
Dyslexia, 29

Ecological realism, 181–185
Education theories
associationism, 76–77, 78–79
behaviourism, 77–78
constructivism, 140–141
nativism, 28
Piaget's theory, 140–141
Vygotskianism, 163–164

Elaboration, 66–67
Empiricism, 47
Environmental changes & adaptation,
40–45, 191–195
Environmental hyperstructures, 201–202
Epigenesis, 42–43, 193
Equilibration, 96, 104–105
Essentialism, 12
Event schemas, 208
Evolution
nativism, 40–45
natural selection, 16
social cooperation, 191–193
Experience, 5, 198
Experimental design appreciation by
children, 118
Experimental methods
conditioning, 52
habituation, 18–19, 34
preferential looking, 18, 19

Face perception by infants, 24–25, 145
Face processing, 9
Face recognition units, 9–10
False-belief tasks, 147
Family resemblances, 68
Feeding patterns, 145–146
Flow charts, criticisms of, 31
Fodor's modularity theory, 15–16
Frames, 90

Gender differences in cognition, 148–149,
150
Gender stereotypes, 91
Generalisation by children, 90–91
Genetics & nativism, 40–45, 214
Genomic regulation, 41–42, 193
Gestaltism, 88–89
Gibsonionism, 181–185
Grasping, 98, 99–100

Habituation experiments, 18–19, 34
HAM (Human Associative Memory), 57
Hidden units, 176, 177
Hierarchical associations, 60
Hierarchical models, 44
Homunculus, 1
Human Associative Memory (HAM), 57

Self-organising systems, 185–190
Semantic networks, 55–61
Semiotic function, 106–108
Sensorimotor intelligence, 97, 98–103, 107–108
Seriation development, 110–111
Sex differences in cognition, 148–149, 150
Shape constancy in neonates, 19–20, 36–37
Similarity perception, 82
Size constancy in neonates, 20
Social associationism, 151–154
Social behaviour
  development, 113–114
  innateness, 24, 144–146, 148
Social cognitive theory, 152
Social constructivism, 154–168
Social cooperation, 168, 191–193
Social covariation, 206
Social learning in infants, 24
Social learning theory, 152
Social marking, 123–124
Social nativism, 144–151
Social regulations, 193–194
Sociobiology, 149, 150–151
Sorting, 67, 69
Space conception, 101–102, 112
Spatial reasoning, 148–149
Speech, internal vs external, 162
Speech development, 107
  & behaviour, 159–160, 193
  Bruner's theory, 162
  Chomskian theory, 3, 4
  Vygotskianism, 159–163
Speech perception 12
Speech preferences in infants, 24, 145
Speech rate, 8–9
Stabilised retinal images, 200
State-space diagrams, 187
Stereotypes, 91
Stimulus-response associations, 50–51
Symbol-grounding, 39

Symbolic play, 107

Taxonomic reasoning, 207–208
Taxonomic structures, 207
Teaching see Education theories
Theory-of-mind, 24, 147–148, 150
Thought & inner speech, 162
Thought development, 85, 108–109
Time conception, 112–113
Tools & Vygotskianism, 156–157, 158, 163
Tracking by infants, 98–99
Triad sorting, 69

Units as concepts, 56
Universals, 4
Utilitarianism, 49

Verbal thought, 162
Violation of expectation paradigm, 20–22, 37
Visual acuity of neonates, 34
Visual categorical perception, 11
Visual cliff, 183
Visual conception, 202–204
Visual cortex, 199
Visual hyperstructures, 203–204
Visual stabilisation, 200
Visual tracking by infants, 98–99
Voice preferences in infants, 24, 145
Vygotsky's theory, 154–163
  compared to Piaget's theory, 165–168
  criticisms, 165
  cultural tools, 156–157, 163
  & education, 163–164
  tools, 156–157, 158, 163
  zone of proximal development, 163

Walking pattern, 186
Wason selection task, 124–125
Working memory, 8–9

Zone of proximal development, 163